IRISH TRAVELLERS
Representations and Realities

Michael Hayes

The Liffey Press

Published by
The Liffey Press
Ashbrook House
10 Main Street
Raheny, Dublin 5, Ireland
www.theliffeypress.com

A catalogue record of this book is
available from the British Library.

ISBN 1-904148-79-4

Printed in Spain by Graficas Cems

Contents

About the Author

Dr Michael Hayes (Mícheál Ó hAodha) lectures on a number of History, Politics and Social Studies courses at the University of Limerick incorporating Traveller, Roma and Migration Studies. He has published six books about the socio-cultural history and development of a number of different (traditionally nomadic) groups within the Irish Traveller community: *The Candlelight Painter* (2004); *Parley-Poet and Chanter* (2004); *Canting with Cauley* (2005); *A Compendium of Fairground Speech* (2005); *Counter-Hegemony and the Irish "Other"* (2006); *Otherness and Identity in Modern Ireland: The Case of Irish Travellers and the Immigrant Roma* (2006). He also works in the area of asylum and the asylum process – in particular the policy implications and effects of present-day asylum procedures as applicable within the EU and Ireland. He has been involved in community work with Travellers, asylum-seekers and other marginalised groups in Liverpool and in Limerick for the past twelve years.

Acknowledgements

Sincere thanks to Dr Eugene O'Brien, Head of English, Mary Immaculate College, Limerick; Dr Brian Coates, Director of Cultural Studies, Bhasha Research and Publications Centre, Baroda, India; Dr John McDonagh, Lecturer, English Department, Mary Immaculate College; and Professor Pat Coughlan, Head of English, University College Cork, for their breadth of knowledge and support. An expression of thanks is also extended to An Chomhairle Oidhreachta (The Irish Heritage Council) for their financial support in relation to this publication. I am grateful to Brian Langan and David Givens of The Liffey Press for all of their work. A special word of love to my wife Caroline and children.

I ndílchuimhne ar mo dheirfiúr Caitríona
agus máthair mo chéile, Patricia.

In memoriam, my siscár Caitríona
and my beór's nadhrum, Patricia

In memory of my sister Caitríona
and my mother-in-law Patricia.

To my father and mother and the people who came before

Preface

This book is an introduction to a relatively new subject area within the canon of Irish Studies. Traveller Studies and its corollaries, Romani Studies and Diaspora and Migration Studies, are all disciplines with which modern Irish society is only now beginning to engage on a more serious and sustained level. This book traces a number of common themes relating to the representation of Irish Travellers in popular Irish culture and how these themes have impacted on aspects of the evolution of State policy as pertaining to Travellers in Ireland. The book also examines the level of cultural recognition that exists both of Irish Travellers and of their community's history and culture. A particular focus of this book is on the development of the non-Traveller (or mainstream's) perception of Travellers as an "outsider" group in Irish society, a negative "Other" who are perceived as a "problem" that needs to be solved.

The past decade has seen the emergence of a canon of literature by Helleiner (2000) and Fanning (2002), to name but two recent studies, which has attempted to reconstruct the history of anti-Traveller prejudice or racism and aspects of lived Traveller experience through an engagement with social history, oral history and other archival sources. It is hoped that this book will also act to supplement the existing sources and enable further theorisation of the way in which Irish Travellers have been discursively constructed in both Irish archival sources and the discourse that is Irish public life generally.

The early chapters of the book examine historical and nineteenth-century attempts to define Irish Travellers and "locate" them amongst a pantheon of Travelling groups in the Europe of the nineteenth century. It gives an overview of some of the early debates concerning the possible origins of Irish Travellers and attempts by nineteenth- and twentieth-century scholars and cultural "enthusiasts" to define them. It surveys the traditional approach of the quasi-Victorian and primitivist movement known as Gypsiology and the discourses of philological and "racial" classification that attempted to locate Irish Travellers amongst a hierarchy of different travelling groups. The book proceeds to an analysis of those modern academic definitions, some elements of which are said to define Traveller culture. It provides an overview of recent debates concerning the definition of Travellers in terms of racism, ethnicity and cultural attributes and examines the importance of these debates to the struggle for Traveller self-determination in the increasingly multicultural society that Ireland is becoming.

A particular focus of this book is on the discussion of the concept of the "Other" or Otherness as it has been analysed both historically and within the realm of the theoretical, and the way in which "Othering" in an Irish context related to a definition of Irishness that accompanied independence, a construction that was monologic. A history that was unitary or homogenous in nature was a natural path to follow for a postcolonial nation where history itself was both an adaptive mechanism and a form of cultural legitimation. However, the teleological version of Ireland's history had a particularly negative impact for those minorities and groups who had always, to a certain extent at least, inhabited a position on the margins of Irish society. This book examines the consequences of this exclusion of the Other, including Irish Travellers, from this homogeneous and constructed definition of Irishness, and how this exclusion has posed difficulties for Traveller cultural determination in the modern and increasingly State-oriented era. This rather essentialist version of Irish history which was promulgated on independence meant that reductionist views of the Irish as represented under colonialism were frequently transferred to the "Other" (including Travellers) within Irish society, as discussed in Chapters 6 and 7. The workings of this process are examined in detail in subsequent chapters with reference to the only purposeful survey of attitudes to Travellers taken prior to the large-scale transformation of Ireland into an urbanised society — the 1952 Irish Folklore Commission's Questionnaire on Travellers.

The book's final chapters give an overview of the Traveller fight for self-determination and cultural recognition and the manner in which this struggle has endeavoured to undo previous representations of Travellers, in particular those representations which "constructed" Traveller identity within a regime of degradation and inferiority and encompassing attributions of primitivism and the anti-social. This latter section of the book examines the intimate link that exists between the category definitions or representations of a particular group and the way in which the government and society respond to that group. The underlying intention of this book is an effort to elucidate the "constructed" nature of Traveller identity in modern Ireland. More importantly still are the effects that this construction has had on the treatment of Travellers in Irish social policy and the serious consequences which a "manufactured" identity have had for the perceived status of Travellers as a distinct group within Irish society.

Note: In the chapters relating to the Irish Folklore Commission's Tinker Questionnaire, Iml. = Volume (Refers to Volume number in the Irish Folklore Commission archive). For example (Iml. 97: 51) refers to Volume 97, page 51.

Introduction

This book attempts to trace the evolution of a discourse of Otherness concerning the figure of the Traveller in Irish popular tradition and interweaves this discourse with academic knowledge and theorisation of Travellers as it has evolved in the nineteenth and twentieth centuries. Drawing on a discourse of difference as outlined through a mythological and stereotypical depiction of Travellers in Irish popular tradition, I attempt to pinpoint the complexity and relativity of what is taken as the *truth* about Travellers.

A group's history is nearly always predicated on historical origins which can be identified and located. The case of Travellers in Ireland and the way in which they have been defined and represented by the dominant society is particularly interesting and complex since they are an indigenous group who fall outside much of the theoretics of race and yet at the same time are acknowledged to be a group of Irish people who suffer a particular form of social and cultural ostracisation. Having traced the way these knowledges or discourses of representation created power relations of inequality, this volume attempts to analyse the way in which this "regime of truth" in relation to Travellers seeped into the official or State arena in the research of sociologists and anthropologists from the 1960s through to the 1980s. By tracing the evolution of the Traveller image in the realms of folklore and Gypsiology it is possible to trace the creation of a stable framework for the representation of Travellers which permeated some of the earliest modern studies of the Traveller "issue", a framework or construct which defines Travellers within a degraded discourse incorporating such notions as irrationality, the uneconomic, the anti-social and the primitive.

This book traces some of the earliest scholarly interest in Irish Travellers. These nineteenth-century investigations into the group then referred to as Tinkers originated outside the Irish cultural milieu and were really an offshoot of a range of debates concerning the origins and cultural make-up of another group of nomads, the Anglo-Romany Gypsies, a group who were considered purer, more exotic and more culturally interesting than the Irish Travellers as defined by the Victorian Gypsilorist/Orientalist and racialist schema prevalent in nineteenth-century Britain. Ironically, the first attempts within Ireland to study Travellers can be seen to have been an offshoot of a cultural project which was similar in many respects to that of Britain's Gipsylorists. This was the very ambitious and still under-appreciated project of reclamation or "re-Gaelicisation" that was the aim of the Irish Folklore Commission and the recording work they undertook during the 1930s and 1940s. While the Folklore Commission's interest in Travellers remained fairly limited in scope and was confined to just a few folklore collectors — Pádraig Mac-Gréine in Longford, Mícheál MacEnrí in Mayo, Seán McGrath in Clare — it nevertheless identified Travellers as a cultural isolate who had their own language and culture, and had furthermore preserved certain aspects of Irish cultural tradition that were believed to be disappearing quickly in both the Traveller and settled communities. Their research had no obvious influence on Irish public policy as related to Travellers but did result in the issuance of the 1952 "Tinker" Questionnaire — the only ethnographic survey of Traveller representations as defined by settled community respondents yet undertaken in Ireland.

These two small bursts of cultural interest in Travellers — i.e. Gypsiology and the Irish Folklore Commission were followed in Ireland by a State-led approach which downplayed any cultural significance attached to Travellers and examined the Traveller issue from a viewpoint whereby Travellers were perceived as a "problem" to be solved in terms of legalistic and assimilationist strategies. It can be argued that this is still the State's approach despite much latter-day rhetoric concerning rights and cultural self-affirmation.

The assimilationist thrust of the 1963 Report of the Commission on Itinerancy is examined. This remains the most influential modern governmental report issued in relation to the Traveller issue in Ireland and it was overt in recommending that Travellers be assimilated into the "settled" community as a solution to their "problem" status. The Report viewed Travellers as a group who were an impediment to progress, economic expansion and the promotion of tourism in Ireland. The views put forward in this Report were very much in step with the sociological theoretics of the time incorporating "culture of poverty" and modernisation theories, theories which recommended the assimilation and rehabilitation of Travellers. This was the first official report ever produced by the Irish State in relation to the Traveller issue and it is one which continues to have profound ramifications for Travellers and the maintenance of their cultural tradition to this very day. I analyse the serious consequences which the cultural politics of these early discourses were to have when they were seen to provide legitimisation for the attitudes and practices of the majority society and the instigation of government policies in relation to the education, "rehabilitation" and assimilation of the Traveller community.

Subsequent to this discussion is an examination of the advent of a more modern theoretical and rights-based approach to the Traveller issue as elucidated in recent decades, including the discussion of Travellers' rights within the framework of such concepts as ethnicity and racism. An analysis of some of the principal Traveller cultural attributes that are said to bolster this increasingly rights-based approach to Traveller self-definition is undertaken and is linked to a discussion concerning the late-twentieth-century prominence given to the discourse of Otherness in the Western tradition.

Having sketched the evolution of the question of Otherness or difference as it applies in the Western tradition, this book attempts to situate the specificity of anti-Traveller "Othering" within the Irish framework. The historical evolution of Irish Othering within the colonial and post-colonial and nationalist traditions is outlined and it is argued that Irish Travellers were one of a number of minority groups whose history was written out of the official and relatively homogenous version of Irish history which was promulgated on Irish independence. This was a teleological version of Ireland's history that incorporated a glorious Celtic past that was weak and yet unbroken despite centuries of colonisation. By analysing this teleological approach to the representation of Ireland's past it is possible to elucidate some of the difficulties experienced by a very small and primarily non-literate group such as the Travellers in attempting to articulate a sense of their identity in modern Ireland.

This book is not intended to be an exhaustive evaluation of the literature on Irish Travellers or the theories that attempt to explain the existence of Traveller culture and the current position of Travellers in Irish society. While an overview of modern explanations of Travellers in terms of racism, post-colonialism, theories of modernisation, the subculture of poverty, theories of the "Other" etc. is provided, the focus is on uncovering the relationship between truth, knowledge and power in the establishment of the Traveller image. One of the primary concerns of this volume is the establishment of this image, the Traveller "subject" — and the link between the discourse that circumvents the figure of the Traveller and those material effects on the lives of Travellers as shaped by institutional behaviours and attitudes.

When taken as a whole this book can be viewed as a brief attempt to trace the evolution of a range of discourses encompassing the figure of the Traveller in Irish culture. It is an effort to examine the evolution and production of a number of "knowledges" concerning Irish Travellers from the late nineteenth century to the present day. The story of Irish Travellers has been told many times already through a different range of voices and disciplines. It is arguable, however, that many of these previous "knowledges" portray the "truth" about Travellers — the purported reality of what Travellers are and where they came from — through the limited perspective that is the identification of causally connected events which are actually a consequence of wider cultural and social changes — modernisation, nation-building, capitalism, the shift from a rural to an urban economy and sedentarism, etc. The "invisible" and for the most part (unknown) history that is the story of the Travellers is given a new unity through the description of societal trends and historical events which explain Travellers within a seemingly logical category or pattern that leads to their stigmatisation, exclusion and attempted assimilation. It can be argued, however, that this teleological approach to Traveller history and culture replicates previous schema of thought pertaining to Irish history as a whole.

In this volume, the history of a group who were considered different or excluded to the margins of Irish society and public discourse is seen to be an element of the postcolonial attempt to emphasise an unbroken and "continuist" view of Irish history that was often ethnocentric in the extreme.

An attempt has been made to highlight the importance of human agency (whether it is Traveller or "settled") in the construction and reproduction of social processes, thereby acknowledging the polysemous and ambivalent nature of cultural interaction between different communities in the same country.

I have attempted to acknowledge the multiplicity of voices that contribute to the reproduction of social and cultural processes, what Jones and Hanham (1995) refer to as "the possibility of multiple outcomes derived from similar processes due to the complexity of social relations embedded in spatially differentiated contexts" (Jones and Hanham, 1995, cited in Warf, 2002: 29).

The historical processes that have given rise to different representations of the Travellers are complex. Consequently this volume endeavours to uncover those relationships between know-ledge, truth and power that have served to define those (frequently negative) nuances that make up the Traveller image — the primitive, the uncivilised, the victim, the parasite, etc. The concern, therefore, is not with the exposition of some "real" or definitive truth about Traveller culture that is hidden beneath its external manifestations. Instead an attempt is made to uncover the manner in which representations and stereotypes concerning Travellers are constructed and have seeped into the collective conscience. While these representations and their import may often be denied or detested, it is nevertheless the case that they have taken on a life of their own and embedded themselves into the innermost level of those collective ideations that shape Irish society. This book is just one attempt to highlight the manner in which these often superficial and ill-informed representations of the Traveller have been created and maintained through a subtle series of unequal power relations that have coalesced over time into what Foucault (1977) defined as a "regime of truth":

> Each society has its regime of truth, its "general politics" of truth — that is, the types of discourse it accepts and makes function as true; the mechanisms and instances that enable one to distinguish true and false statements; the means by which each is sanctioned;

the techniques and procedures accorded value in the acquisition of truth; the status of those who are charged with saying what counts as true. (Foucault, 1977; in Faubion, 1994: 132)

The regime of truth which I examine here is a relational one. It is one which is fashioned in those interstices that are the "capillary points" between the Self and the Other. Coming to an understanding of this truth involves a negotiation with the forces that have shaped this truth and their motivations and terms for doing so. It also necessitates a comprehension of the effects of representation on this "truth" that is fashioned through the interplay between discursive and material effects and with respect to a range of attitudes, policies, behaviours and types of governance. I have tried to demonstrate that the regime of truth as ascribed to Irish Travellers through the median of suspect scholarship, anecdote and unfounded theory and stereotype has had a very real significance in Travellers' lives, their self-definition as a separate minority group and even the very maintenance of their cultural self-identity. Relatively little attention has, as yet, been paid to the theorisation of Traveller anti-prejudice and the cultural politics that underlie those texts which rely on the comforting bulwark that is stereotype. The stereotypical as theorised by Bhabha (1994, 1996) evolves from a position of stability and pre-judgement. It evolves from a pre-conceived idea that must of necessity be constantly re-articulated. It evades that aspect of the text which is the source of cultural production. It neutralises the now widely acknowledged tenet that the dynamics of a text depend on who is talking, "what is left unsaid and within what is said, on the choice of words, and the way they are combined into sentences and an overall description (Inglis, 1998: 203).

The manner in which individuals give meaning to their "experience" or what they perceive to be the "truth" is dependent on a complex process the interrogation of which has only begun in recent decades. It is those "Devices of 'meaning production' — grids of visualisation, vocabularies, norms and systems of judgement" which "produce experience, they are not themselves produced by experience" (Joyce, 1994; cited in Barry et al. 1996: 130).

The constructions of Travellers which I discuss here have congealed over the past century to become a stock of knowledge, a truth that has an apparent legitimacy by virtue of the very fact that it has self-perpetuated and reinforced itself over a considerable period of time. A careful analysis of the decades of representation encompassing discursive formations and imposed interpretations exposes the false nature of many of the judgements that "gave birth to those things that continue to exist and have value for us" (Foucault, 1979: 146). This powerful regime of truth cannot be easily discredited, not even from the minds of those who would do so, such is the power with which it "constructs" and the manner in which it dominates Travellers in the process of knowing them (Ashcroft, 1999: 57).

That the relational and contingent aspect of this "regime of truth" concerning Travellers should be exposed is important. It is only through such an attempt that it may be possible to discover a "new politics of truth" (Foucault, 1977), a new discourse and a more productive understanding of Travellers, their culture and their relationship with the rest of Irish society.

Chapter 1

Nineteenth-Century Approaches
to Traveller Studies

THE LITTLE THAT WE KNOW

Irish Travellers are an indigenous minority who have traditionally lived
on the margins of mainstream Irish society and who are frequently referred to as an ethnic minority or group in contemporary sources. It is
estimated that there are at least 28,000 Travellers living in the Republic
of Ireland with a further 1,500 in Northern Ireland. There are also significant communities of Travellers who claim Irish descent living in
Britain and the United States. They are distinct from the surrounding
population due to a range of differing cultural attributes. These include
family structure, language, employment patterns and a preference for
mobility that is inherent in the very ascription they attach to themselves.
These cultural attributes function to reproduce their way of life and ensure their survival on the margins of what is in modern times an often
hostile majority community.

Irish oral history from the earliest times is replete with references to
"fir siúil" (*travelling men, wanderers, lit: "walking men"*) and "mná
siúil" (*travelling women*). Some of these people were bards, musicians or
herbalists. Others were tradesmen such as travelling metalworkers, tinsmiths, horse dealers and fairground entertainers. Some were journeymen labourers. Others again were "professional" beggars or combined a
trade or occupation with occasional begging. Some of these people travelled alone, others travelled with their immediate family or in larger extended family groups. At least some of these people were the antecedents
of the group known until recently in Ireland as "tinkers", now called

Travellers. The one element which united all of these different people was the fact that they were nomadic for all or part of the year. This nomadism has always set Travellers apart from the majority sedentary population.

This study is an attempt to understand the image of Irish Travellers as defined by the majority society. Central to this study are the descriptions of Travellers provided almost exclusively by members of the Irish settled community in the early 1950s. The primary source material for this study is the archives of the Irish Folklore Commission, a body of material which includes a Questionnaire on Tinkers that was circulated to members of the settled community in 1950. It is my argument that the representation of Travellers, as incorporated in the general attitudes expressed by the Questionnaire respondents, translated Travellers into a dramatic spectacle of cultural Otherness. Travellers are described using a series of discursive strategies and popular stereotypes, incorporating an array of suspicions and superstitions. These same reductionist stereotypes have been the subject of constant re-articulation in Ireland over many centuries and have been used to justify Travellers' exclusion from "regular" society. They have also been used to support the majority society's view that to "solve" the Traveller issue, it is necessary that Travellers be assimilated and that their nomadic culture, an apparent anachronism in the modern nation-state, should be outlawed.

One of the most powerful forces the modern nation-state has had in its battle against Travellers is the power of definition, the power of the written word in particular. This is an area which is of particular significance in the current climate given the claims for ethnic status being pursued presently by some Traveller activists in Ireland. Because Traveller culture has primarily been non-literate, how their culture is defined is frequently beyond the control of Travellers themselves. Travellers are at a disadvantage when attempting to negotiate their struggle for identity and recognition in a society which is increasingly state-oriented and where the power of the media and the presentation of "image" is paramount. Travellers themselves have scarcely been able to exercise any influence on the way in which their identity has been constructed over the past century or so. Indeed it is the case that the Traveller image, as defined by non-Travellers, has become institutionalised in Ireland in the same way that the image of the Roma (Gypsy) people, part-negative and part-romantic, has become so institutionalised in Western tradition that it has become part of the Western cultural heritage. The survival of Traveller culture, while depending primarily on the powers of the Travelling community to withstand the forces of assimilation and acculturation to the majority society, is also largely dependent on the attitudes of the majority culture towards it. This is why it is important to examine the attitudes (both official and non-official) of the majority society, to the minority culture, the central theme of this book.

THE ORIGINS QUESTION

Irish Travellers have themselves no standard theory as to their origins. Cultural legitimacy has often been predicated on historical origins and therefore the question of Traveller origins has in recent decades assumed a more prominent role in debates about Traveller rights and Traveller/settled relations. Commentators in both the Travelling and settled communities have attributed Traveller origins to a number of sources which may have operated either individually or jointly. Theories regarding these origins can be divided — roughly — into three principal schools of thought. Traveller emergence as elucidated by one strand of opinion includes the possibility that Travellers are descended from:

1. Peasants driven from the land by changing economic conditions, conflict or famine.

2. Peasants who were forced onto the road by some sort of social disgrace.

3. Native chiefs dispossessed by English colonial policies during colonisation (e.g. Cromwell's clearance policies).

This school of thought is indicative of many contemporary constructions of Travellers in Ireland. Travellers are considered to have fallen from a previous "settled" or "mainstream" existence, i.e. they were either victims of their own inadequacy or victims of colonial oppression. The fact that this theory holds sway in modern Ireland has very serious implications from a sociological point of view, implications that affect both the Travelling and settled communities. It can serve as a justification for anti-

Traveller racism (see Helleiner, 2000) and act as a catalyst for assimila-tionist policies as implemented by the Irish State (see McDonagh, 1994).

A second idea places Traveller ethnogenesis at an earlier juncture and hypothesises that Travellers are the descendants of pre-historic groups who were displaced by successive invasions in Ireland. Writers who have posited this position include McCormick (1907), MacNeill (1919), Puxon (1967) and O'Toole (1972).

Finally, a combination between the first two hypotheses has been suggested. Binchy (1993) cites Michael Flynn, a medical doctor who has traced the genealogies of several Traveller families in the Irish midlands. Flynn argues that Traveller origins may be located somewhere between the two main prevailing theses:

> I liken the situation to a conveyor belt stretching back into an-cient times carrying the traveller population. There would have been a steady trickle of families dropping off and settling in houses while other persons or families would "hop onto the con-veyor belt", or drop out from society, or take on some of the for-mer crafts or occupations of the travellers . . . (Flynn in Binchy, 1993: 13)

This latter viewpoint has some support among Travellers themselves, as indicated by Traveller musician, Pecker Dunne:

> Where did we come from? I've often asked myself that question. . . . Some say that the Travellers left their houses and started trav-elling. They left old shacks at the side of the road because they couldn't make a living anymore. People say that it was the land-lords and the evictions that were the cause of this. That is only one part of the story though. Some people have always preferred to live their lives on the road. If you go back and read the old stories you will find Travelling people mentioned all the time. When the Gaelic culture was stronger in Ireland travelling was a normal part of the life then and no-one passed any heed to it. Some people travelled for a living and some people preferred to stay in the one place and make their living there. Many poets and healers have always travelled. So too have many musicians like myself. There have always been Travellers in Ireland because some people have

always preferred to travel so as to make a living. It's the same in a lot of other countries too. You go to any country and you'll find a group of people who preferred to travel to make a living. Look at the aborigines in Australia, the Red Indians in America, the Romany Gypsies in England. There is no way that all the Travellers in Ireland were the product of eviction and famine. Some of us were but not all of us. The Travellers are in Ireland a long, long time. We have been here for centuries — we sure have! (Dunne and Ó hAodha, 2004: 32)

The latter strand of belief, implying an ethnogenesis as a consequence of a range of historical factors, may be the most likely hypothesis. It is unlikely, however, that one will arrive at a definite solution as to the nature and reason for Traveller ethnogenesis. That Irish people took to the roads at various times and for varying reasons is without question. Whether they became part of an already extant Traveller community cannot easily be ascertained. What is a known fact, however, is that the conventional wisdom in Ireland today finds favour with some version of the colonial expulsion theory: Travellers are considered to have left a previously settled existence and are most likely the remnants of Ireland's colonial past. Since the question of group origins is often considered a marker of cultural legitimacy this hypothesis has far-reaching consequences for the position which Travellers occupy in modern Irish society. This version of Traveller history was not always the dominant one, however. In the nineteenth century there were a number of alternative discourses concerning the origins of both Travellers and Gypsies.

The Traditional Approach to Gypsiology

The question of group origins as a marker for cultural legitimacy was the backdrop to the very first studies of Travellers and Gypsies. In the western world the study of Traveller and Gypsy history and culture was a relatively peripheral interest for much of the nineteenth century and the early half of the twentieth century. In the English-speaking countries of Western Europe the main source of interest for Gypsies and, to a much lesser extent, Travellers was the *Gypsy Lore Society,* then based in Liverpool, England. Originally founded in 1888, this Society was a "pseudo-academic" group of linguists, scholars, artists and hobbyists who in their day were regarded as England's leading authorities on Romany Gypsies. Its first members included the explorer Sir Richard F. Burton and Archduke Joseph of Austria-Hungary. Later members included the artist Augustus John, the Celtic scholar Kuno Meyer and for a brief period the Irish poet William Butler Yeats. The members of the Society recorded dialect, folk-tales and songs from various bands of Romany Gypsies in Britain and in parts of Eastern Europe. Many aspects of the Society were similar to those of its closest Irish counterpart, the Irish Folklore Commission, whose earliest manifestation *The Folklore of Ireland Society (An Cumann le Béaloideas Éireann)* was founded in Dublin in 1927. Like the folklore movement in Ireland, the British Gypsiology movement included elements of primitivism and romanticism in its approach to the study of "Gypsiology" or "Gypsydom" as the members more frequently referred to it. Gypsies and their culture were of particular interest to the Society's members (known as Gypsilorists) because they inhabited a sphere of existence that was perceived to be external to capitalism and state control.

The Society had as its aim the collection of information on the cultural and linguistic practices of Gypsies and the recording of this information before what they saw as the inevitable death of this "primitive" culture. Delaney (2000) has highlighted the particular nature of this primitivism, a primitivism whereby difference as encapsulated in the figure of the "doomed primitive" was often used as a synonym for underdevelopment. According to this hierarchical model of human development, societies and/or cultures could be divided into those which were advanced or primitive, a demarcation which overrode the historical specificities of that which was culturally heterogeneous.

The designation of the status of "doomed primitive" to certain nomadic groups such as the Roma Gypsies has continued as a phenomenon into the modern era. Delaney (2000) highlights the modern utilisation of this mode of categorisation by referring to recent photographic projects undertaken on the Roma Gypsies in the countries of the former Eastern Bloc. Photographers such as Ljalja Kuznetsova (in Kazakhstan) and Josef Koudelka (in Slovakia), have provided powerful contemporary reflections on the Roma people, the trope of "doomed primitive" as applied to Gypsy people resurfacing once again. The Gypsy Lore Society[1] was very much of its time in its concern to record "a decaying language and culture" that was in their view on the point of disappearance, faced as it was with the inevitable march of "progress" (Mayall, 1988: 5). The intellectuals who shaped the folkloristic discourse of the GLS were for the most part members of the urban middle class, all of whom took a strong position against the materialism of the modern, urban industrial world. Their fascination with Gypsies stemmed in part from their search for a pure community of people, unblemished by the ravages and corruption of modernity.

This emphasis on a purity of community was situated within the context of race and in this regard the Society was very much a product of its time. Ideological notions of race were current throughout Europe at this period and were frequently invoked in a British context in discussions of minorities such as the Irish (in Britain), the Jews and the Gypsies. These notions of race had also been used as ideological bulwarks in the colonisation of a number of European countries including Ireland, and also served as an explanation of religious, economic and environmental differences as evidenced between different countries (Miles, 1989). The Gypsilorists attempted to distinguish between (and classify) whom they considered to be "true Gypsies" and other wandering/Travelling people. This preoccupation with racial classification led the leading intellectuals of the GLS to construct a racial classification of their own to delineate which Travellers/Gypsies they themselves considered worthy of particular study. This hierarchy was based on alleged exotic origins, skin colour and the use of the so-called "puro jib" or "pure" Romany. At the top of this "racial" hierarchy came the "true-blooded" ("tatcho") Romany Gypsies while much further down the ladder came the Scottish Tinkers and Irish Tinkers. The allegedly "pure-blooded" Romany Gypsies who had migrated from India originally were regarded by the Gypsilorists as real Gypsies — i.e. the most noble, peaceable and culturally interesting of all of the travelling groups then travelling in Britain — while the Scottish Tinkers were seen as lesser-regarded, indigenous Travellers who had some intermixture of Romany blood. The Irish Tinkers were also suspect

---

[1] I will subsequently refer to the Gypsy Lore Society using the abbreviation GLS.

due to their indigenous origins and were one of the lowest groups on the exotic and cultural purity scales created by the Gypsilorists.

This preoccupation with racial classification characteristic of the British scholarship of the late nineteenth century meant that the members of the GLS used the information they collected on Gypsy linguistics and cultural practices to search for what was the central concern of Gypsiology at this time, i.e. the proof of the racial origin of the true Gypsies then resident in Britain. Basing their theories on the philological work of the eighteenth-century German linguist Grellman (1783), the membership were in general agreement that the Gypsies had originated in India before subsequently migrating across Europe. The Gypsies then resident in Britain were thus "racialised" as non-Europeans. GLS members echoed the racialist discourse of colonialism and the "exotic" discourse of Orientalism, both of which were fashionable at this period, by researching the "exotic" cultural attributes inherent in Gypsy culture, which were perceived to resemble those of various populations within India.

Particular emphasis was placed on those cultural attributes, including purity rituals and linguistic similarities that were common to certain Gypsy groups and which seemed to hark back to their homeland in India. It was assumed that the Gypsy presence in Europe was the consequence of a movement from India. The Gypsilorists also assumed that this "original" and separate culture, complete with a pure Indian language and a unique racial character, was now under threat of dilution as a consequence of the Gypsy migration from East to West; hence the necessity to record its most salient cultural characteristics. The exact location in India from which this exodus occurred and the timing of this selfsame exodus were major sources of debate within the ranks of Gypsiology. It was as part of this debate that the Irish Travellers, referred to in the GLS literature as tinkers, made a brief appearance. The 1888 preface to the first issue of the *Journal of the GLS* outlined the three central hypotheses regarding when the Gypsy migration westwards took place. These included:

- That the Gypsies had entered Europe in 1417 shortly after they left India;

- That the Gypsies had left Persia in approximately 430 AD and had entered Western Europe at a later period; or

- That the Gypsies had been in Europe for two thousand years as metal workers.

The latter theory, which situated the Gypsy presence in Europe in a much older timeframe, negated the first British written reference to Gypsies, referred to as "Egyptians", which dated to the year 1505. The word "Gypsy" was itself a derivation from "Egyptian". Clébert (1967) claimed that "all mountebanks and travelling showmen found themselves dubbed 'Egyptians' well before Gypsies or 'Tsiganes' were publicly recorded in western Europe in the fourteenth century" (1967: 27). Many of these Gypsies when first arriving in Europe presented themselves as pilgrims from "Little Egypt" (presumed to be the Middle East) who were fleeing persecution (de Vaux de Foletier, 1961: 20–21). These early "Egyptians", as recorded in Britain, were associated with exotic occupations including fortune-telling, which they exercised "with crafte and subtyltie" according to a statute of Henry VIII proclaimed in 1530 (cited in Okely, 1984: 53).

Both the persecution and Egyptian angles of the story were further elaborated upon by an association with religious personages. It was said that the Gypsies had been forced to flee along with Joseph and the Virgin Mary. "Egyptians" were also associated with "exotic" occupations including fortune-telling which it was assumed they brought with them from the East. These myths ensured an initial welcome for the migrant Gypsies on their first arrival into Europe, a welcome that was short-lived, however, as Gypsies and other Travellers have been the objects of persecution or prejudice in most European countries from the sixteenth century onwards (Acton, 1974: 61).

The theory that the Gypsies had been working as metal workers in Britain as long ago as the year 1505 could be demonstrated by the earlier references in official records to "tinkers". It is worth noting that the term "tynker" was a trade name in England as far back as the year 1175. The extent to which this term referred to a distinct cultural category of people, however, is still unclear. So too is the possible connection between "tinkers" and those referred to as Gypsies, Egyptians and the Irish, all of whom were travelling throughout Britain in kin-based groups during the period when British vagrancy came under particular state scrutiny and repression. Beier's (1985) work on the phenomenon of "masterless men" in sixteenth-century Britain indicates that whatever cultural or social differences may have existed between these different Travelling groups, they were of no interest to the British authorities, who applied increasingly repressive legislation to them. For example, all of these Travellers were declared rogues according to a Poor Law enacted in 1596 which targeted "tynkers wandering abroade" as well as "all such persons, not being Felons, wandering and p'tending themselves to be Egipcyans or wandering in the Habite Forme or Attyre of counterfayte Egipcians" (Mayall, 1988: 189).

Okely (1984) has questioned the evidence regarding the cultural demarcation of the different travelling people of this era and suggested that there is a great deal of ambiguity regarding the categories of people defined as "vagabonds", "tynkers", "Egyptians", etc. Okely is sceptical as to the foreign origin of many "Egyptians". She suggests that the term "Egyptian" may have been a term of self-ascription utilised by "indigenous" wanderers who wished to appear exotic or an ascription or "label imposed by persecuting outsiders" (1984: 54). Irrespective of these various possibilities it was the fact of a possible historical link between these "Egyptians" (Gypsies) of the sixteenth century and the tinkers of the Middle Ages which stimulated an interest amongst the Gypsilorists in the possible links between contemporary "Gypsies" and "tinkers". Thus the brief upsurge of interest in "tinkers"/Irish Travellers exhibited by the GLS was in reality only an offshoot of a larger debate regarding the origins and migration of the Gypsies to Western Europe and to Britain in particular.

While the GLS had created an artificial "racial" hierarchy in terms of which nomadic groups were deemed the most "pure", "authentic" or worthy of investigation, the Society's publications at this period nevertheless indicated some confusion about the exact status of the "tinkers", whether these tinkers were Scottish or Irish. For the Gypsilorists there was frequently confusion as to whether the Scottish or Irish tinkers should be regarded as Gypsies, or as some type of indigenous or "mixed" nomadic group. In this aspect the GLS echoed the popular discourse of the late nineteenth century when terms such as "tinker" and "Gypsy" were often used interchangeably and in an often-confused fashion. Despite the fact that "tinker" origins were shrouded in doubt, the British

Gypsiologists did not hesitate to postulate theories to explain any differences that they perceived existed between the different groups. In any case, they were still inferior from a cultural-interest point of view in the eyes of the Gypsilorists and consequently were ranked lower on the racial/purity hierarchy as devised by them.

Philological Analysis

Philological analysis had been the primary tool of GLS members in their situating of Gypsy genesis in India and GLS members asserted that proof of Irish Traveller/tinker origins could also be established through philological enquiry. This could be done, they believed, by a careful examination of those few wordlists of the tinkers' language, known in academic parlance as Shelta, which had been recorded by the Society's members. The Society considered itself well-positioned to undertake such linguistic enquiry, as it included in its ranks two leading Celtic scholars, the renowned Celticist Kuno Meyer and Welshman John Sampson.

While Shelta had been adopted as the academic name for the Travellers' language from an early date, Travellers themselves refer to the language as spoken today as Gammon or Cant. The name Shelta originated with an early member of the Gypsy Lore Society named Charles Leland (1882), who "discovered" Shelta when speaking to an Irish Traveller in Wales and who stated that his informant called the language "Shelta" or "Sheldru".

The justification for the philological analysis of Shelta as undertaken by the Gypsilorists on Shelta has two aspects. On the one hand the Gypsilorists felt the need to justify their interest in the language of a travelling group who were lower on the rungs of the racialist/cultural purity scales, as they themselves defined them, than were the Romany Gypsies. The racial hierarchy aside, Gypsilorist attitudes to Irish Travellers differed little from the contemporary racism of the English upper-class towards the Irish in general. The justification for investigative work into Shelta was primarily that it served as an adjunct into the primary purpose of the Gypsy Lore Society, i.e. recording the evidence that the Romany Gypsies were culturally and racially superior to other groups. The differentiation of the "gentle Romany" from the "swinish Saxon" (Borrow in Binchy, 1993: 107) or "Celtic vagrant" (Sampson, 1891: 204) was con-

sidered a legitimate process within the Victorian obsession with a hierarchical structuring of the various Travelling groups.

The second justification for this philological enquiry concerned the
"exoticist" and Orientalist attitudes that were prevalent among the Victorian Gypsilorists. It was necessary to "exoticise" the Irish Travellers to
furnish them with some semblance of cultural legitimacy thereby justify-
ing scholarly enquiry into them. This was achieved by hypothesising on
their antiquity as a group with reference to possible Pictish and bardic
origins. The possibility that the Irish Travellers had Pictish antecedents
was the first theory to be mooted as part of this philological project. The
Travellers'/tinkers' language Shelta was first discovered in 1876 by ama-
teur folklorist and one-time President of the Gypsy Lore Society, Charles
Leland. He tells of coming across an itinerant knife-grinder in Bath, England, a man selling ferns in Aberystwyth, Wales and an Irish tramp in his
home state of Pennsylvania in the US, each of whom mentioned the use
of Shelta. These people had also suggested that this "secret" language
was far older than Romani and was habitually spoken by Irish tinkers.
Writing in his book *The Gypsies*, published in 1882, Leland described
his excitement on discovering a fifth Celtic language and suggested that
it might even be the lost language of the Picts, a suggestion that was later
mooted by Gypsilorists such as MacRitchie and Sampson:

> It is one of the awfully mysterious arcana of human stupidity that
> there should have existed for a thousand years in Great Britain a
> cryptic language . . . that I should have discovered it . . .the most
> curious linguistic discovery of the century, the fifth British Celtic
> tongue! (Leland in Macalister, 1937: 153)

Leland's theory was given some support by the Welsh Gypsilorist John
Sampson (1891) who also posited a possible Pictish origin for the Travellers. He claimed that one of the old names for the Irish tinkers was the
Creenies, which he claimed was a corruption of "na Cruithne", the Irish
for "the Picts" (1891: 220–1). A note appended to Sampson's article by
his editor, David MacRitchie mentioned a "peculiar caste" in Wigton-
shire, also known as the Creenies, who it was said were the descendants
of "some savages that came over from Ireland" (1891: 221).

The Gypsilorists' claims for a Pictish origin for the Travellers had anecdotal evidence only to support it. Modern linguistic research on the structure and etymology of Shelta indicates the unlikely nature of this theory of origin. Anthony Grant (1994) who has analysed the structure of Shelta, has pointed out for instance that "our knowledge of Pictish is exiguous and our understanding essentially nil, so that any claims of Pictish influence cannot be substantiated for want of incontrovertible evidence" (1994: 184). Since the grammar and syntax of Shelta has an English structure, most scholars who have examined Shelta are now of the opinion that Shelta was formed in the modern period, possibly at that juncture when the language shift from Irish to English was taking place (see Grant, 1994; Ó Baoill, 1994; Ó hAodha, 2001, 2002a, 2002c). Indeed, Dónall Ó Baoill (1994) who is the only bilingual (i.e. native Irish and English speaker) Irish scholar to have examined Shelta in detail to date, hypothesises that Shelta must have been created at a time when its original speakers were bilingual, having a knowledge of both Irish and English, i.e. some time within the last 350 years or so.

The fact that the English language was spoken by high-ranking Irish at the close of the sixteenth century and by the rest of the Irish population at an even later date gives credence to this view. The temptation to explain Traveller origins with reference to the Picts fitted into the "racial purity" and exoticist hierarchy of the Gypsilorists. Tinkers, whether classed as Irish or Scottish, were suspect due to their indigenous origins and consequently they were amongst the lower groups on the "exotic" and "cultural purity" scales created by the Gypsilorists.

For this reason it is possible that the references to Pictish origins were a solution to a Gypsilorist dilemma, i.e. how to accept a nomadic group possibly generated from within the sedentary society. If the presence of the group could not be explained by its migration from a distant exotic location, then some indigenous exoticism might be emphasised in order that the Travellers might be viewed positively. The essays of the various Gypsilorists writing for the *Journal of the Gypsy Lore Society* at this juncture also hint at the existence of a certain element of competition between the different Gypsilorists as to who was better acquainted with the most exotic Gypsies or Travellers.

That Gypsy and Traveller groups sometimes internalised exoticist views of themselves, including the myth of the true or full-blooded/pure Gypsy, and then fed these myths back again to Gypsilorists and others involved in Gypsy Studies is quite likely, as pointed out by Acton (1974) and Ó hAodha (2002b). There is evidence that this happened in the case of the "Pictish" theory of Traveller origin, in particular in the case of the Scottish tinkers. The Scottish Gypsilorist McCormick (1907) gave an example of how this exoticising worked when he wrote of a famous Scottish tinker named Billy Marshall, who allegedly claimed descent from some "Pictish kings" rather than any Indian ancestry. The allegedly more favourable genetic inheritance conferred by Romany/Indian ancestry is implied by McCormick's patronising statement that "many of Billy's worst 'peculiarities' are not Romani characteristics, and must be attributed to his Pictish blood" (1907: 19). For a short period after Leland's "discovery", occasional sightings of Irish tinker groups were reported in the pages of the *Journal of the Gypsy Lore Society*.

It was not until John Sampson commenced his researches into tinker origins and linguistics in 1890, in part as a by-product of the Gypsy origins debate, that attention to the tinkers' language known in academic parlance as Shelta and the collecting of this language became more focused. Sampson was also the first scholar to raise the possibility of bardic influence on the formation of Shelta, a possibility that would permit the Gypsilorists to exoticise the tinkers in much the same way as Leland had exoticised them using the "Pictish connection". Sampson collected Shelta from an Irish tinker living in Liverpool and concluded that Shelta was Celtic in origin. He suggested that Shelta was originally derived from a "prehistoric Celtic" — this despite his admission that much of the vocabulary appeared of more recent origin and included many modern Irish words, which had been transformed so as to be rendered unintelligible to non-speakers by the use of various methods of word disguise (Sampson, 1891: 207–8). In Sampson's view, this linguistic research provided proof of the independent origins of the two separate groups known as Irish tinkers and English Gypsies, thereby acting as a justification for the Traveller purity hierarchy which the Gypsilorists had created.

Sampson's analysis subsequently became the Gypsilorist orthodoxy regarding the ethnogenesis of the tinkers, negating in the process the earlier conclusions of another leading Gypsilorist and expert on the Scottish tinkers named David MacRitchie (1889), who had claimed that the Irish tinkers were a more diverse group of people and included a Romany intermixture. Sampson, whose knowledge of Irish was limited, was helped to develop this view by the leading Celtic scholar of his era, the German Kuno Meyer, to whom he passed on the Shelta material which he had collected for analysis. Meyer (1891) concluded that Shelta was indeed of Irish origin. He suggested that Shelta was a language of great antiquity and traced its genesis to sometime before the eleventh century. He suggested that Shelta had not necessarily originated with the tinkers, although they were now its only speakers.

> . . . though now confined to tinkers, its knowledge was once possessed by Irish poets and scholars, who probably were its original framers. (1891: 258)

Meyer demonstrated the linear relationship that existed between substantial elements of the Shelta vocabulary and the Irish language. Irish words had been "disguised" by a number of linguistic "transforming" devices including metathesis, apocope, the reversal of syllables and the use of prefixes. Since it was necessary to fit the tinkers into this "exoticist" Gypsilorist hierarchy neither Sampson nor Meyer evinced much interest in those elements of Shelta vocabulary which did not emanate from the Irish language but had been incorporated instead from other "secret" languages with which Shelta was in contact including Anglo-Romani, Scottish Travellers' Cant or English Cant.

The principal interest of the Gypsilorist linguists in Irish Travellers and their language was in the light they could throw on the Gypsies and their enthnogenesis. Therefore Sampson and Meyer did not overly concern themselves with the question of Tinker origins and culture. The dismissive attitude evinced towards tinker culture in general accorded with the rather lowly rung they inhabited on the *racial purity* scale invented by the Gypsilorists. Sampson justified his interest in tinkers, in part, by appealing to philanthropy:

> The Tinker has already been introduced to us by Mr MacRitchie [the Society's president] and he is undoubtedly a good fellow,

and worth knowing, there can be no impropriety in further cultivating his acquaintance. Although his less reputable connections
may perhaps cause him to be somewhat coldly received by the
more exclusive of our members . . . yet he still comes of a good
old stock, rich, if in nought else, in hereditary and developed
characteristics . . . an inviting field for the labours of the mission-
ary and social reformer. (Sampson, 1891: 204-221)

Sampson even extended the "racial purity" hierarchy further by creating
further "racial" classifications of his own within the Shelta-speaking population based on their knowledge of the language and whether they were
"full-blooded tinkers". To his mind the tinker who spoke a language derived from "prehistoric Celtic" was undoubtedly a cut above the many
English nomads, including hawkers and knife grinders, who also spoke
Shelta. The Shelta spoken by the "knife grinder, street hawker, and other
shady characters" was a lesser form of language, however. It was "corrupt" and "scarcely a tithe of the words in daily use by the Irish 'tinker' are
intelligible to his English half-breed cousin" (Sampson 1891: 208). While
their studies of Shelta allowed the Gypsilorists to racialise tinkers as
"Celts" in much the same way as they had racialised Gypsies as Indian, it
did not happen that the tinkers were allocated a higher rung on the cultural
purity scales. The "racial" hierarchy created by the GLS placed the tinkers
only slightly above the "half-bloods" (i.e. those who were half-Gypsy and
half-English) or other English Travellers, often referred to as "vagrants".

Despite their belief that some aspects of Shelta indicated its possible
antiquity as a language, the tinkers and their culture were still regarded in
an ambiguous light by the Gypsilorists. Sampson linked the tinkers' language with their perceived social status:

. . . [the Tinker's] moral and social code, like his language, is certainly of the backslang order (1891: 220).

This was also clear from comments of Kuno Meyer, who felt the need to
explain his interest in Shelta thus:

I would scarcely have taken much interest in Shelta, if it were
nothing but tinkers' cant, fabricated from Irish in modern times, of
a kind not superior to the backslang of costers and cabmen. It was

the fact of there being evidence to the great antiquity of Shelta that made me want to know more about it. (Meyer, 1891: 261)

The ambiguous status of the tinkers in the eyes of the Gypsilorists manifested itself not only in relation to linguistic factors but also in relation to other cultural attributes, including nomadism. The literature of Gypsiology at this period exoticised the group of people referred to as the "true" Romany Gypsies not only in terms of genealogy and linguistic inheritance. Their nomadism was also seen to be "true" because it was a nomadism that was racially determined. This was in contrast to other travelling groups including tinkers and tramps whose nomadism was generally perceived to be a consequence of degeneracy and opprobrium.

After the initial burst of enthusiasm, as a consequence of the debate on Gypsy origin, little further interest was evinced by the Gypsilorists in the possible origins and genesis of the tinkers themselves. Since the tinkers were for the most part non-literate, it was assumed that their use of Shelta was a remnant of the Gaelic past from whence they had emanated. It was thought that they were just the inheritors of a linguistic link with an older culture, one which included the use of perhaps many secret languages by those occupational groups (including druids and stonemasons), aspects of whose lifestyle may have been suppressed by the dominant society.

The only other known "secret" language or "cant" to have survived in Ireland into the twentieth century in addition to Shelta was *Béarlagair na Saor* (the Language of the Stonemasons). Although the name given to this language indicated that it was the cant used by stonemasons, it seems to have been spoken by a much wider range of people including pedlars, beggars, knife-grinders, horse-trainers, etc. From the evidence that has been recorded it seems to have consisted largely of innovated words or modified Irish words used in an Irish grammatical framework.

The question of "monastic" influence on these "secret" languages was mooted by scholars like Meyer and Macalister. In fact Macalister (1937: 257) would maintain that the language of today's Irish Travellers (formerly known as Tinkers), Shelta, is just one of a number of "secret" languages apparently devised or inspired by medieval Irish monks and comprising vocabularies formed from the engineered interaction of Irish Gaelic with other languages including Latin, Greek, Hebrew and English.

Charles Leland, the original "discoverer" of Shelta, summarised the Gypsilorist orthodoxy in an article written in 1891:

> [Shelta] appears to have been an artificial, secret, or Ogam tongue, used by the bards and transferred by them, in all probability, to the bronze workers and jewellers — a learned and important body — from whom it descended to the tinkers. (Leland, 1891: 195)

Repercussions of the Gypsilorist Theories

The "racial purity" classifications of the Gypsilorists could be dismissed as the fashionable obscurantism of a group of late-Victorian gentlemen if it were not for the very real and dangerous effects their theorising had on public policy towards Gypsies and Travellers in Britain as the twentieth century progressed. Unlike the folklorists of the Irish Folklore Commission, some of the Gypsilorists held positions of influence in British social life and also had a role as advisers to the government on policy issues concerning Gypsies and Travellers in Britain. Sampson, Leland and others were the first lorists to put forward the concept of "racial" and "exoticist" classifications relating to Gypsies and Travellers. After the Second World War, however, there emerged a second-generation of Gypsilorists who accepted these classifications with apparent ease.

In his work *Gypsy Politics and Social Change* (1974) Acton has described the practical effects of these exoticist classifications on the Gypsy and Traveller communities in Britain in the second half of the twentieth century at a period when the British state imposed increased controls on nomadism and the Gypsy/Traveller way of life. Many county councils and local government officials in Britain accepted the thesis of "racial purity" as promulgated by members of the Gypsy Lore Society, including Brian Vesey-Fitzgerald, Rupert Croft-Cooke and Edward Harvey, from just before the Second World War and for some time afterwards. This categorisation of Gypsies into sub-groups as undertaken by the Gypsilorists of the British Gypsy Lore Society allowed local authorities to build up their own inventories of how many "true" Romany Gypsies as opposed to "mumpers, half-breeds, didakais and tinkers" there were in a particular area of the UK. These bizarre classifications would have been amusing except for the devastating results they had for Gypsies and Travellers still living on the road, particularly in the period immediately after the Second World War.

The belief that the "true-blooded Gypsy" was a dying breed lived on in the literature of Gypsiology and officialdom alike and the romantic idealised Gypsy of literary and Gypsy-lore fame became a millstone around the necks of those Gypsies and Travellers agitating for their rights. So-called Gypsy experts such as Edward Harvey and Brian Vesey-Fitzgerald continually warned in their writings of the demise of the "real" Gypsy and the upsurge of those whose claims to a Gypsy lifestyle were at best spurious. Writing in the *Journal of the Gypsy Lore Society* in the late 1940s both Harvey and Vesey-Fitzgerald continued to propagate the romantic and primitivist myth of the "true" Gypsy and warned of the demise of this "true" Gypsy type in Hampshire's New Forest, an area inhabited by Gypsies for centuries. Their thinking was to influence those various bodies responsible for local affairs. A 1960 report of the Hampshire Association of Parish Councils, for example stated:

> The old Romany stock is diluted and there has been an infiltration of "poor white". The majority of these people have wandered all their lives. Though, in the past, they had their proud traditions, they, and we too, as thinking people, are faced with the problem that besets a decadent stock. They belong to neither past nor present. (Cited in Acton, 1974: 191)

The continuing strength of the racial stereotype allowed local authorities to either avoid their responsibilities towards Gypsies and Travellers on the pretext that they would help "real" Romanies but not the crowd of "pretenders" and "mixed-breeds" who were then on the road. In many instances the reports of the true Gypsy's demise aided county councils and local authorities in their efforts either to totally assimilate Gypsies and Travellers or to practise so-called "rehabilitation" on them, at the same time absolving themselves from any charges of racial oppression. Some local councils such as Kent conducted surveys in the 1950s and attempted to distinguish between the number of so-called "true" Romanies and others — a process with uncomfortable echoes of the categorisation of Gypsies into sub-groups and their subsequent "ethnic cleansing" by the Nazis in the concentration camps only a few years before. To marvel at the longevity of the Gypsilorist stereotype tradition, and the frighteningly precise nature in which the cult of the "true Gypsy" persists from one generation of public policy-makers to another, all we have to do is read the comments made by then British Home Secretary Jack Straw in 1999:

> Now the first thing we have to say is that people have got to stop being sentimental about so-called travellers. There are relatively few Romany Gypsies left, who seem to be able to mind their own business and don't cause trouble to other people, and then there are a lot more people who masquerade as travellers or Gypsies, who trade on the sentiment of people, but who seem to think because they label themselves as travellers that therefore they've got a licence to commit crimes and act in an unlawful way that other people don't have. . . . In the past there has been rather too much toleration of travellers. (Jack Straw, British Home Secretary in a BBC radio interview, 22 July 1999)

Unsurprisingly, groups campaigning for social rights and cultural autonomy for Gypsies and Travellers are increasingly reassessing the role which the Gypsilorist tradition played in the perpetuation of erroneous stereotypes and myths, many of which are still in common currency and many of which have justified economic and cultural discrimination against Gypsies and Travellers.

Chapter 2

Cultural Legitimacy and Bardic Links

The initial Gypsilorist interest in Irish Travellers/tinkers faded away during the first few decades of the twentieth century. It was not until the late 1930s that an interest in Traveller culture and Shelta resurfaced. It was Traveller language which once again acted as a catalyst for this renewed interest. In 1937 the Scottish Celtic scholar R.A.S. Macalister gathered the previous research of Meyer and Sampson into book form and produced *The Secret Languages of Ireland*, a work that remains to this day the only comprehensive study of Shelta and the other Irish "secret" languages written to date. He agreed with the theories of both Meyer and Sampson that the genesis and formation of Shelta could not have occurred solely within the occupational group known as tinkers. He surmised that the linguistic inventiveness inherent in Shelta might have been the product of either travelling monks expelled from their monasteries or lay masters of the verbal arts who joined the myriad of other itinerants on the Irish roads, including the tinkers.

Macalister disagreed however with aspects of the linguistic analysis undertaken by the earlier Gypsilorists. While Meyer and Sampson had surmised that Shelta was a language that might have dated as far back as the eleventh century or earlier, Macalister demurred. Since Shelta's structure and syntax was based primarily on the English language and since the English language was first spoken only by a few high-ranking Irish nobles at the end of the sixteenth century (and by most other Irish at a later date), Macalister concluded that Shelta probably originated in the modern era, a view that has been reinforced by more recent studies of the language (see Ó Baoill, 1994; Ó hAodha, 2002a, 2002c; Cauley and Ó hAodha, 2005). Macalister also posited a mixed ethnogenesis for Irish

Travellers. He devoted an entire chapter of his 1937 book to examining the way in which the caste-like underworld in ancient Ireland operated. This caste-system was a hierarchical one and included kings, nobles, non-noble freemen, etc. At the bottom of this hierarchy was a group comprising those who were unfree, slaves or homeless vagabonds. This latter group had no civil rights under the Gaelic system, were nomadic and wandered between classes in an effort to forge a living wherever they could. Some of them were entertainers "who specialised in acrobatic and clownish performances . . ." (1937: 124). Macalister believed that modern Travellers were the descendants of people from this group.

However, modern Travellers were also in his view descended from another group of people. These were the scholars and druids some of whom became redundant with the arrival of Christianity in Ireland. Some of these scholars had also formed guilds of poets who wandered from house to house, paying for their board with poetry and harp-playing, some of them attaching themselves to the nobles of the great houses. Macalister echoed Meyer (1891: 1909) in proposing these poets in conjunction with travelling monks as the antecedents of many of the literary "disguise" techniques found in the Travellers' language Shelta.

The likely cross-fertilisation between "literary" Travellers and travelling craftsmen was highlighted by the first Irish-born scholars to take an interest in Travellers and their culture. Pádraig MacGréine or "Master Greene" as he was known to the Travellers in his home county of Longford worked as a folklore collector on behalf of the Irish Folklore Commission during the 1930s. He discovered Shelta while collecting folk tales from a well-known Traveller woman storyteller from the Midlands named Owney Power and wrote a number of articles during the 1930s on this topic for *Béaloideas, the Journal of the Irish Folklore Commission* (MacGréine, 1931, 1932, 1934). He called for further research into the "traveller-folk" because of their importance as repositories of Irish tradition (MacGréine, 1931: 186). He noted that:

> . . . these "travellers", the *bacaigh* [Irish: literally "lame person",
> beggar, wanderer, etc.] of an earlier time, the poor scholars — the
> Irish *scolares vagantes* — had been the medium for the spread of
> folk tales and all manner of traditions. (1931: 186)

MacGréine's call for further research into the Travellers was taken on by the Irish Folklore Commission in 1937 when "Travelling People" was included as one of the many topics about which Irish children wrote short paragraphs for the *Bailiúchán na Scoil* (Irish Schools Collection). This Collection was carried out by the Irish National Schools at the request of the Irish Folklore Commission between the years 1937 and 1938, where schoolchildren were given the task of making a collection of folklore as recounted by their family and neighbours.

MacGréine's views were taken into account in an even more comprehensive way in 1952 when the Irish Folklore Commission issued the *Tinker Questionnaire* (under study in this book) to its folklore collectors in an effort to document aspects of the Tinker way of life, "before it is too late" (IFC *Tinker Questionnaire*, 1952: 5). The Questionnaire included questions about tinkers under a list of topics including: "Generic Names", "Local Tinker Groups", "Areas Within Which Tinker Groups Operate", "Customs and Superstitions", "Religious and Social Practice", "Visits and Local Encampments", "Crafts and Means of Livelihood", "Behaviour", "Physical and Other Characteristics", "Tinker Personalities", "Tinker Society" "Languages", "Origins and History", "Sayings, Proverbs or Songs about Tinkers". There was a good response to this Questionnaire, with over 800 pages of material forwarded to the Commission by its various respondents. The primary socio-historical value of the Questionnaire is the insight it gives us into the relationship between the Irish settled and Travelling communities mid-way through the twentieth century. The Questionnaire is a particularly useful insight into the perceptions that the settled community held of Travellers. It demonstrates the negative stereotypes and false images of Travellers held by those in the settled community who were prejudiced against them. The Questionnaire is one-sided in nature since it was only the views of the settled community which were looked for by its compilers. However, it is still a very useful source of information on Traveller trades, Traveller families, their travelling patterns and the range of societal attitudes and prejudices prevalent among the settled community at this period.

Almost contemporaneous with the issuance of the IFC's *Tinker Questionnaire* was the work of another IFC folklorist, Seán McGrath. He collected specimens of the Traveller language Shelta and information on other aspects of Traveller culture, including folklore, in County Clare throughout the early 1950s. The style of McGrath's writing echoes in many ways the nostalgic and primitivist tone that suffused much of the writings of the British Gypsilorists who idealised the "true" Gypsies.

McGrath's views were an important forerunner of the new orthodoxy of colonial dispossession and the drop-out theory, which were adopted in official Irish discourse as the explanation of Travellers' origins from the 1960s onwards. The fact that he formed his researches into a number of radio talks which he gave on the national radio station Raidió Éireann also in the early 1950s, meant that his views had a much wider audience than those folklorists like Pádraig MacGréine who had come before him and who simply published their material in *Béaloideas*. McGrath (1955) was of the opinion that a large proportion of the Travellers were the descendants of those evicted during the Famine or those small landowners who were evicted during Cromwell's reign of terror in 1649. In his view only "genuine" tinkers were of interest because they were "symbolic of an older Ireland" (1955: 19).

However, he was in doubt about how many genuine tinkers were still living on the Irish roads. By a remarkable coincidence McGrath echoed the racial classifications of Britain's Gypsilorists, the "second generation" of whom were contemporaneously still engaged in a "racial" classification of Gypsies and Travellers in Britain. Because of their roles as advisers to the government on policy issues concerning all British Gypsies and Travellers, the "racial" and "exoticist" classifications of British Gypsilorists were to have a profound effect on British local government policy towards Gypsies and Travellers until well after the Second World War. While Irish folklorists like McGrath were not to have any public policy role like some of the British Gypsilorists, it is almost uncanny how the style of McGrath's writing echoes the nostalgic and primitivist tone that suffused much of the writings of the Gypsilorists who idealised Britain's Gypsies. Take the following quote, for example:

> Despite the apparent increase in the tinker population, the older type steadily seems to disappear . . . there are vagrants on the Irish road today, and they are a shame and a disgrace to the genuine tinkers of the country. (1955: 8)

While MacGréine had promulgated the value of all Travellers as a repository of an older Irish traditional culture, McGrath saw only a few of the Travellers as worthy of investigation, since, in his view, only a few of them were actually "old-style Travellers" and therefore heirs to an "older Ireland".

While folklorists like McGrath did not have any influence on government policy *vis-à-vis* the objects of their study, as did his counterparts in the British Gypsy Lore Society, it is likely that his views were common enough among certain strands of the Irish intelligentsia in the 1950s. His views on the worth of the Travelling population still on the Irish roads and his view of Traveller origins were soon to become the dominant ones in Irish public discourse. The Irish Folklore Commission deserves a certain credit for its issuance of the 1952 Tinker Questionnaire and the zeal of its local investigators like Pádraig MacGréine, who highlighted the importance of Traveller culture to the project of national reclamation. There is no doubt, however, that the fact that the Commission undertook no systematic survey of the lives or folklore of any group of Travellers, as elucidated by Travellers themselves, can now be seen as a grave oversight on their part. While one can allow for the grave lack of resources by which the IFC was hampered, and the particular difficulties that might have been inherent in recording nomadic Travellers, it is difficult not to suspect that the fact that no attempt was ever made to record Travellers themselves might also have been in part a "political" decision — a decision that may have been influenced to some extent by the anti-Traveller prejudices prevalent at the time.

Chapter 3

Twentieth-Century Approaches
to Traveller Studies

REPORT OF THE COMMISSION ON ITINERANCY

The first major Irish report of consequence regarding Irish Travellers was the 1963 government *Report of the Commission on Itinerancy*. This report was the first official enquiry by the state into the Traveller issue and was to have far-reaching consequences by virtue of its subsequent influence on public policy. This was particularly the case in relation to the question of the settlement and/or assimilation of Travellers. The Report included the first systematic collection of information regarding the living conditions of Irish Travellers. This information was itself of minimal importance to the conclusions of the report.

The inaugural meeting of the Commission included a reminder from Charles Haughey, the then parliamentary secretary to the Minister for Justice, that "there can be no final solution of the problem created by itinerants until they are absorbed into the general community" (1963: 111). The terms of reference of the Report were therefore predetermined from the very beginning. The settlement and absorption of Travellers into the "settled" community was set down as a prerequisite. The Report's terms of reference included the following:

> To enquire into the problem arising from the presence in the country of itinerants in considerable numbers;
>
> To examine the economic, educational, health and social problems inherent in their way of life;
>
> To consider what steps might be taken:
>
> to provide opportunities for a better way of life for itinerants;

to promote their absorption into the general community, pend-
ing such absorption, to reduce to a minimum the disadvantages
to themselves and to the community resulting from their itinerant habits; and

to improve the position generally;

To make recommendations (Report of the Commission on Itinerancy 1963, 110)

Every facet of the 1963 Report was turned against the notion of the survival or reinforcement of Traveller culture. In fact the conclusions
reached by the Report were to provide a justification for the exact opposite. The Report's goal was the settlement of Travellers on the grounds
that their way of life was no longer socially or economically viable. The
continuance of the Traveller way of life was seen as a hindrance to the
modernisation and economic expansion of Ireland. Since Travellers inhabited land which was targeted for development, their camps were considered a hindrance to progress. Traveller camps were also thought to be
a hindrance to foreign investment, and the elimination of these camps
was considered a panacea for the growing tensions over land use between Travellers and the "settled" community. The "settlement" of Travellers therefore was seen as another rung of the national project of economic modernisation, a project initiated in 1958 by the Irish state's *First
Programme for Economic Expansion.*

For both social and economic reasons it is clearly undesirable that a
section of the population should be isolated and follow a way of
life which is harsh, primitive and of low economic value both to
those who follow it and to the nation, and, most important, which
tends to create a closed and separate community which will become increasingly inferior to the rest of the national population and
from which it will be increasingly difficult to escape. (1963: 104)

The Report therefore presented Traveller settlement as beneficial for the
Irish population as a whole, the Traveller community notwithstanding.
Settlement would be the first step in an inclusionary project comprising
"rehabilitation" and their hoped-for eventual "absorption" into the "settled community". "Justification" for settlement was also supported by a
pessimism regarding the economic sustainability of Traveller culture.

Neither the complexity of the Traveller economy, where tin-smithing was only one of a variety of combined economic activities, nor the continually evolving nature of Traveller economic sustainability were taken into consideration by the Report's compilers. Neither was the contribution of women and children to the Travellers' family-based economy alluded to except with reference to the context of farm labour. The peddling and begging activities of women and children and their contribution to the Traveller economy as a whole were also ignored. Instead the survival of the Traveller economy was equated solely with the tin-smithing trade:

> The Commission are satisfied from their investigations . . . that
> the trade of the tinsmith, which so many of them claim as a skill,
> cannot except in a few areas, of itself provide a sufficient income
> for an itinerant family. (1963: 72)

The Report equated Traveller poverty with itinerancy at every opportunity and the settlement of Travellers was presented as a boon for them, such was the perceived squalor of their existence. Arguments for settlement were supported by descriptions of Travellers' allegedly appalling living conditions. Applications for houses from Travellers were to be given priority as the Traveller community "were living in totally unfit and overcrowded conditions" (1963: 61). The Report described Travellers' tents as "completely unfit, unhygienic and unhealthy . . ." while the suitability of their wagons for accommodation purposes was deemed "questionable" (1963: 61).

The Report itself was compiled primarily by non-Travellers and did not attempt any sociological or anthropological understanding of Traveller culture. Amongst the sources of information listed as contributing to the Report were visits to itinerant encampments in Ireland and oral evidence as received from local gardaí, local officials and local residents. The report did not pronounce judgement on any of the reasons why some Travellers lived in destitute circumstances. Neither did it critique the external factors in Irish society that contributed to discrimination against Travellers in the spheres of health, accommodation and education, or the poverty of structural resources at the state's disposal so that disadvantage might be tackled. The Report noted that the Traveller way of life was different to that of the "settled" community in so far as Travellers appeared to have little involvement in most of the major institutions of Irish society. Any charges that the conclusions of the Report amounted to a policy of settlement and absorption or were discriminating against the cultural ethos of Travellers were obviated by the assertion that the overwhelming majority of Travellers themselves were in favour of settlement; this despite the fact that no Traveller actually sat on the Commission. Perhaps the strongest justification of all for the settlement and assimilation of Travellers lay in the Report's lack of any meaningful analysis of what constituted Traveller history or culture. The report situated Traveller history and ethnogenesis anywhere between the "last century" and a "few centuries" ago (1963: 34). Traveller ethnogenesis was thus firmly situated within the context of colonial dispossession, thereby absolving the Irish government of any blame for the Traveller problem.

Social policy in relation to Irish Travellers has in the modern Irish state been linked to their perceived status as a distinct group within Irish society. Perhaps the most significant statement in the Report then was the following, where the Commission failed to recognise that there even was such an entity as a Traveller community:

> Itinerants (or travellers as they prefer to themselves to be called) do not constitute a single homogenous group, tribe or community within the nation, although the settled people are inclined to regard them as such. Neither do they constitute a separate ethnic group. (1963: 37)

Having provided extensive "justifications" for the rightness of a settlement programme for Travellers and its mutual benefits for both Travellers and the settled community, the Report went on to outline the more stringent legal measures by which its proposed assimilationist policies might be enforced. The inducement for settlement would be reinforced by increased legal penalties relating to the straying of animals, begging, the use of tents and wagons. Legal penalties were also instigated to curb nomadism, including the necessity for Travellers to sign on for unemployment benefit more frequently than the settled population and increased penalties for the existence of illegal encampments, encampments in which the majority of Travellers lived at this period (1963: 104). The Report recommended the setting up of Itinerant Settlement Committees, whose remit it would be to help Travellers to settle in local communities.

This *Report of the Commission on Itinerancy* is undoubtedly the most important public policy document ever written about Travellers in Ireland. It marks the beginning of a purposeful examination of Travellers in both the public and academic spheres. It was the catalyst for an assimilationist ethos which found expression in such publications as the aptly titled *Settlement News*. The Report was a watershed for local government in relation to Travellers because it heralded a new penalisation of the nomadic lifestyle. The decades since the 1960s have seen the systematic blocking-off of traditional campsites and a widespread failure to implement state guidelines on culturally appropriate accommodation for Travellers, factors which have in effect acted as the death-knell for nomadism on any large scale.

THE SUB-CULTURE OF POVERTY

The first major sociological study of Irish Travellers ever undertaken in Ireland has almost certainly had more far-reaching consequences for Travellers on a practical level than any academic work done either before or since its appearance. The theoretical framework proposed by Patricia McCarthy in her thesis entitled *Itinerancy and Poverty: A Study in the Sub-culture of Poverty* (1971) was adopted by policy-makers and was a contributor to the assimilationist trend of Irish local government policy as it has been applied to Travellers ever since.

McCarthy's research on Traveller lifestyle and the effects of the poverty trap this lifestyle allegedly entailed served to bolster the principal findings of the Government *Report of the Commission on Itinerancy* published eight years previously. McCarthy's theory was congruent with mainstream trends in social policy as prevalent throughout the 1970s. She adapted Oscar Lewis's (1963) "sub-culture of poverty" thesis to her research question and found Traveller society to be one where alienation and grinding poverty were with few exceptions the norm. Lewis had argued that the culture of poverty was self-perpetuating, the younger generation being socialised into the values and attitudes of being poor. This cycle of deprivation was found in underdeveloped societies or communities and was typified by a cash economy and high unemployment. According to Lewis these latter values inhibited the inculcation of the modern values that were necessary for social and economic development.

Fatalism was a key aspect of the sub-culture of poverty, the poor learning to cope rather than escaping from this lifestyle.

McCarthy adopted Lewis's theory as an interpretative device to explain Traveller culture. She considered Travellers' destitution and marginalisation from the dominant Irish society to be something that was institutionally reinforced. Factors reinforcing the culture included the organisation of Traveller family relationships and economic patterns. Lewis, who had engaged in anthropological work in deprived South American communities, had listed a large number of traits which he considered peculiar to the poor, specifically the long-term and intergenerational poor. These traits included such characteristics as: present-time orientation; inability to defer gratification; poor self-image; a loss of self-respect. McCarthy adapted some of these tenets to the situation of Travellers and identified contributory factors to Traveller poverty, which included the system of social controls operating within the society, child-rearing techniques and a lack of stable employment. In her view Traveller culture was an entity which acted with "the logic of inherited poverty" and she applied the "sub-culture of poverty" tag to Traveller culture, despite the fact that discrepancies and discontinuities in her field-work data sometimes negated her own argument.

Lewis's "culture of poverty" theory can be criticised on a number of fronts including the fact that this theory "blames the victim" while neglecting those external influences which affect economic development. McCarthy did not concur entirely with this aspect of Lewis's theory, preferring to see the roots of poverty in the structures which instigated and support the structures of Traveller society rather than with the people themselves. McCarthy found that the traits synonymous with the "culture of poverty" were a relatively recent phenomenon in the marginalised "sub-culture" that was Traveller society.

McCarthy's "sub-culture of poverty" theory was particularly useful to Irish policy-makers since it provided a justification for the assimilationist bent of social policy as implemented in the latter half of the twentieth century. Of primary importance was her rejection of ethnicity theory as applied to Irish Travellers. Her study was clearly predicated on the assumption that Travellers are not an ethnic group with an entirely separate tradition and culture from those other cultures which it comes into contact with, including the Gypsies:

> It is a basic assumption of this study that the Irish travellers are not Gypsies and do not constitute a separate ethnic group with an entirely separate tradition and culture. Poverty is considered to be basic to the problem of itinerancy in this study. (McCarthy, 1971: 6)

She discussed nomadism and the love of horses as central tenets in the lifestyle of Travellers but did not make any link between the phenomenon of nomadism and ethnicity as subsequent writers did (Okely, 1983; Liégeois, 1994; McDonagh, 1994; Ní Shúinéar, 1994). Rather than acting as markers for a separate ethnicity, she considered Traveller cultural practices like matchmaking, death/wake rituals and storytelling to be borrowings from pre-industrial Irish rural life. Although McCarthy acknowledged to some extent the importance of kinship, she placed little emphasis on the importance which social networks play in Traveller culture and their central role in the persistence of perhaps the most defining attribute of Traveller culture itself i.e. Traveller nomadism (something examined by people like Barth 1975; Okely, 1983; Liégeois, 1994).

McCarthy subsequently repudiated her original classification of Travellers (1971) as a "sub-culture of poverty" group. She later acknowledged Travellers as a separate ethnic group within Irish society (McCarthy, 1994). Travellers are a separate cultural group because they identify themselves as such and because they are almost exclusively endogamous (preferring to marry within the group). She identified a system of Traveller norms which are quite different and quite separate from the surrounding society and which constitute "a cohesive, separate parallel cultural system" (1994: 127). Norms include: "early marriage, close kin marriage, specific rituals around death, ritual cleansing, how relationships between men and women are regulated, how conflict is handled within the group, etc." (1994: 127).

She concluded her later work by stating that the method whereby she had first articulated the "the sub-culture of poverty" theory was fashionable at the time when she wrote her thesis but that she realised now that it was of no benefit to Irish Travellers in shedding light on the *raison d'être* for either their existence or their lifestyle. She also said that the application of her "sub-culture of poverty" theory as applied to the Traveller issue by those in positions of authority in Ireland had been to the detriment of Travellers in both the political and social spheres. It provided validation for some policies which posited permanent settlement and ultimately assimilation as the solution to the Traveller "problem". For this reason in particular it denigrated the Traveller struggle for recognition on a cultural level. Rather than increase awareness of the cultural distinctiveness of Travellers her theory was sometimes used to negate salient aspects of the same culture.

Academic debate on the subject of Travellers coalesced around a number of key concepts towards the end of the twentieth century, concepts including ethnicity, nomadism and racism. I now discuss these key concepts and explain the way in which these concepts have become central in modern debates on Travellers. The application of ethnicity theory to Irish Travellers is an approach which has assumed a prominent role in the articulation of Travellers rights. Another theoretical concept central to Traveller culture is the concept of nomadism. The importance of nomadism as a Traveller cultural value has been increasingly articulated by both Traveller and settled community activists and academics at a time when the repression of nomadism has continued. Racism theory as applied to Irish Travellers has also become a key concept in Traveller Studies. Racism against Travellers in Ireland is a unique phenomenon as it is an example of an endogenous racism despite the fact that the group in question have not been constructed as racially "Other". Anti-Traveller racism, along with ethnicity and nomadism, are concepts which are only now beginning to be seriously theorised.

IRISH TRAVELLERS AND
THE EMERGENCE OF ETHNICITY THEORY

The first anthropological study of Irish Travellers incorporated elements of McCarthy's (1971) analysis whereby Travellers were defined as a "sub-culture of poverty". American anthropologists George Gmelch and his wife Sharon Bohn Gmelch spent a year engaged in participant observation work while living on a Travellers' camp-site in urban Dublin from 1971 to 1972. As a consequence of this research George Gmelch located Irish Travellers amongst the pantheon of pan-European "itinerant outcast populations" (1977: 3). Gmelch used Barth's theory of self-ascription to explain the internal cohesion of Travellers and their maintenance of a separate group identity within the majority Irish society. In his early work, however, he did not pursue Barth's theory of self-ascription to its conclusion and assign ethnic status to Irish Travellers. He believed the Travellers to be descendants of peasants whose nomadism was an economic adaptation necessary for economic survival. For this reason he considered Irish Traveller nomadism in a similar light to that of many other indigenous groups. He made a distinction between this nomadism and that of Britain's Romany Gypsies, who he said travelled more widely. Gmelch used his status as an observer to focus in particular on the way in which Travellers were adapting to the change from a previously rural *modus vivendi* to an urban setting.

Like the Travellers in McCarthy's work the people studied by Gmelch were not representative of all Travellers. Most were poor, some extremely so. George Gmelch connected the economic success or failure of these urban-based Travellers to their adaptation or otherwise to this relatively new and uncertain modern environment, an environment where the old rural-based economic niches of Travellers had disappeared. His analysis of Traveller culture revealed cultural traits including nomadism, begging, increased settlement and its occasional corollary conflict. The ability of Travellers to exploit every opportunity for self-employment had led to the urban adaptation of older practices like recycling and begging. The urban environment had also meant social change for the Traveller community and the implementation of new forms of social control, including an increase in marriage amongst closely related families.

Gmelch echoed McCarthy (1971) in considering individual or group behaviour to be primarily the product of the socio-economic circumstances in which people found themselves. Consequently he concluded that all Travellers should be given the opportunity to settle and find employment, something which had been achieved by only a minority among the Travelling population. He found Travellers to be a "markedly conservative" group. (Gmelch, 1977: 157). This conservatism was intertwined with their marginalised position. Travellers needed to be able to leave this marginal position so that they could find space for "truly innovative change" (1977: 157). He blamed Travellers' poverty and exclusion from mainstream society on their oppression by the majority system, therefore, but nevertheless situated a successful future for Travellers only within the paradigms of the dominant society. He echoed Lewis's "subculture of poverty" theory and saw many facets of Traveller culture as reactive. The cultural traits which he observed, including secrecy, begging and conflict, were in his view only part of a Traveller adaptive superstructure that was in constant negotiation with the majority society. His research echoed the conclusions of McCarthy (1971) in assigning a status to Travellers, a pariah status which necessitated that they be supported in a move from nomadism to assimilation into the settled community.

Gmelch did not appreciate the central role of nomadism in the Traveller culture. He claimed instead that it was this very nomadism which had contributed to the marginalised status of Travellers since it had justified the settled community's decision to exclude Travellers previous to this. His fieldwork also led him to the conclusion that adaptation to the settled way of life was not a uniform process. Some Travellers, the wealthier families in particular, had adapted better than others to settlement. Despite this lack of uniformity it was Gmelch's view that settlement and assimilation remained the best route for the many poorer Travellers whose response to the urbanisation of the 1950s and 1960s had been "dysfunctional" and "maladaptive" (1977: 5–6). This analysis posited settlement and wage labour as a solution to the situation which Travellers found themselves in and had echoes of the "culture of poverty" model put forward earlier by McCarthy. Like McCarthy's analysis, Gmelch's early work can be seen to add support to the sedentarist and assimilationist social policies pursued by the State from the 1960s onwards.

In much the same way that McCarthy later repudiated her sub-culture of poverty as applied to Irish Travellers, the Gmelches changed their position regarding the status of Travellers and the inevitability of Traveller assimilation into Irish society. Subsequent to their fieldwork in the early 1970s, the Gmelches have together written a number of articles (1976, 1990) where they shifted from their original positions while charting the policy changes of both official and voluntary bodies regarding Irish Travellers. Sharon Bohn Gmelch's work (1974, 1975, 1976) prefigured a movement away from her husband's position where Travellers were seen as a pariah group adapting as best they could to urbanisation and marginalisation. She critiqued the blinkered approach of the Irish Government to the Traveller problem, its inability to perceive any room for self-determination within Traveller culture, and the "dependency" culture the Government's policies are likely to promote in the long term. She also critiqued the assimilationist and sedentarist aims of the Irish Itinerant Settlement Movement then in existence and pointed out that it had, in practice, become an arm of the government in implementing policy.

Sharon Bohn Gmelch was one of the first scholars to acknowledge the continuing importance of nomadism in Traveller culture and she criticised the Irish Itinerant Settlement Committee for disrespecting the views of those Travellers who wished to continue travelling. Settlement policies induced a dependency culture, one which was critiqued by Travellers themselves as recounted to Gmelch in the following example where Gmelch interviewed an elderly female Traveller:

> [Travellers have] no respect in themselves . . . the buffers are doing it all for them. Life on the road is full of hardship but I'd rather have it. You get peace of mind doing a day's work, and a good night's sleep. If they want to help . . . give them work and let them do the rest for themselves. (Cited in S.B. Gmelch, 1974: 13)

More recent writing on Travellers by the Gmelches (1990, 1994) charted the progress of Traveller organisations into the political arena and the success or otherwise of Traveller organisations in the articulation of their rights. They also critiqued the assimilationist policy of successive Irish governments, the Irish Itinerant Settlement Committee (now defunct), and examined the evolution of the movement for self-determination amongst Travellers. This analysis included an examination of the way in which new groups such as Mincéir Misli and the National Traveller Women's Forum were increasingly articulating demands for Travellers' rights. The core of the new position adopted by the Gmelches was that Travellers are an ethnic group whose culture is entitled to respect and the possibility of self-determination. This new position was the first academic work in which the concept of ethnicity was invoked in relation to the Irish Travellers.

The move to a full recognition of Irish Traveller ethnicity on the part of the Gmelches was evidenced most clearly in the title of their 1976 work *The Emergence of an Ethnic Group: The Irish Tinkers*. Irish Travellers and similar groups such as Scottish Travellers and Finnish *Zige-nare* are examples of ethnic groups which have emerged from what the Gmelches term "culturally homogenous populations" (1976: 225). Changes in accommodation are the bedrock upon which this emerging ethnicity materialises. While Travellers sheltered in farmers' sheds or derelict buildings for perhaps hundreds of years the arrival of first the tent and then the wagon in the early part of the twentieth century consolidated a new and emerging sense of ethnic identity. The changing nature of Traveller accommodation was the seal which reinforced already existing cultural boundaries between the Traveller and settled populations. Distinctive aspects of Traveller culture which indicate a separate ethnicity include endogamy, the use of carts, wagons and horses for transport and their engagement in specific specialised trades such as tinkering and horse-dealing. Traveller culture has developed in parallel to that of the host majority population over a long period of time, perhaps from as early as the twelfth century, although the oral nature of Traveller culture has meant a reliance on occasional historical references. The Gmelches quote manuscript sources which record the existence of Travellers during the twelfth century.

The Gmelches are not clear as to whether culturally separate boundaries between Travellers and the settled community were only solidified with the arrival of tents and wagons although they allude to the mid-nineteenth-century records of the Poor Law Commission to prove the existence of Travellers as a recognisable group within Irish society even before the arrival of changing accommodation and transport. Evidence for separate ethnicity as put forward by the Gmelches lies neither in the Travellers' filling of particular economic niches within Irish rural society nor in their practice of apparently separate traditional customs, many of which were the same as the rural Irish peasantry at an earlier juncture. The kernel of their ethnicity is to be found in their Barthian self-ascription of themselves and others as separate cultural groups, inhabiting separate loci of communication. The Gmelches paint a picture of an emerging ethnic group, whose adaptation of distinctive accommodation strengthened the boundaries between themselves and the majority population, boundaries that were already evident before the advent of the tent and the wagon in the late nineteenth century.

Chapter 4

Ethnicity and the
Socio-Constructionist Approach

It is without question that one of the major academic growth areas in recent years has taken place in relation to the study of ethnicity and ethnic-
ity-related issues. A raft of theoretical works have appeared in the past
few decades which have provided a bulwark to individual studies of particular ethnic groups. The interaction between the concept of ethnicity
and other prominent societal developments has also been a very important growth area in recent years, with the ethnicity concept being explored in relation to such themes as nationalism and public health. The
overriding issue which all of these studies have to grapple with to one
extent or another is the difficulty of definition, i.e. the questions of who
defines an ethnic group and using what criteria. It has been necessary for
theories of ethnicity and ethnic identity to be formulated in such a way
that they can accommodate a large range of differently originating,
styled and composed ethnic groups, a factor that inevitably leads to considerable debate on the question of ethnic definition. As a consequence
there is a great variance in the meaning of ethnicity and the components
of ethnic identity, depending on the academic commentator in question.

Ethnicity theory as applied to Irish Travellers (it was applied firstly
by the Gmelches (1976)) has followed the socio-constructionist approach
as outlined by anthropologists such as Barth. Barth (1969) identified an
ethnic group as one where the group was largely biologically self-
perpetuating and shared fundamental cultural values. For him the concept
of ethnicity represented the social organisation of culture difference. He
argued that ethnic groups were not groups formed on the basis of a shared
culture, but rather that they were formed on the basis of cultural differ-

ences. He emphasised the continual flux that was central to the reproduction of cultural processes globally. Culture, in a global sense, showed
great variation, a "continual variation . . . characterised by a complex and
patterned continuity" (Barth, 1981: 2). Culture needed to be continually
re-assessed in his view, since its pattern was not one encompassing a
"mosaic of bounded, internally homogenous units". Instead, the ideas of
which culture was composed "overflow and spread differentially and create a variety of clusters and gradients. . . . we must not think of cultural
materials as transmitted traditions from the past, fixed in time, but as ba-
sically in a state of flux" (1985: 2).

According to Barth it was within the contrast between the "us" and
the "others" where the process of ethnicity developed, an evolution that
was organised within "an otherness of the others that is explicitly linked
to the assertion of cultural differences" (Barth, 1985: 2). For Barth, as for
many subsequent theorists of the ethnicity concept, ethnic identity was an
affiliative construct, whereby an individual is viewed by themselves and
by others as belonging to a particular ethnic or cultural group. The cultural values that were fundamental to an ethnic group were realised in an
overt unity of cultural forms. This unity in cultural formation indicated
that the group made up a separate field of communication and interaction.
Self-ascription to this group was a vital component in his theory.

The question of self-ascription was essential to the research of Judith
Okely, an anthropologist who undertook fieldwork amongst Travellers
and Gypsies in Britain during the early 1970s. She applied Barth's theory to explain the ethnicity of the Traveller-Gypsies she encountered
during her research. She also echoed Barth in denigrating the emphasis
on specific cultural traits to "justify" ethnicity. Barth (1969) had stated
that "Socially relevant factors alone become diagnostic for membership,
not the overt 'objective' differences" (1969: 15). Okely argued that
Traveller-Gypsy culture consisted of an ongoing and evolving identity
which defined itself by a process of self-ascription and the maintenance
of specific boundaries with the majority community. Self-ascription was
undertaken on a group basis in Okely's view, a group that would by
definition be larger than the nuclear family:

> Self-ascription should be taken to refer to group ascription rather
> than to that of the lone individual; i.e. if a group of Gypsies or
> Travellers recognises as a member a person calling him/herself a
> Gypsy then his/her Gypsy identity is a social fact. (Okely, 1983:
> 66)

Historically, the attempts of the sedentary society to identify Gypsies or
Travellers have not coincided with the way Gypsies identified themselves and "were often not intended to" (1983: 66). Criteria of definition
which appeared to be objective, such as country of origin, language, race
or occupation often reflected the interests of those in the settled community who were seeking to define Gypsies and Travellers. State authorities
were often engaged in an attempt to find a sufficiently inclusive category
which would cover all nomads or quasi-vagrants, whereas for folklorists
and those charged with making local site provision for a select few, the
concern has been with an exclusive category which would enable them,
for different reasons, to discriminate between an acceptable minority and
a mass of "rejects" (1983: 66).

Barth (1969) had put forward an alternative whereby the continuing
dichotomisation between members of the group and outsiders could allow scholars to investigate the "changing cultural form and content" of
the group and the very nature and continuance of this dichotomy (1969:
14). Using Barth's alternative as a basis, Okely (1983) gave a cogent
argument for jettisoning any method of ethnic categorisation which de-
pended on evidence of a separate identity as a fixed product of history.
While it was important that the majority society recognised and respected the separate ethnicity of the minority group, it was not important
how the dominant society defined that identity:

> Some cultural traits may be symbols of identity, others not. The
> important traits may also change over time. . . . Aspects of Gypsy
> culture may resemble aspects of the wider society. But cultural
> similarity . . . does not necessarily weaken the permanent feature
> in the Gypsies' identity: namely their conception of themselves as
> a distinct group. Some aspects of Traveller culture and values
> serve to reinforce the division, for example nomadism, self-
> employment, dress, language, and rituals of cleanliness. But none
> of these is sufficient. (1983: 67)

Okely (1975, 1983) was also dubious about the distinctions made between the different Travelling groups she encountered during her fieldwork in Britain and the uses to which such distinctions are put. She theorised that Travellers and Gypsies are ethnic groups but questioned the
apparent necessity for distinguishing between the different Travelling
groups, and said that such a concern with categorisation and the maintenance of specified distinctions between groups could aid a divisive
agenda which suited elements in both the settled and Traveller-Gypsy
communities while simultaneously acting to the occasional exclusion of
other Traveller-Gypsies. The divisiveness that she encountered between
different Traveller-Gypsy groups was often in the context of claims regarding descent. This divisiveness had no bearing on ethnicity as defined
by the principle of self-ascription, however:

> Ascription by the individual is subsidiary to the group's continuing
> self-ascription. . . . Sometimes a group will denigrate another's
> claims. But this should be understood within the context of rivalry
> between groups. The principle of descent is not refuted where one
> group of Gypsies deny the birthright of others. (1983: 68–9)

While competition between different groups might be at the root of occasional divisiveness amongst Traveller-Gypsies in the context of ascription,
the divisive agenda perpetrated by the official designations as instigated by
the authorities of the state was more serious:

> The English and especially the Welsh Gypsies are given the exotic
> Indian or Romany origin, while it is said that the Irish and Scottish
> Travellers or Tinkers are "merely" descendants of vagrants and
> victims of the Great Famine or the Highland Clearances. It is con-
> veniently forgotten that the first "Egyptians" were recorded in nei-
> ther England nor Wales, but in Scotland. (1983: 18)

The frequent official designation of Welsh and English Traveller-
Gypsies was a romantic one, a likely consequence of the permeation of
Gypsilorist literature into the arena of public policy. This was a romanti-
cism based on the perceived exotic or cultural "purity" of these Gypsies
and Travellers as defined according to the racialist classifications of
Gypsiology of previous decades.

Okely found that Scottish and Irish Travellers in Britain were placed in the despised Tinker/Traveller class with Irish Travellers in particular being perceived to be more unruly and more frequently in conflict with the British authorities. As a consequence "the Irish label was conveniently attached to *any* Travellers coming up against the authorities" (1983: 19). She also found there to be considerable intermarriage between all Travelling groups in Britain and a consequent manipulation (by the state and by the groups themselves) of both national labels and the "real Romany" identity according to context. Accordingly she used the term "Traveller-Gypsy" throughout her book to emphasise the fluidity of the application of such sobriquets as Gypsy, Traveller, Romany, etc., and the preference of many members of these groups to refer to themselves as Travellers.

While the Gmelches had first argued for the ethnicity of Irish Travellers in 1976 it was only in the late 1980s that it became an issue of academic and policy debate in Ireland. The debate on ethnicity in the policy sphere was instigated by the work of John O'Connell, the founder of Pavee Point. He analysed the case for the definition of Travellers as a distinct ethnic group in a number of unpublished papers, presented at meetings of teachers, social workers and other professionals in the mid-1980s. These papers were subsequently published in the early 1990s and included an identification of various "models of Travellers" as well as an analysis of how the exploration of Traveller ethnic identity could be conducted in an imaginative way, particularly within the school setting. His exploration of intercultural and anti-racist policy as applied to minorities such as Travellers revealed striking parallels with policy developments in other European countries, developments which have been elucidated by scholars such as Okely (1983) and Liégeois (1994). O'Connell criticised social policy employed in relation to Travellers in Ireland and the popular constructs of Travellers underpinning these policies. In his 1994 paper *Reach Out: Report on the "Poverty 3" Programme, 1990–1994*, he critiqued five different underlying models of Travellers, all of which served to validate the assimilation and rehabilitation of Travellers. He focused particularly on two models of Travellers which had informed social policy in Ireland and which had reinforced stereotyping practices and prejudice towards Travellers on the part of the settled community.

The *Social Pathology* model, a strain of which can be identified as far back as the first written records of Travellers in the twelfth century, maintained that Travellers were drop-outs from settled society and that their nomadism was a form of vagrancy. According to this model, Travellers were in need of reformation, through charity and assimilation. *The Sub-Culture of Poverty Model* perceived Travellers as a group in need of rehabilitation and state aid. This model viewed all Travellers as marginalised from the settled community and subsumed in a body of inherited practice so that they were incapable of adapting to, or taking advantage of a changing society. He identified this latter model as that which is still currently preferred in the discourse of modern Ireland. Neither model acknowledged the existence of a Traveller culture, one that was deserving of respect, preservation or affirmation on any official level.

The model of ethnicity which O'Connell proposed led to much debate in the theoretical sphere. He used a *Human Rights Model* to identify Travellers as ethnic. Like other academics who have studied Travellers and Gypsies, O'Connell posited that ethnicity was a socio-cultural phenomenon, one which was constantly negotiated by each succeeding generation of Travellers. Echoing the Gmelches (1976) and Okely (1983), O'Connell (1994a) argued that the salient features of this ethnicity were transmitted between the Traveller generations and made themselves manifest in boundary situations. He explained Traveller ethnicity as follows. Travellers are:

> An identifiable minority: they regard themselves and are regarded by others as distinct; they have a long shared history; they have values, customs, lifestyle and traditions associated with nomadism; they have a language (Gammon or Cant) and express their identity in a range of arts and crafts and work practices; they adhere to a popular form of religion in the Catholic tradition. Furthermore, [they] . . . share a history of oppression and discrimination. (1994a: 15)

An analysis of the constituent elements of Irish Traveller ethnicity was undertaken by Ní Shúinéar (1994). She prefaced her essay with Barth's definition of an ethnic group as understood from an anthropological perspective:

> The term "ethnic group" is generally understood in anthropologi-
> cal literature to designate a population which is biologically self-
> perpetuating, shares fundamental cultural values realised in overt
> unity of cultural form, makes up a field of communication and in-
> teraction, and has a population which defines itself, and is defined
> by others, as constituting a category distinguishable from other
> categories of the same order . . . (Barth, 1969: 11)

Ní Shúinéar (1994) analysed the question of Traveller ethnicity by taking
the primary definitions of ethnicity as outlined by Barth and questioning
whether Irish Travellers fulfilled these criteria. She found that Travellers
did indeed fulfil these criteria and consequently were a group that fulfil
"all the objective scientific criteria to qualify as an ethnic group" (1994:
54). She also found the itemised characteristics as described by Barth
indicative of "racial difference, cultural difference, social separation,
language barriers, and spontaneous and organised enmity" (1994: 54).
The fact that Travellers were a *self-perpetuating* group was clear from
their propensity to intermarry. Self-perpetuation was linked to *racial difference*, another criterion of ethnicity as outlined by Barth. Ní Shúinéar
linked intermarriage with physical distinctiveness and found that Travellers were physically distinctive from the settled community. She alluded
to genetic studies of Travellers (Crawford and Gmelch, 1974; Crawford,
1976) which appeared to corroborate this view. Travellers also met the
criteria of shared fundamental cultural values and its concomitant *cultural difference*. The core values which met these criteria included:

> self-employment, occupational flexibility, priority of social obli-
> gations based on kinship over everything else, nomadism as a
> functional corollary of the above and as a value in itself, strict
> segregation of pure and impure, versatility, adaptability, and skill
> in the delicate art of living among and supplying the market de-
> mands of the non-Traveller majority, without losing their Travel-
> ler identity. (Ní Shúinéar, 1994: 55)

Ní Shúinéar also found *overt unity of cultural form* and, by implication,
social separation to be characteristic of Traveller culture. "Cultural
form" covered a multitude of phenomena including accommodation,
speech patterns and group rituals such as religious ceremonies and artis-

tic expression. "Traveller versions of all of these are distinctive — identifiably Traveller; that is how and why Travellers are 'different'" (1994: 56). That Travellers operated within their *own field of communication and interaction* was also Ní Shúinéar's view. Travellers interacted with the settled community in a wide range of contexts including trade — the selling of carpets, collecting scrap — but also in the context of hospitals, social welfare, schools, religious occasions. However, this interaction was not a truly meaningful one in Ní Shúinéar's view:

> Travellers and settled people meet head on rather than side-by-side; they do not work or drink or live or play or go to school together. The settled community is very anxious indeed to keep Travellers well out of its "field of communication and interaction". (1994: 57)

Barth's inclusion of *language barriers* as a constituent element of distinctive ethnicity was also discussed by Ní Shúinéar. She found Travellers' use of English to be unique and worthy of more serious consideration. Travellers' English was so distinctive that "uninitiated" settled people often had difficulty understanding it "even when Travellers are trying their best to be understood" (1994: 58). Travellers' own language, known as Cant or Gammon was another constituent that came under the rubric of *language barriers*. Ní Shúinéar alleged that the conventional wisdom regarding Traveller language "is that Travellers' language is a kind of schoolboys' backslang deliberately made up out of bits of scrambled Irish in order to conceal skullduggery from decent settled folk" (1994: 58). This view of Traveller language ignored much evidence to the contrary. Cant or Gammon formed the syntactical underlay for Traveller English. It had also proven a lot more tenacious than the Irish language had for the general population. Irish Traveller emigrants to the US had chosen to hold onto Cant or Gammon rather than to Irish, a language that was equally incomprehensible to the American settled population.

A further criterion of ethnicity, that of *self-ascription*, was also met by Travellers. They were clearly a group whose membership defined itself and were defined by others as belonging to that group. A corollary of group ascription was the Barthian ethnic constituent defined as *spontaneous and organised enmity*. This was obvious in relation to Irish Travellers,

Ní Shúinéar citing the daily newspapers as a good resource for examples of "pickets, marches, and mob attacks on Traveller camps, to the institutionalised harassment of evictions and the deliberate blocking off and destruction of any and all possible camp sites by boulders . . ." (1994: 59).

Ní Shúinéar's 1994 essay defining the constituent elements of Traveller ethnicity was one of the few instances in the modern academic literature where the assumption of Traveller ethnicity was counterchallenged. McLoughlin challenged Ní Shúinéar's assertions in the same publication *Irish Travellers: Culture and Ethnicity* (1994). McLoughlin (1994) acknowledged that the claim to Traveller ethnicity had been a powerful catalyst for debate between Travellers and the settled community concerning a range of issues which needed discussion and had brought Travellers and certain sections of the settled community into communication with one another. She found the concept of Traveller ethnicity problematic, however, in many other aspects. She pointed out that Travellers themselves were divided on the issue, with the National Council for Travelling People split on whether Travellers ought to pursue a claim to ethnicity or not. Her greatest reservation, however, lay in the *value* of the ethnic claim to Travellers in the long term:

> Ultimately the claim of some Travellers that they constitute an ethnic group is a most conservative claim. None of the structures, institutions and practices within Irish society which serve to perpetuate inequality, poverty and lack of access and its corollary of social exclusion are addressed in this assertion. Equal participation in the bounty of the state should be available to all Irish citizens and not on a special claims basis. (1994: 79)

McLoughlin then challenged Ní Shúinéar's checklist approach under the headings of racial distinctiveness, shared cultural values, etc. She expressed a grave sense of unease on the question of "racial difference". She considered biological theories of race to be "a dangerous starting point in any group's search for identity or solidarity" (1994: 80). Apart from being very difficult to prove, the biological theory and its corollary, the idea of a pure race, had in the twentieth century supported a eugenics movement and violence that had had long-term negative repercussions on a global scale. On the question of *shared cultural values* McLoughlin pointed out that:

> The common bond in any group of individuals is a sense of shared cultural values. This does not make them an ethnic group. (1994: 80)

McLoughlin gave the example of a religious order to show how a group of people could dedicate their lives to a certain community role while sharing certain fundamental values and commitments, a fact which did not make them an ethnic group. Shared cultural values were values that were usually subject to negotiation:

> shared cultural values are usually negotiated between members of the group. Even in the most conservative and defensive of groups they are not totally rigid and immutable. It is therefore not the cultural values per se but the consensus of the individuals as to these shared values that determines group membership. (1994: 80)

McLoughlin also disagreed with Ní Shúinéar on the question of *social separation* as a constituent element of ethnicity:

> Social separation is the fundamental impulse in the organisation of all societies. The majority of societies known to us have some type of social hierarchy where intermixing amongst the different strata is difficult . . . The social separation felt by many Travellers is part of a larger class separation. Their feelings of exclusion, marginality and social isolation are replicated within many poor communities. (1994: 81)

McLoughlin made the important observation that the social separation which Travellers experienced was not self-imposed and was not something that was seen as desirable by Travellers. Rather the separation was imposed upon Travellers by outside forces. This was consequently a worrying issue as this separation denied Travellers access to basic civil rights, rights which Travellers were themselves increasingly pursuing through the taking of cases before the Irish Council for Civil Liberties.

McLoughlin also questioned two other Barthian concepts which Ní Shúinéar (1994) had utilised to bolster her argument for Traveller ethnicity — the concepts of *language* and *spontaneous and organised enmity*. McLoughlin questioned whether the existence of Traveller language was a prerequisite to claiming racial distinctiveness and pointed to the position of the Irish language minority in Ireland who had never used a different language to claim racial separateness. McLoughlin admitted that prejudice and discrimination exists and is a daily fact of life for Traveller families, but said that intolerance was not confined to Travellers since the formation of the Irish state. Religious minorities had also at certain times felt barely tolerated in Ireland, as had deserted wives, single parents and illegitimate children. Intolerance was still widespread in modern Ireland:

> the neverending intolerance of our society can daily be seen in the treatment of "undesirables", drug addicts, persons recovering from mental illness, the homeless. Because they are powerless, poor, disorganised and inarticulate, the infringements in their human rights and civil liberties rarely merit public comment. (1994: 83)

Despite such challenges, there is now an increasing acceptance — in academia at least — that Travellers meet the legal and sociological criteria to constitute an ethnic group. McDonagh and McVeigh (1996) outlined the legal parameters whereby Travellers were considered an ethnic group in Britain and argued that this definition should also be extended to Ireland. They referred to the notion of ethnicity given definition in the *Mandla v Lee* judgment of the British Courts, a judgment which led to the legal recognition of Irish Travellers and Gypsies in Britain as ethnic groups. Travellers were an ethnic group when ethnicity was "legally defined in terms of the 'cultural stuff' which makes it up" (McDonagh and McVeigh, 1996: 9–10). McDonagh and McVeigh (1992) analysed the implications of this judgment for Travellers and found their shared history and nomadism to be the cultural criteria that defined their distinctiveness as an ethnic group:

> according to these criteria of ethnicity, Travellers are an ethnic group in Britain and in Ireland, north and south. They fulfil the two "essential characteristics" of ethnicity; they have a long shared history of which they are conscious as distinguishing them from other groups; and they have a cultural tradition of their own, not specifically associated with religion but rather with nomadism ... (1992: 355–7)

Chapter 5

Nomadism — The Cultural Kernel

PATHOLOGISING NOMADISM

While the most recent government policy document in the Irish Republic, the *Report of the Task Force on the Travelling Community* (1995) did not contain an explicit recognition of Travellers as an ethnic group, it accepted that Travellers had a separate culture and identity, a move which could be viewed as a *de facto* recognition of Traveller ethnicity. Traveller nomadism is seen as the kernel of ethnic identity in most of the academic work on Traveller ethnicity undertaken to date. Barth (1975), Okely (1983, 1994), Liégeois (1994), and O'Connell (1992b, 1994a, 1994b) all list Traveller nomadism as a central constituent factor in the ethnicity of Travellers. Travellers are commercial and economic nomads as defined in Acton's (1974) definition of an economic nomad:

> a man [sic] who, aware of the geographical and seasonal variations in the prices of goods and services, regularly moves his household to take advantage of these. (1974: 254)

Traveller flexibility and adaptability in terms of their economic base are characteristic of their nomadism as identified by both Acton (1974) and Okely (1994). Okely (1994) describes the way in which Travellers adapt to niche opportunities in the wider economy:

> They do provide occasional goods and services where there are gaps in the dominant system of supply and demand. They must follow the shifts in the wider economy and make the necessary adaptation (1994: 5)

Acton (1974) includes Traveller nomadism in a continuum which embraces the nomadism of pastoral groups such as the Masai of Kenya or certain Persian tribes. These groups are made up of "those who exploit these advantages, who turn their mobility into a form of asset, like skill or material capital" (1974: 257).

Okely (1994) defines Traveller nomadism in a more complex manner. Their nomadism does not fall within the classical definitions of what constitutes a nomad, because it is uniquely interdependent with the wider economy:

> Gypsies, Tsiganes, Tinkers or Travellers are a unique group around the world. They do not fall into the classical anthropology of nomads, for they are interdependent with a wider sedentary economy. They do not live in the wild off natural produce as hunter-gatherer nomads, nor do they depend mainly on animal herds as do pastoral nomads. (1994: 4–5)

She finds Traveller nomadism to be an important constituent in the inter-relationship between the Traveller and settled communities:

> . . . the group's culture is not self-contained. The Travellers' economy is directly dependent on the wider economy, even though self-employment gives a measure of freedom from non-Gypsies through mobility and flexibility. The group's beliefs and rituals are not an abstract totality floating separately from the material circumstances and relations of production with non-Gypsies. . . . This absence of autonomy should not preclude the understanding that the group's beliefs and practices have coherence and form a meaningful whole. (1994: 34)

Despite this interdependent relationship nomadism is the Traveller cultural attribute which is the greatest source of tension between both communities and the attribute which is most frequently pathologised. Traveller nomadism is pathologised by both the settled community and the state. For the settled community it appears to be an anachronistic survivor from an earlier era which has no place in a so-called "modern" society.

The state's pathologisation of nomadism draws sustenance from longheld prejudices and fears relating to the migrant dispossessed and the potential challenge they might pose to the social and political order.

Contemporary pathologising of nomadism on the part of the state can draw on a rich history of fear and prejudice against those who are perceived as uncontrollable, trouble-makers or marginal to the dominant order. As a consequence, Traveller nomadism is seen as deviant when it could simply be perceived as the symbol of an opposing cultural system, as explained by Okely (1983):

> Deviants from the dominant system and self-ascribed minorities are not, as the functionalists would claim, exceptions which merely reinforce the general rule. They can be seen as images of opposing systems. In practice, Gypsies or Travellers, who are dependent for their livelihood on non-Gypsies who are the majority, can remain only a minority. But such reasoning does not suffice. The Gypsies' symbolic work is seen as subversive, although their number is small. (1983: 37)

Celebrating the diversity that nomadism embodies is what makes the legal enshrinement of the concept of Traveller ethnicity so important to the struggle for Traveller equality. The debate concerning Traveller ethnicity is:

> not a sterile academic debate but one about justice, equality and the right to self-determination. If Traveller ethnicity is recognised, Traveller disadvantage is explained in terms of discrimination and the main priorities for action are tackling this discrimination and "celebrating diversity"; if Traveller ethnicity is denied, Traveller disadvantage is explained in terms of pathologising Traveller culture and the main priorities are getting rid of this "less respectable" culture through sedentarisation, assimilation or other more violent genocidal strategies. (McDonagh and McVeigh, 1996: 7–8)

Traveller nomadism is premised on the self-ascriptive basis of the ethnic group as outlined by Okely (1983). Nomadism, often referred to as simply "travelling", emerges as a theme in most of the creative, autobiographical or rights-based literature produced by Travellers themselves, whether it be Travellers' life stories such as *Traveller Ways, Traveller Words* (Pavee Point, 1992), Travellers' poetry (O'Reilly and Kenny, 1994), Travellers' film such as *Nomadism, Now and Then* (Pavee Point, 1994), etc.

O'Boyle's (1990) study of value orientations in Traveller folktales also confirmed nomadism as central to Traveller identity and self-expression. Nomadism, she argued, was the central value knitting together Traveller folktales. The major socio-economic changes which had occurred in both settled Irish and Traveller communities, including the increased legislative control on nomadism, had not altered the core value-orientations of the stories to any significant degree. The chronology of events within the stories was relatively unimportant and it was their present-time orientation which was paramount. Commercial concerns based on the core values of self-employment and nomadism were prominent to a large degree in the narratives and the rewards or successes of the tales' protagonists were to be enjoyed immediately. This sense of transience and immediacy as characteristic of a group with an ever-changing and nomadic mindset also transferred its way into the narrative style. Traveller storytellers exhibited a more rumbustious or muscular style as compared with settled storytellers, a style that was defined by a sense of immediacy and present-time orientation. McDonagh (1994), who is himself a Traveller, provided one of the most powerful frameworks within which to consider the phenomenon of Traveller nomadism. He deliberately drew a distinction between "nomadism" and "travelling" so as to distinguish between the travelling of Travellers and settled people, whom Travellers often refer to as "country people".

> Many country people who call themselves "settled" may in fact travel more than some Travellers, but that does not make them nomadic. . . . Country people travel to get from A to B. But for Travellers, the physical fact of moving is just one aspect of a nomadic mind-set that permeates every aspect of our lives. (1994: 95)

Nomadism has three principal and overlapping constituents in Travellers' identity. These are economic, social and cultural and nomadism is essential to the very survival of the Travellers as a minority group:

> Travellers must travel to earn their living, be it by scrap collection, hawking, or recycling waste. Travel is essential to our economic survival. (1994: 95)

The ethic of self-employment overrides the nature of the actual work which Travellers undertake:

> Being your own boss is the important thing — being free to fit your work into the often unpredictable demands of the extended family. What you actually work at is of very little importance; you look for opportunities and make the best of them. (1994: 95)

McDonagh echoed the research findings of Okely (1983) and Ní Shúinéar (1994) with his emphasis on the rejection of paid employment and the coterminous nature of Traveller work space and family space. Traveller and Gypsy history was one where they have:

> . . . refused to become proletarianised. In Britain's industrialised capitalist economy the Travellers are one of the few groups who have remained independent of one of its fundamental features: wage labour. Travellers only occasionally employ others and they have avoided being employees. . . . Self-employment is bound up with Gypsy identity. There is shame attached to a wage-labour job . . . (Okely, 1983: 53)

The nomadism of Travellers is part of a community identity which is based on kinship:

> Country people organise every aspect of their lives . . . on the fact of sedentarism, the fact that they live permanently side by side with a fixed group of people. Travellers . . . organise every aspect of their lives around family ties. . . . The Traveller's very identity requires "keeping in touch" and this in turn requires travel. (McDonagh, 1994: 98)

The support system provided by the family network is a "pull" factor for Traveller nomadism. McDonagh listed the avoidance of serious conflict when arguments arose as a "push" factor. Nomadism functioned in a dynamic way and was coterminous with the entire range of Traveller cultural values. Today the concept of nomadism is frequently referred to as the "nomadic mindset" because of the societal changes that have affected Travellers' travelling patterns. Liégeois (1987) referred to the importance of nomadism's psychological dimension for Travellers. Nomadism was also "a state of mind" (1987: 53). McDonagh (1994) pointed to the dangers and potential crises that accompanied the forced settlement that have characterised the Irish state's attempts to assimilate Travellers. The repression of nomadism resulted in such problems as a lack of suitable marriage partners, and the breakdown of social controls and extended family support systems: "The policy of forcing Travellers to stay put, and that in large, mixed groups, has eaten into Traveller social structure, economic base and cultural identity" (1994: 107). He quoted Liégeois's (1987) document *Gypsies and Travellers*, written for the Council of Europe:

> When travel becomes just a dream, a long-delayed dream for the Traveller, despair and its effects set in (illness, breakup of the family, aggressiveness and delinquency). The result is a crisis in the society . . . (1987: 54)

McDonagh's (1994) personal summation of the cultural significance of Traveller nomadism is both simple and powerful:

> Nomadism entails a way of looking at the world, a different way of perceiving things, a different attitude to accommodation, to work, to life in general. (1994: 1)

NOMADISM, SEDENTARISM AND RACISM

It can be argued that racism is a constant and pervasive theme in the literature on Travellers. Prejudice against Travellers is entrenched in Irish society. They have a pariah status (Gmelch, 1977); they live in "caste-like isolation" (McCarthy, 1971: 1). MacGréil's research into Irish prejudice (1977, 1996) chronicles a substantial deterioration in attitudes towards Travellers since the early 1970s. Irish Travellers are treated as a lower caste in society (1996). Many recent writers have categorised the discrimination affecting Travellers as racism (O'Connell, 1992a, 1997); Acton, Okely, Ní Shúinéar, McDonagh, McLoughlin and others in Ó Síocháin et al., 1994; MacLachlan and O'Connell, 1999). This view concurs with modern approaches to the concept of race whereby racism is no longer seen as referring to a class or group of people or as an elaborate method for classifying or arranging peoples (see Hannaford, 1996) but as something which is socially defined and constructed, socially imagined rather than pre-given and immutable (see Banton, 1998; Husband, 1982; Malik, 1996; Miles, 1989; etc.).

The bulk of the theoretical work on anti-Traveller racism has been undertaken by non-statutory organisations and community-based activist groups. Anti-Traveller racism has been addressed by Traveller organisations like the Irish Traveller Movement, Pavee Point and anti-racist organisations such as Harmony. However the issue of anti-Traveller racism has only been properly addressed in two main contexts. One context is that of explaining that a minority ethnic group such as Travellers experience racism. Another is the detailing of the different forms of racism that are experienced by Travellers.

This emphasis on advocacy has meant that the issue of anti-Traveller racism and why it happens remains relatively under-theorised. Acton (1994) has highlighted what he identifies as an inherent racism in the very nature of scholarly enquiry into the perceived distinctions between different groupings of Gypsies and Travellers. He argues that academic attempts to locate distinctions between different groups originate in a denial of the realities of slavery and genocide as inflicted on Gypsies/Travellers in both the sixteenth and twentieth centuries. He advises those interrogating the ascriptions by which nomadic people define themselves to remember the importance of understanding the nature and context of such definitions, and their fluidity, as and when imposed by Gypsies/Travellers themselves. What Gypsies/ Travellers are doing when they refer to themselves as one and not the other may depend on the context in which they find themselves and the dangers or opportunities inherent in such situations. In his earlier work Acton (1969) had discussed the way in which Travellers/Gypsies may have been manipulated. Their assertions regarding status ranking within groups – i.e. the ideal of the "true" Gypsy or inter-group status rankings – are also a protective mechanism in response to the influence of Gypsiology and the categorisation of Gypsies and Travellers into sub-groups as undertaken by the Gypsiologists of the Gypsy Lore Society:

> Gypsies certainly did learn some things from the "Romani Rais" (Romany "king" or "gentleman") which they incorporated into their own culture and fed back to later generations of Gypsiologists. Most Gypsies have a stereotype of their own about "a man

who's writing a book about Gypsies" and know just how to deal
with him. (1969: 90)

Ó hAodha (2002b) has discussed further the extent to which the racist
stereotype tradition of the "true" Gypsy lived on in Britain, in particular,
and the way in which it was manipulated not only by Travellers and
Gypsies but also by the settled authorities, often to the detriment of
Travellers and Gypsies in the area of public policy. Acton (1994) out-
lines how the racist legacy of Gypsiology and the ascription of "true"
Traveller or Gypsy status impacts on current debates regarding Irish
Traveller ethnicity when he says:

> The assertion that "Irish Travellers are not Gypsies" is also not
> without a political agenda. If the attribution of minority rights is
> predicated on a distinct ethnic identity, and the possession of a
> distinct ethnic identity is only allowed upon proof of "exotic"
> "racial" origins, then it can be argued that because Irish Travel-
> lers "are not Gypsies", they are therefore "not an ethnic group"
> and therefore discrimination against them is not racist and general
> arguments about the oppression of Gypsies by Europeans have no
> relevance. (1994: 40)

Historically, racism was associated with notions of "race" and attempts to
distinguish between groups of people on a biological basis. By ranking
different human groups hierarchically on the basis of alleged biological
characteristics it was possible to validate differential treatment. European
colonial discourse utilised the concept of "race" to justify the exploitation
of colonised peoples and their resources. Racist ideologies never alluded
to their real *raison d'être* which, according to McVeigh, was:

> ordering the world to make sense of it; ordering the world to ex-
> ploit it; ordering the world to control it. (1996: 10)

The logic of biologism as a justification for racism was questioned subsequent to the Second World War and the widespread slaughter of Gypsies, Jews, Slavs and Poles. It was found that there was no biological or
genetic basis that would explain the social differences between different
groups of people previously identified as "races". UNESCO issued a de-

finitive statement on the absence of scientific justification to support racist doctrines in 1967:

> racist doctrines lack any scientific basis whatsoever . . . racism falsely claims that there is a scientific basis for arranging groups hierarchically in terms of psychological and cultural characteristics that are immutable and innate. In this way it seeks to make existing differences appear inviolable as a means of permanently maintaining current relations between groups . . . racial prejudice and discrimination in the world today arise from historical and social phenomena and falsely claim the sanction of science. (Montagu, 1972: 160–3)

Despite this clear denunciation, older discourses of racism continue to have strong roots in modern culture, as the belief that the concept of race has no scientific validity has yet to permeate widely and has not been fully accepted as of yet in many cultural contexts. Even where the older biologist approach has been discarded, racism can still thrive in other forms, as McVeigh (1992a), one of the leading theorists of anti-Traveller racism, maintains:

> just because "race" has disappeared as a concept with explanatory efficacy there is no implication that racism can be simultaneously discarded — thus racism exists with or without biological notions of "race". (1992a: 357)

A new racism based on perceived cultural incompatibility has become prevalent with the recent widespread emigration from East to West and from Islamic countries to those countries that were traditionally Christian. This racism based on cultural incompatibility is not as immediately obvious or identifiable as the old biologistic form:

> . . . the new racism becomes less tangible than traditional racisms as other elements enter the discourse. (McVeigh 1992b: 357)

O'Connell (1994) alludes to the widespread tendency to deny the existence of racism "despite evidence of a racialisation process in both media and political discourse" (1994: 49). He traces the various phases or approaches of the Irish government to the Traveller issue. The assimilationist *Report of the Commission on Itinerancy* (1963) is followed by a revision in thinking on the question of absorption and settlement in the *Report of the Travelling People Review Body* (1985) a report in which O'Connell identifies "a great reluctance to name discrimination as an issue" (1994: 51). Extensive lobbying by Traveller support groups resulted in a change in the 1990s and the *Report of the Task Force on the Travelling Community* (1995) devotes a full section to the issue of discrimination in the areas of health, education, accommodation, training, youth service provision, culture and Traveller/settled relations. O'Connell finds a strong resistance among the Irish public to calling the treatment of Travellers racism. A mistaken tendency exists to define racism only in terms of skin colour, a tendency which has increasingly been refuted by academics such as Husband (1982). Instead racism is:

> more than a prejudicial attitude. It involves a pattern of social relations, structures and an ideological discourse which reflects unequal power between groups. (O'Connell, 1994: 53)

Racism includes an ideology of superiority in O'Connell's view, an ideology that rationalises the oppression of another group. While it involves the perpetuation of negative stereotypes and assumptions it constitutes more than simply a set of attitudes. It is also an *"abuse of power by one group over another group"* (1994: 55). O'Connell (1994) sketches the racialisation process as it applies through the Irish media by reference to some recent newspaper articles about Travellers, all of which imply the inferiority of Travellers. He examines how racism impinges on Travellers' daily lives in terms of accommodation, social welfare and educational provision. As part of this discussion he outlines the strategies by which Traveller support groups can combat racism including the development of national and pan-national alliances with other minority ethnic groups, which can increasingly be fostered through the auspices of the European Union. McVeigh (1997) highlights the specificity of anti-Traveller racism by calling it sedentarism. Sedentarism is:

> that system of ideas and practices which serves to normalise and reproduce sedentary modes of existence and pathologise and repress nomadic modes of existence. (1997: 3)

Sedentarism is in one sense a new racism. As a new racism it highlights particular aspects of another culture, aspects which are rendered pathological, dangerous or non-productive. In its highlighting of perceived incompatibility between the sedentary and nomadic modes of existence it is a more subtle but equally invidious form of racism. Sedentarism is also an old racism because contemporary moral panics about Travellers, Gypsies and more recently New Age Travellers draw on very old phenomena. McVeigh (1997) argues that sedentarism can only be understood with reference to the past because the contemporary pathologising of nomadism draws on:

> a long history of establishment fears about the travelling dispossessed and the threat they pose to the moral and political order. (1997: 2)

Contemporary anti-Traveller racism incorporates a legitimation of repression based on a series of pathologising stereotypes that render Travellers problematic and culturally incompatible. In this view, Travellers are:

> criminals by "nature", they come from outside the community, they are dirty, they are dishonest, they are immoral and amoral, and, most importantly, they are "nomadic". (McVeigh, 1997: 2)

It can be argued that stereotypes regarding those who live a nomadic lifestyle have achieved a fixed status with the advent of the modern nation-state. The pre-modern era saw those who were nomadic as an external threat because state-formation was in its infancy:

> states in process of formation feared spies and trouble makers, migrants and marginal groups. Gypsies regarded as a threat in this context, became the focus of suspicion (McVeigh, 1987: 89)

Modern anti-Travellerism as made manifest in sedentarism increasingly views the nomadic threat as an internal one according to McVeigh (1997). The second half of the twentieth century has seen virtually every European state enact stricter legal controls on Travellers and their nomadism (see Acton, 1974; Hancock, 1987; Kenrick and Puxon, 1972):

> If modernism was about ordering and controlling, then the nation-
> state became the key mechanism for securing order and control.
> And no-one threatened the emerging hegemony more than the
> nomad whose mode of existence was the very antithesis of this
> project. (McVeigh, 1997: 13)

McVeigh considers contemporary anti-nomadism to be a reflection of a
historical juncture when there was a "much more real and extensive
'threat' posed by nomads to sedentary societies" (1997: 7) and cites the
work of writers such as Khazanov (1995) and Chatwin (1987) as further
evidence for the threat that sedentary societies once felt from nomads.
Prejudice against Travellers because of their nomadism cannot be simply
explained away as the pathologising of a group who are different. It is also
indicative of an unease which lies at the heart of the evolution of the modern state. While nomadism is today regarded as an anachronism this was
not always the case. McVeigh points out the likelihood that the seden-
tary/nomad distinction was much more ambiguous at certain junctures in
the past and "it is possible that everyone was semi-nomadic" (1997: 5).
The transition from nomadism to sedentarism that accompanied modernity
and the nation-state was not as successful as is sometimes thought and
"there is much evidence to suggest that the transition was actually associated with a profound sense of loss and unease" (1997: 7). McVeigh alludes
to biblical myths such as the story of the Fall, myths which concern no-
madic/sedentary difference and whose subtext reveals a sense of loss and
envy among the sedentarised majority in society. Developments in agricul-
ture required sedentarisation and introduced the concept of organised and
scheduled work into social life. As McVeigh (1997) argues, these developments ensured a more secure food supply but they also "entailed the end
of nomadic freedom — the expulsion from the Garden of Eden" (1997: 8).

Contemporary constructions, as incorporated in media impressions of
Travellers, sometimes depict Travellers as living a life that is easy and
replete with freedom — "a free and easy life" — when the reality is that
sedentary repression and discrimination has resulted in the exact opposite. This is another indicator of this sense of unease on the part of the
sedentarised. McVeigh argues that sedentarism is and was much more
than an explanation for often-localised anti-Traveller racism. Nomadism
was often the justification for the brutal repressive measures that accom-

panied the colonisation of indigenous peoples. The logic of sedentarism is "not simply to repress or discriminate against nomads but to get rid of them altogether" (1997: 16), whether this is achieved by sympathetic assimilation or repressive extermination.

The sympathetic assimilation that has characterised the policies of many European countries since the 1950s and 1960s is presented in a more humane and less overtly anti-nomadic manner. However, the sedentarist aims of these policies, as encompassed through forced settlements, have as their intention a similar outcome:

> Nomadism in itself might no longer be expressly prohibited, but legislative systems designed for settled society could have much the same effect. (Fraser, 1992: 283)

Sedentarism and repression may simply have assumed a different form. The *Porraimos* or Romany Holocaust (1941–1945), where up to 1,500,000 Roma were killed, was the nadir of the then-frequent attempts by European states to exterminate, sterilise or deport all Travellers and Gypsies within their borders. Consequently McVeigh underlines the importance of theorising the roots of sedentarism and anti-Traveller racism in Europe:

> It is important to remember that anti-nomad prejudice and discrimination has been (and remains potentially) a prelude to genocide. (1997: 13)

The theorisation of anti-Traveller racism in a European context has been accompanied by a new theorisation of the way in which Travellers have been constructed in Ireland, particularly since the foundation of the Irish state (MacLaughlin, 1995; Helleiner, 2000). MacLaughlin (1995) links the exclusionary discourse as applied to Irish Travellers to similar discourses in the history of European nationalism and colonialism. He argues that the bourgeois nationalism of nineteenth-century Ireland deliberately constructed the Travelling community as the "Other", intentionally excluding the same community from Irish identity as defined by the emerging state.

> On the one hand, Irish nationalism, simply considered as a strug-
> gle for control of territory, has striven to control population and
> to produce an Irish "people" as a political community. On the
> other hand the Irish nation was forged as a historical system of
> exclusions and dominations. It became a place where the patriar-
> chal values of the rural bourgeoisie occupied pride of place . . .
> (MacLaughlin, 1995: 72).

An anti-Traveller racism that was once "deeply embedded in the social
fabric and agrarian history of Ireland" (1995: 73) has acquired new ad-
herents in Irish towns and villages with the increased urbanisation of Ireland. This racism, like sedentarism, is rooted in the belief that the way of
life of Travellers is an anachronism and a throwback to a less civilised
era in Irish history. It is this racism, McLaughlin argues, that is at the
root of the economic, social and geographical exclusion of Travellers
from Irish society.

Helleiner (2000), an anthropologist, uses archival research as well as
existing biographies to reconstruct aspects of the history of Irish anti-
Traveller racism. She also analyses how Travellers have engaged with this
racism which acts to exclude them while simultaneously working to recreate their own identity and distinctive way of life within the constraints
which society imposes on them. She reconstructs the directions taken by
anti-Traveller racism from the turn of the century to the period of her
fieldwork, which she undertook while living in a Traveller halting site in
Galway city between 1986 and 1987. She argues that the true nature of the
historical relationship between the Travelling and settled communities has
been obscured by the tendency on the part of settled community spokespeople and political representatives "to collapse the past into an ever-
receding present" (2000: 50). She also questions the claims by these representatives that tensions between Travellers and non-Travellers are a relatively recent phenomenon. The ongoing denial of a longer history of anti-
Traveller prejudice has supported "dominant models of an anti-racist and
homogeneous post-colonial Irish nation" (2000: 52).

In addition to examining the dynamics of this prejudice within a
modern socio-anthropological framework, Helleiner interrogates the
ways in which anti-Traveller racism has been historically produced and
reproduced within the wider processes of colonialism, nation-building

and capitalist development. In her discussion of these processes she particularly explores how anti-Traveller racism was articulated within the wider constructions and social relations engendered by class, generation and gender. She locates anti-class-based Traveller racism within the context of changing agrarian relations within Ireland at the end of the nineteenth century and the attendant emergence of a nationalism associated with what Foster termed "rural embourgeoisement" (1988: 439)

Using ethnographic and archival sources which relate to Galway, Helleiner discusses anti-Travellerism as it related to the implementation of settlement policy for Travellers in the city, policy which was a feature of most Irish cities. She argues that conflicts over land use were the instigation for the development and imposition of settlement policies for Travellers in Galway and in the Irish state generally. She situates the state's introduction and development of a comprehensive national Traveller settlement policy in the 1960s within the context of the opening up of the Irish economy to global capitalism and the Irish Government's political project of economic and social "modernisation" as associated with the *First Programme for Economic Expansion* of 1958. Helleiner also finds that class-related interests and the interests of property owners in particular had a large bearing on the how the settlement policy was implemented in Galway, particularly in relation to the speed of settlement and the location of Traveller accommodation.

Relations of class amongst Travellers themselves also had a large bearing on the discourse and implementation of settlement. Traveller patterns of mobility and accommodation complicated the dominant discourse, which equated housing with settlement and camping with mobility, and this complexity was frequently a hindrance to Traveller mobilisation on a political level. Anti-Travellerism was at its most fundamental level motivated by the twin drivers of class and self-interest, particularly as relating to the interests of the propertied class, but the true nature of this anti-Travellerism as fostered by local and national politicians was hidden behind political rhetoric which identified Travellers as a threat to non-class-based categories, including "urban" or "rural" dwellers or "women and children" and the "social order" of the Irish state itself.

Helleiner drew upon feminist theory to examine how early anti-Traveller discourse constructed the alleged Traveller threat in terms of a masculinised Traveller population threatening non-Traveller women in their homes. Anti-Traveller racism in the political sphere also had a strong basis in the rhetorical construction of Traveller childhood. A re-curring theme in the discourse of anti-Travellerism was couched in terms of helping Traveller children who were victims of a harsh and primitive lifestyle. Politicians advocated intervention into the Traveller problem and increased control of Travellers so that Traveller children might avoid becoming victims of a harsh adult Traveller lifestyle of camping and mobility.

Anti-Traveller racism in Helleiner's view is an example of a long-standing and endogenous Irish racism, one which predates the more re-cent rise in anti-immigrant and refugee racism. Travellers differ from colonised indigenous populations elsewhere because they have not been constructed as racially "Other". Stories relating to the question of Travel-ler origins told about and by Travellers have however focused not on "where" they are from so much as on "when" and "why" they emerged as a distinct group within Ireland. This emphasis on the "when" and the "why" has meant that the imputed origins of Travellers as incorporated in the many differing origins accounts have often been "deeply stigmatis-ing" and thus central to the reproduction of anti-Traveller racism (Helleiner, 2000: 30).

Chapter 6

Otherness and the Construction of "Difference"

THE "OTHER": SOME THEORETICAL PERSPECTIVES

The concept of the "Other" or Otherness has been analysed through a range of varied discourses including the historical, the socio-cultural, the anthropological, the psychoanalytic (see Freud, 1938, 1950a, 1950b, 1957, for example), the linguistic and the philosophical (see Lévinas, 1996; Volf, 1996). While the question of the "Other" or Otherness may have not have been a term which carried much significance in Irish academic circles during the 1950s and 1960s when folklorists such as Seán McGrath were writing, it can be said with little fear of contradiction that it was the search for Otherness, albeit Irish and Gaelic and primarily through the reclamation of the folklore and tradition-rich heritage of Ireland's Irish-speaking regions, which was in reality the fundamental impulse underpinning much of the valuable work undertaken by the Irish Folklore Commission and its devoted collectors.

"Othering", "difference" and how difference is constructed came to the fore as a question in Cultural Studies particularly during the second half of the twentieth century. It is an issue with which social and academic analysts continue to have a strong engagement, partly as a consequence of the increasingly globalised nature of the world, one where human migration is an issue of considerable social and political significance.

Of particular interest to academics who have recognised the importance of this question of Otherness has been a re-engagement with the manner whereby aspects of the Enlightenment and the formation of European/Western identity were heavily predicated on the articulation and creation of the "Other". This analysis has included an examination of the role which ideology (see Eagleton, 1991; Said, 1993) played in the internalisation of values that accompanied colonialism and the legitimisation of ideas about the "Other" so that these ideas appeared "natural".

Many theorists have identified the concept of Otherness and "difference" as essential to the very question of meaning itself. Otherness and the way in which "otherness" or "difference" elucidates meaning has dominated French thought especially, where a linguistic and structural analysis of otherness was attempted by de Saussure at the turn of the twentieth century. French analyses of Otherness have focused on the philosophic, the linguistic and the psychoanalytic, in particular. De Saussure (1915) Lacan (1977) and Derrida (1974, 1978, 1982) all became dominant influences on the cultural movements known as structuralism and post-structuralism, movements for which the analysis of the relational and binary aspects of the question of Otherness were of primary importance.

The French theorisation of the Otherness question highlighted the necessity for "difference", a difference without which meaning itself cannot exist. Meaning depends on the difference between opposites, particularly those oppositions which are binary e.g. black/white, masculine/feminine, etc. It is possible to understand what black means, because it can be contrasted with its opposite — white. This view of "difference" or "otherness" as an element of the human condition which exists prior to meaning came to dominate the thought of many intellectuals who attempted to theorise and conceptualise not only Otherness but the question of the human psyche and its very relationship with society in the twentieth century (See Cixous, 1975; Kristeva, 1982, 1991; Lacan, 1977).

Lacan outlined the complexities inherent in any attempt to map the self, the Other and their relationship with reality as produced in any linguistic text. For Derrida, the complexities of the self meant that attempts to define meaning based on the difference between opposites were fraught with the dangers of over-simplification and reductionism. Derrida (1974) attempted to deconstruct the binary oppositions upon which much of Western literary and philosophical debate had been premised and showed that a relationship of power was inherent within the nature of these binaries. Hall (1997) outlined Derrida's deconstruction of these power relationships in the following manner:

> There is always a relation of power between the poles of a binary opposition (Derrida, 1974). We should really write white/black, men/women, masculine/feminine, upper class/ lower class, British/alien to capture this power dimension in discourse. (1997: 235)

The theorisation of the "Other" as incorporated through the dialogue that is language was examined by the Russian linguist Mikhail Bakhtin. For Bakhtin the "Other" was essential to meaning because of the dialogic nature of human interaction. Meaning was dialogic because everything we say or mean is modified by the interaction with another person or "the Other". "The Other" was essential to meaning because:

> the word in language is half someone else's. It becomes "one's own" only when . . . the speaker appropriates the word, adapting it to his own semantic expressive intention. (Bakhtin, 1981 [1935]: 293–4)

Psychoanalytic theory's emphasis on the formation of the self also provided certain insights into the formation of "the Other" and the dialectical relationship that exists between the "self" and "the Other" (see Freud's "object relations theory" (1938)), with a particular emphasis being placed on the unconscious dialogue that takes place between the self and the "Other", an internalised dialogue which much psychoanalytic theory considered flawed and incomplete. Psychoanalytic theory was used by scholars such as Fanon (1986) to explain racism, arguing that a high proportion of racial stereotyping and violence against the other had its roots in the refusal of the white "Other" to give due recognition to the black person, or he who had come from "the place of the other" (see Bhabha, 1996; Hall, 1997). Perhaps the most significant contribution of psychoanalytic theory to the debate concerning Otherness, however, lies in the insights it furnished into boundary mechanisms and their formation, an area that continues to be explored in the discipline of anthropology. Douglas (1966) and Kristeva (1982) described the negative feelings which accrue from boundary subversion and the disturbance of what is a perceived set cultural order.

Kristeva and fellow French scholar Cixous (1975) also used the concept of the "Other" to theorise on gender relations and what they saw as the primarily troubling discourse that is the binary opposition of man/woman. For Cixous the founding binary opposition of the couple man/woman was an exemplar of the sexist hierarchisation that constituted much of Western thought. Anthropologist Mary Douglas drew on sociological research into symbolic systems by the French scholar Emile Durkheim (1938, 1964) and the French anthropologist Claude Lévi-Strauss (1964, 1971) to argue that social groups impose meaning on the world by organising and classifying things into particular groups. The notion of the "Other" was fundamental to this classification process as it was normally defined in the form of binary oppositions.

A disturbance of this cultural order was inevitable when hybridity manifested itself, a disturbance applied particularly to materials or groups who were to be liminal or whose status appeared ambiguous. Groups such as Travellers or mulattoes who belonged to the mainstream and were at the same time liminal to it were seen to inhabit an indeterminate, unstable or dangerous cultural locus. Since stable or mainstream cultures required that groups stay in their appointed or classified position they imposed symbolic boundaries to keep their categories "pure" and reinforce their own meaning and identity. Douglas argued that the response to the transgression of these symbolic boundaries or taboos was an attempt to eradicate that which was considered impure, dirty or out of place. The mainstream society attempted to drive away that which it perceived as impure or abnormal.

This idea was developed further by Kristeva (1982) who saw this rejection in terms of a retreat that was in essence an attempt at purification. Many cultures simply retreated from or exhibited alienating tendencies towards the "Other" who took the form of foreigners, intruders or those "others" who were perceived as different and outside the norm. Babcock (1978) further developed this theorisation by analysing the seminal role of the symbolic in boundary relations between that which is considered a "normal" part of the cultural order and that which is considered "outside" or Other. Her insights can be seen to be particularly pertinent to the question of Settled/Traveller relations as evidenced in Ireland. Babcock argued that the double-bind inherent in symbolic boundaries was central to all cultural reproduction since its taboo nature made the "Other" both attractive and repellent at the same time:

> . . . symbolic boundaries are central to all culture. Marking "dif-
> ference" leads us, symbolically, to close ranks, shore up culture
> and to stigmatise and expel anything which is defined as impure,
> abnormal. However, paradoxically, it also makes "difference"
> powerful, strangely attractive precisely because it is forbidden,
> taboo, threatening to cultural order . . . what is socially peripheral
> is often symbolically centred. (1978: 32)

While the question of Otherness has been theorised across a range of cultural dynamics, particularly as it applies within the realm of the symbolic,
less attention has been paid to the way in which theories of the "self" and
"other" link to particular cultural and national contexts and within discourses such as racism, colonialism and post-colonialism. What is very
evident in the work of theorists who have written on the question of the
"Other" is the primarily negative or disruptive attribution which the
"Other" holds in the development of Western thought. Cultural identities
such as those which depict the Traveller, the Jew or the migrant as "Other"
have been formed and legitimated through a complex process that incorporates the representation of these cultural types in both myth and historical
discourse. Historical discourse, it can be argued, tends towards the specifi-
cation of social identities while at the same time frequently presenting
these cultural identities in a manner which appears fixed, pre-given or immutable. Yet it can be argued that identity itself is a form of myth. Historians like Healy (1992) have highlighted the problematic that is the concept
of identity as presented through historical discourse:

> History is not some unmediated story of events. It is a construct,
> often a narrative of interested parties who seek to prove a thesis
> of how events have been shaped. (1992: 15)

The "Other" as constructed in the neo-conservative Western European
tradition has generally been perceived in negative terms. The culture of
the "Other" ("their culture") is perceived as different from that of the
"us" in a myriad of ways including religion, race, behaviour, language,
age, gender, etc., traits that generally embody negativity as defined by
the fictive homogeneity that is the "us".

Contemporary studies of the "Other" as situated within a historical or
materialist context draw to a large extent on Edward Said's (1978, 1986,

1993) work on Orientalism. In this work the relationship between the Orient and the Western world rests on a discursive formation of the Orient as "Other", a formation that was invested in both materially and culturally by the colonial powers of the West. The creation of the "Other" as a zone of differentiation was in many ways the means by which an identity for Europe was created and installed. "Nations themselves are narrations" wrote Said in his book *Culture and Imperialism* (1993: xiii). The formation of colonial and imperial attitudes towards the Orient was one of the methods used by both the colonisers and the colonised "to assert their own identity and the existence of their own history" (1993: xiii). European culture and politics cooperated in the nineteenth and early twentieth century to justify the colonial project so that the identity of Europe and the Western world was, in many ways, articulated and installed through the creation of the "Other".

Adorno and Horkheimer (1973) used both Marxist and psychoanalytic theory to explain the central role that the Enlightenment project played in the construction of the "Other", the development of the "nation-state" and the establishment of European identity through a process of differentiation. In *Dialectic of Enlightenment* (1972), they exposed the double-bind which, as they perceived it, lay at the very heart of the Enlightenment project. The Enlightenment advocated humanism, universalism, rationalism and the virtue of reason. However, reason, as theorised by Adorno and Horkheimer, was a two-edged sword. It was the instrument through which humanity could free itself from nature and yet it was simultaneously the means by which Europe subjected the "Other" to domination. The Enlightenment spawned both the rational and the irrational as exemplified in "new" and discriminatory attitudes towards "Others" such as a range of migratory peoples and the Jews.

> The Enlightenment of modern times advanced from the very beginning under the banner of radicalism; this distinguishes it from any of the earlier stages of demythologisation. When a new mode of social life allowed room for a new religion and a way of thinking, the overthrow of the old classes, tribes and nations was usually accompanied by that of the old gods. But especially when a nation (the Jews, for example) was brought by its own destiny to change to activities, and objects of worship were magically trans-

formed into cracies, derided and execrated character traits may be deciphered as the marks of the violent outset of this or that stage of progress in human flesh, the suspicion of fanaticism, laziness and poverty, behaviours which were metamorphosed from the adequate and necessary into abominations. This is the line both of destruction and civilisation. (1972: 62)

While promulgated as a "civilising" and "radical" project the Enlightenment was also conservative. While all peoples could, in theory, share power, the new democracy was predicated on the premise that they abided by the rules that defined the dominant group. Rules were used to define and construct the "Other", a process which elucidates the heavy debt that Western imperialism owes to the philosophy of the Enlightenment. Imperialism as implemented by the West involved the creation of a myth about the coloniser and the colonised, a myth that included the personae of the "us" (the coloniser) and the "them" (the colonised). By focusing on a range of individual works which defined the Orient, Said (1993) analysed the manner in which the Western powers overcame some of the resistance to their colonising projects. He found that a mutually enhancing relationship had been created between culture and the imposition of empire whereby countries engaged in imperialistic projects defined the superior culture as belonging to the dominant nation or state, differentiating the "us" from the "them" with an accompanying xenophobia. Culturally, this was achieved through the concept of the "Other", a process whereby the colonised country was represented through the language and ideas of the coloniser. Said (1986) says that the colonised were left:

> to assert a dignified self-identity in opposition to a discourse which defines them as, variously, barbarian, pagan, ape, female; but always subordinate and inferior. (1986: 7)

Eagleton (1991) elucidated the power of ideology in the internalisation of imperial values by subject peoples, a process that achieved a certain legitimacy because of its being made to appear natural, universal, obvious and unquestionable. Ideology, incorporating the coloniser/colonised myth, justified imperialism, an imperialism that was frequently couched in terms of a religious, moral, or civilising enterprise.

What persuades men and women to mistake each other from time
to time for gods or vermin is ideology. (Eagleton, 1991: xiii)

The written record of the coloniser often depicted the colonised as being
grateful for the imperialist project which had "saved" them from barbarism
or oppression. The imposition of imperialistic ideology and myth was also
achieved by the constant repetition of certain national representations and
stereotypes, as happened in the case of Ireland and the Irish people.

THE "ANTI-IRISH TRADITION": A BRIEF OVERVIEW

The discursive image of Travellers as defined by the "settled" community cannot be divorced from a tradition of anti-Irish prejudice that has
strong roots in the colonial history of Ireland. As Irish people Travellers
were subject to the same cultural conditioning and discursive stereotyping as others. The colonial tradition made no distinction between Travellers and other Irish people with the result that Travellers remained
largely invisible in the historical record. Modern-day debates concerning
Travellers' cultural legitimacy and Travellers' rights return almost in-
variably to the question of Travellers origins and what evidence is available in Irish historical records. The most prevalent view of Travellers'
origins also situates them firmly within the framework of Ireland's colonial history. More often than not they are considered to be a people who
left a previously settled existence as a consequence of the dislocation
that was an inevitable outcome of the colonial project. The negative
stereotyping of Irish Travellers which became dominant in the public
discourse of the latter part of the twentieth century in particular can ar-
guably be viewed as an extension of a deeply inculcated anti-Irish tradition, a more extreme version of the anti-Irish "Othering" tradition which
existed during the centuries of British colonisation. The "Othering" of
Irish Travellers as evidenced in modern Ireland can, as with the Othering
of groups such as the Jews in Europe, also be linked to the formation of
the new nation-state in Ireland.

A process whereby the Irish people came face-to-face with the self-
definition of their national identity occurred with the formation of the
new nation-state in twentieth-century Ireland. A very deliberate political
agenda had underwritten representations of Ireland, as produced by the

British, and as current in the pre-independence era. The British had "translated" the Irish using self-interested representations that were primarily negative and essentialist. Curtis (1984) and Peart (2002) have demonstrated the way in which the agents of English colonisation had both the power and authority to impose a representation of the "Other" on the Irish that was self-interested. From the earliest times, nomadism, beggary, backwardness, superstition (later Popery), anarchy, sexual profligacy and violence have been portrayed as general characteristics of the Irish by those who "othered" them. Strabo, whose geography dates from the first century AD and who wrote in the classical literary tradition of the time, used elements of fantasy that depicted Ireland in a pejorative light. Some of the earliest critical views of the Irish were a consequence of the Church's wish to establish greater orthodoxy in practice throughout Western Europe. This became intermeshed with more materialist, colonial ambitions. Leerssen (1996) outlines how the bull *Laudabiliter* issued by Pope Adrian IV in 1155 acted to condone English territorial ambitions in Ireland. The desire to reform Irish morals and imbue Irish Church affairs with increased orthodoxy meant that the English presence in Ireland under the stewardship of Henry II was envisaged as a lesser evil:

> *[ut pro dilatandis ecclesie terminis, pro vicorium restringendo decursu, pro corrigendis moribus et virtutibus inserendis, pro Christiane religionis augmento, insulam ille ingrediaris.]*

> (that you should enter that island for the purpose of enlarging the boundaries of the church, checking the descent into wickedness, correcting morals and implanting virtues, and encouraging the growth of the faith in Christ). (Cited in Leerssen, 1996: 34)

Negative attitudes on religious grounds towards indigenous Church structures were common justifications for conquest and persecution at this juncture in Europe generally. The works of the Anglo-Norman churchman Giraldus Cambrensis who wrote his treatises *Topographica Hibernica* and *Expugnatio Hibernica* in the late 1180s acted as a religious justification for the invasion of Ireland. In much the same way as Grellmann, Cambrensis created a prototype of the negative Irish "other" that was to last for centuries. His taxonomy of the cultural attributes which defined the typical Irish person cast a long shadow over English perceptions of the Irish. He considered the Irish to be inferior in every respect to their Norman colonisers and classified their barbarity in both economic and social terms. He considered the nomadic pastoral (herding) economy of the Irish to be inferior to that of their English counterparts and castigated their social customs, including their sense of dress and their preference for beards and long hair. The marriage customs and religious practices of the Irish came in for particular condemnation, indicating that he found it necessary to undermine the widespread European view of Ireland as a centre for civilisation and learning:

> This is a filthy people, wallowing in vice. Of all peoples it is the least instructed in the rudiments of the faith. They do not pay tithes or first fruits or contract marriages. They do not avoid incest. (Cited in Curtis, 1984: 5)

Other characteristic tenets of the Irish character in Giraldus's view were their animal-like natures, including slyness, nomadism, treachery and a repugnance for rules. It is fascinating to observe the consistency with which such stereotypes, as applied to Irish people generally, were subsequently transferred from the majority Irish population onto the Traveller "Other":

> This people then is one of forest-dwellers and inhospitable; a people living off beasts and like beasts; a people that yet adheres to the most primitive way of pastoral living. For as humanity progresses from the forest to the arable fields, and thence towards village life and civil society, this people, spurning agricultural exertions, having all too little regard for material comfort and a positive dislike of the rules and legalities of civil intercourse, has been able neither to give up nor to abandon the life of forests and pastures which it has hitherto been living. (Cited in Leersen, 1996: 35)

These aforementioned traits all coalesced in a reductionist archetype of the Irish as an essentially corrupt and sensual people who had an inherited propensity for degeneracy.

In addition to being considered barbarous and uncontrollable, the Irish were also represented as morally suspect and criminally deviant in the writings of those tasked with the colonial project, including Sir Philip

Sidney and the poet Edmund Spenser. Sidney damned the entire Irish populace in the following terms:

> Surely there was never people that lived in more misery than they do, not it should seem of worse minds, for matrimony among them is not regarded in effect than an conjunction between unreasonable beasts, perjury, robbery and murder counted allowable. Finally, I cannot find that they have any conscience of sin; for neither find I a place where it should be done, nor any person able to instruct them in the rules of a Christian. (Cited in Johnson, 1980: 15)

Discursive techniques as outlined by Said in *Orientalism* and as employed in stereotypes such as those promulgated by Sidney can be seen as part of a technique employed to subdue the colonised. By describing the colonised through the use of rigid representations which depicted them as inferior, it seemed possible to "know" the Irish and "manage" them in some way. Knowledge and power were inextricably linked in this form of stereotyping, which also served to strengthen the self-image of the coloniser and justify the colonial project in terms of intervention and civilisation.

The subduing of the resistance on the part of the colonised often entailed brutality and killing. Resistance to colonisation on the part of the Munster Irish, whether military or cultural — in the form of the maintenance of Gaelic customs — was met with murder, as outlined by Sir Humphrey Gilbert, military governor of Munster and a half-brother of the better-known Sir Walter Raleigh. Those massacred included many travellers and poets amongst the large population for whom nomadism was a normal part of the Gaelic way of life:

> I slew all those from time to time that did belong to, feed, accompany or maintain any outlaws or traitors; and after my first summoning of a castle or fort, if they would not presently yield it, I would not take it afterwards of their gift, but won it perforce — how many lives soever it cost; putting man, woman and child to the sword. (Cited in Ranelagh, 1981: 86)

Said outlines the dehumanisation that accompanied the "knowing" gaze of the coloniser. This dehumanisation "justified" colonisation under the cloak of benevolent interference whereby a morally superior "race" codified a knowledge bank of ideas about a supposedly "inferior" "race", a "justification" that legitimated extermination in much the same terms as the Nazi Holocaust of the mid-twentieth century:

> . . . this Eurocentric culture relentlessly codified and observed everything about the non-European world or presumably peripheral world, in so thorough and detailed a manner as to leave no item untouched, no culture unstudied, no people and land unclaimed. All of the subjugated peoples had it in common that they were considered to be naturally subservient to a superior, advanced, developed, and morally mature Europe, whose role in the non-European world was to rule, instruct, legislate, develop and at the proper times, to discipline, war against and occasionally exterminate non-Europeans. (Said in Mariani et al., 1989: 6)

The English historian Christopher Hill links the rationalisation of English colonisation in Ireland between the fifteenth and seventeenth centuries with more modern examples of ethnic cleansing and the imposition of new forms of "civilisation":

> A great number of civilised Englishmen of the propertied class in the seventeenth century spoke of Irishmen in tones not far removed from those which Nazis used about Slavs, or white South Africans use about the original inhabitants of their country. In each case the contempt rationalised a desire to exploit. (1970: 113)

The eighteenth century saw the continuation of the Irish stereotype tradition as outlined by leading British intellectuals as a justification for colonisation and exploitation. Peart (2002) links this pattern to an internal dynamic evident in the cultural conditioning that was imposed on Ireland. Ireland and the Irish were viewed in terms of English cultural images that were considered negative — i.e. wild, uncontrollable, barbaric — mirror-images which emanated from the English hierarchical system. The English upper classes, who were the creators and controllers of this discourse, also had little time for the working class in their own country. Historian John Plumb (1969) described English eighteenth-century attitudes towards the working class in the following terms: "It was a general conviction that the working man was a savage, unprincipled brute" (1969: 158).

The English upper class frequently ascribed their alleged superiority to their ancestry and their supposedly superior bloodlines. The nineteenth century also saw the advent of "scientific" theories of racism, theories which accompanied the British expansion into areas like the British West Indies, Canada, South Africa, Australia and India. The idea of Anglo-Saxon superiority was increasingly seen in terms of pseudo-scientific theories of race as promulgated by scholars and intellectuals and as accompanying movements such as Gypsiology (described in Chapter 1 of this book). Nineteenth-century theorists divided the human population into a hierarchy of "races", frequently on the basis of external physical features. External features were said to hold the clue not only to physically inherited differences but also to differences in terms of "nature" or "character". Inevitably, Anglo-Saxons were placed at the top of this hierarchy with allegedly more inferior races such as the Celts and the Jews further down. At the bottom of the hierarchy were races such as black people, Gypsies and Travellers. The binaries which accompanied colonial justifications for the "civilisation" and takeover of certain peoples were part and parcel of these bizarre hierarchies. Anglo-Saxons were symbolic of traits such as thoughtfulness, emotional restraint and a propensity for abiding by the law and clean living. On the other end of the scale, less highly-ranked races such as the Celts were described by anatomists such as John Knox in terms such as the following:

> Furious fanaticism; a love of war and disorder; a hatred for order and patient industry; no accumulative habits; restless, treacherous and uncertain . . . (Cited in Curtis, 1968: 70)

English contempt for the Irish was a part of a continuum that included the advent of a figure known in theatrical circles as the Stage Irishman, a discursive character that was to become the vehicle for the portrayal of Irish people by both Anglo-Irish and English playwrights for the two centuries prior to Irish independence. The stock character of the Stage Irishman portrayed the Irish as ingratiating rogues who encompassed a range of vices including laziness, cunning, drunkenness and mendacity. As with similar archetypal representations of the Irish in previous centuries this figure was trapped within a range of pre-determined character traits that emanated from a very old and consistent discursive tradition. The Stage Irishman was a character who performed as outlined by the discursive tradition. He was both wild and unreliable and exuded an ungovernability that was a further justification for the exploitation that accompanied the English colonial presence in Ireland. That this anti-Irish "Othering" discourse was exceptionally successful is attested to by Curtis (1984) who examined the evolution of anti-Irish "Othering", culminating in the infiltration or "naturalisation" of this discourse within the fabric of the English language itself. Curtis notes that "The very word Irish is enough to provoke roars of laughter from television studio audiences, and is used in everyday conversation to describe behaviour that is confusing or illogical" (1984: 45). Words like "paddywagon" and phrases like "throw a paddy" or "take the mickey" all attest to the internalisation of anti-Irishness within English so that this discourse has been naturalised within both English and Irish society.

By tracing the stereotype tradition that locates Irish identity within a reductionist framework, I have endeavoured to examine the way in which notions of English "identity" relied on representations of the Irish as the English "not-self". The subaltern position of the Irish in this discourse resulted in their demonisation as a consequence of being discursively constructed according to a series of endemic binarisms. A discursive technique such as that outlined here employs inequities in representational power and stereotypes which become reified so as to perpetuate a sense of absolute difference between the coloniser and the colonised. The reiteration of this stereotyping process for hundreds of years morally strengthened the colonialist enterprise through the continual representation of the colonised as fundamentally inferior. This discursive tradition can be seen as a form of cultural conditioning, one which inculcated an ideology of domination. Eagleton (1991) explained the process whereby ideology acts to legitimise a form of domination by a political power intent on promoting "beliefs and values congenial to it . . ." (1991: 5). The dominant power achieved this objective both by naturalising/universalising certain beliefs so that they assumed the status of universal truths and through the denigration and exclusion of any counter-hegemonic ideas that served as a challenge. The universalisation and inculcation of the values of the dominant group utilises the power of sub-conscious thought by incorporating enticing ideas that are constantly re-peated. Tolson (1996) outlines the role of the unconscious in the inculca-tion of ideology on the part of a subject people:

> Ideology (is) as much unconscious as conscious, as much irra-tional as rational. That is, if ideology consists of arguments, con-taining propositions, these don't simply take the form of ideas which we may or may not find convincing. They also have the force of repeated patterns of behaviour in which we more or less unthinkingly participate. (1996: 163)

Ideology's reliance on repeated patterns as encompassed in a reductionist stereotyping tradition is evidenced in writings on the subject of Ireland and the Irish from Cambrensis's twelfth-century religiously motivated images to the bizarre racialist categorisations of Knox in the nineteenth century. These writers created a myth which pertained to themselves (the dominant group) and those Others (those they considered subordinate such as the Irish and those people who were considered inferior on the hierarchical scale). This myth was reiterated constantly so that it became a form of cultural hegemony, internalised by coloniser and colonised alike. That this "constructed" myth was exceptionally successful was due in no small measure to the reiterative nature of this form of cultural he-gemony, a form of hegemony that came to be transferred to other subal-tern groups when the project of colonisation had ended. As Gramsci (1971) put it, "repetition is the didactic means for working on the popu-lar mentality" (1971: 340).

Chapter 7

"Othering" and the New Irish Nation-State

I have briefly traced the development of the Irish "Othering" tradition as encompassed in a reiterative and reductionist discourse because Ireland's history of colonisation has meant that the "official" version of the Irish people (including Irish Travellers) and Irish history is, it can be argued, itself a form of "Othering". Healy's statement regarding the "manufactured" or mediated nature of much of the historical record can be seen to be particularly pertinent to Irish history: "History is a construct, often a narrative of interested parties who seek to prove a thesis . . ." (Healy, 1992: 15). That the interpretation of history and definitions of nations or self are the subject of competition or struggle on the part of various contending interests has been outlined by a number of historians. Hawthorn (1994) has outlined the way in which these competing interests condition "processes of definition (of self and others) perception and interpretation" (1994: 116).

Contending interests in the form of the colonial discourse have also resulted in the probability that a realistic depiction of Ireland as it was in the past is extremely difficult to recreate. The only records that we have — written representations of Ireland as recounted by primarily colonial chroniclers — are confusing and suspect. Discussing the dubious nature of representations of Ireland in both the sixteenth and seventeenth centuries, for example, Kiberd (1995) has pointed out that the "notion of Ireland" as depicted in the writings of this era can be viewed "largely as a fiction" (1995: 83). This discursive and often-false discourse concerning Ireland and the Irish can, I argue, be extended to encompass an equally discursive depiction of Irish Travellers that is available in Irish popular tradition through the lens of folklore.

The primary subject of this book — the discursive image of Travellers as defined by the "settled" community — is intimately intertwined with this anti-Irish "Othering" tradition that I have briefly outlined. Travellers were Irish people who were subject to the same cultural conditioning and discursive stereotyping as others. The colonial tradition made no distinction between Travellers and other Irish people with the result that they are largely invisible in the historical record. Travellers are also situated within the historical framework of colonial "othering" because the dominant view of their origins today is that they are people who left a previously settled existence and are most likely the product of Ireland's colonial past, colonial violence and eviction in particular. In addition to this it can be argued that the negative stereotypes and constructions of Irish Travellers which became dominant in the twentieth century are simply an extension of the anti-Irish "Othering" tradition which existed during the centuries of British colonisation.

The "Othering" of Irish Travellers as evidenced in modern Ireland can, as with the Othering of groups such as the Jews in Europe, also be linked to the formation of the new nation-state in Ireland. The formation of the nation-state in twentieth-century Ireland involved a new mediation on the part of the Irish people with the question of self-definition. A political agenda had motivated the propaganda-driven representations of the Ireland in the era prior to independence. The English had "translated" the Irish using self-interested and essentialist representations. However, a new essentialism manifested itself in the discourse of self-identity that appeared in the early years of the twentieth century and on independence. Colonialism's efforts to deracinate, assimilate, and "civilise" the Irish meant that the new discourse of Irish identity became bound up with notions of authentication rooted in a pre-colonial, prelapsarian past that was equally essentialist. I argue here that this "new" Irish essentialism which accompanied the discourse of the emergent nation-state employed an ideological framework of "control" or "representation" that was quite similar to that which had accompanied British imperialism. This new essentialism was reductive by nature and consequently it obscured the existence of heterogeneity in Irish culture including subaltern groups such as Irish Travellers. As a marginalised and stigmatised group within Irish society Travellers became a useful projective outlet for those stereotypes and types which the "newly nationalist" Irish population wished to jettison and to categorise as "not us".

The 1952 Tinker Questionnaire was one small part of the emergent nation-state's attempt to re-nationalise and "re-Gaelicise" Ireland. The representations of Travellers as outlined in the Irish Folklore Commission material are thus an element of the Irish sense of self and other. They express the contradictory feelings held by those Irish people engaged with the project of nation-building towards their own society and towards the "others" within that society. The representation of the Traveller as "Other" can be seen as one element in the expression of the collective conscience of Irish society as it attempted to jettison a long-evolved and often-negative discourse and appropriate a new form of cultural nationalism. Leerssen (1996) has elucidated the importance of a collectively defined identity to the effort of self-definition in the form of nationhood or nationalism:

> A "nation", which nationalism considers to be the natural unit of human society, is a group of individuals who distinguish themselves, as a group, by a shared allegiance to what they consider to be their common identity; and "nationality" can be considered as the focus of a nation's allegiance, the idea (indeed, the self-image) of its common identity, the criterion by which a "nation" defines itself as such. (1996: 18)

To understand the emergence of this new cultural nationalism that accompanied the work of the Irish Folklore Commission and projects such as the Tinker Questionnaire, it is necessary to locate this nationalism's emergence within a historical framework. The end of the nineteenth century had seen the growth of Irish nationalism as promulgated by the emerging Catholic class and a consequent challenge to the hitherto governing classes of the Protestant Anglo-Irish ascendancy. This challenge was extended into the cultural sphere where both groups now competed to define what was "really" Irish through different appropriations of Irish history. The claims of the Protestant Anglo-Irish ascendancy class had much of their basis in the Celtic Literary Revival. In this movement a pre-colonial Celticism that played down the Ascendancy class's involvement in the structures of colonisation was put forward as the basis for a new Irish cultural nationalism. This Celticism included strong elements of the discourse of Gypsiology discussed in Chapter 1. Indeed Celtic Revivalists like W.B. Yeats, Douglas Hyde and J.M. Synge all had strong leanings towards Gypsiology and the theories discussed therein. Both the Gypsiologists and the Celticists deplored what they saw as the death of traditional rural life. For them the Gypsies and the rural Irish were repositories of spirituality and mysticism, untainted by the materialism of urban culture. Gypsies and other wanderers as described by the Celticists and Gypsiologists were people who lived in a "time-warp". They were survivals of an ancient past that was largely unaffected by either colonialism or industrialism.

According to this discourse, tinkers, beggars and other wanderers were the true heirs of an older and more traditional Ireland. Helleiner (2000) says that the artists and intellectuals of the Celtic Literary Revival often used the figure of the wanderer to critique what they saw to be the emerging Ireland. This was an Ireland that in their view was characterised by increased materialism and repressive sexuality as encapsulated in Catholicism. The wandering life as encapsulated in the life of a Traveller was presented as a romantic symbol of escape from the perceived repression and hypocrisy of post-Famine Irish society in plays such as Synge's *The Tinker's Wedding* (1904) and *The Shadow of the Glen* (1910), and Lady Gregory's *The Travelling Man* (1905). Wanderers as depicted in these plays were sometimes a symbol for the position of the Anglo-Irish writer in the then Irish society. This position became increasingly precarious as a different and contradictory understanding of Irish history as envisaged by the hitherto dominated Catholic intelligentsia came to the fore. Irish cultural nationalism became increasingly radicalised with partition and the foundation of the new Irish state.

The new Irish state saw cultural nationalism in different terms to that of the old Anglo-Irish elite. Foster (1988) suggests that one of the central preoccupations of the nascent Irish state was self-definition against Britain in both the political and cultural arenas. Ó Gilláin (2000) analyses the importance which these "new" cultural nationalists placed on de-Anglicising Ireland. Douglas Hyde's seminal lecture *The Necessity for de-Anglicising Ireland* (1892) was a succinct summary of the direction which cultural nationalists would now take. For Ireland to assume a preeminent position in literature and the intellectual sphere, it was necessary for Ireland to re-Gaelicise itself. In Hyde's view, Daniel O'Connell had overseen the death of Gaelic civilisation, "largely, I am afraid, owing to his example and his neglect of inculcating the necessity of keeping alive racial customs, language and traditions" (Hyde in Ó Giolláin, 2000: 115).

Ireland's rich Gaelic past would be the font for this new cultural nationalism, because "though the Irish race does not recognise it just at present", it was this past that had prevented the Irish from being fully assimilated into an Anglocentric worldview (Hyde in Ó Giolláin, 2000: 115). Hyde's views on the nexus between folklore and nation-building were reflected in the contemporary thinking of the day. Orvar Lofgren says that "cultural matrices were freely borrowed across national frontiers"; matrices that made up "an international cultural grammar of nationhood, with a thesaurus of general ideas about the cultural ingredients needed to form a nation" (Lofgren, 1993: 217). This international "grammar" was one that could be transformed into a specific national lexicon. Folklore was one of the means whereby people could get to know those parts of Ireland where Irish was the vernacular and where Gaelic culture was still in the ascendancy. Folklore could also act as the inspiration for a new literature, which, unlike the Anglo-Irish revival, would be an "authentic" literature that was "true" to its roots of origin.

The establishment of structures for the preservation of folklore, then, became ancillaries to the new state's attempt to "re-Gaelicise" Ireland. The Folklore of Ireland Society (*An Cumann le Béaloideas Éireann*) was founded in Dublin in 1927 by a number of prominent cultural activists including the Kerry writer Pádraig Ó Siochfhradha and Séamus Ó Duilearga, the editor of its journal, *Béaloideas*. By the end of the 1930s the Society had about a thousand members, the bulk of whom were members of the emerging Catholic middle class. These included several dozen volunteer fieldworkers who in their spare time tracked down and recorded local storytellers. The focus of the Irish Folklore Commission was on the recording of Ireland's stories, popular beliefs and traditions, but the primary locus for this collecting was what were perceived to be the "culture-rich" Gaelic-speakers of the Gaeltachtaí or Irish-speaking districts. Various possibilities for Travellers' origins and existence as a separate group were posited in the folklore of the "settled" community as recorded by the Irish Folklore Commission's 1952 Tinker Questionnaire. What these various possibilities had in common however was that Travellers were perceived to be a group whose identity was concomitant with that of the majority Irish community. Although it was acknowledged that Travellers inhabited a separate locus within Irish society, little credence was given to the evidence that this separate existence might have included a separate and unique culture.

The all-encompassing nature of the nationalist discourse that accompanied the foundation of the nation-state obscured complexities relating to the history and image of certain minority groups, including Travellers. Lee (1989) points out that post-independence Ireland sought knowledge but was reluctant to seek knowledge about itself. Rather than engaging in any real analysis of Irish life, the new state participated instead in a public myth of a traditionally harmonious Catholic Ireland, a myth that was itself a response to a particular political climate and a particular historical inheritance. The creation of the Free State in 1922 held the potential for a section of the Irish people to create a new identity for themselves, one which would distinguish them and separate them from the British. The attempt to do this was flawed, however, and any expectations for extensive social and economic change in the era following partition were not realised. It can be argued that the characteristic which defined the first four decades of the new Irish state above any other was an emphasis on continuity. Little overt change was evident from the society that had existed prior to 1922, a fact that was due in strong part to the tenuous nature of those foundations on which partition and the newly created Free State had been based. In such a climate it was almost inevitable that any radical efforts at change would be seen as profoundly threatening. Breen et al. (1990) who provide a good overview of the post-partition period, argue that securing the new nation-state was the most important priority in the post-1922 era where the state could "see the potential for chaos everywhere" (1990: 2). Consequently the newly independent state attempted to establish nationalism/republicanism on a basis of mass homogeneity and conformity. McLoughlin (1994) describes some of the negative aspects of this endeavour:

This sense of Irishness came "naturally" from the dominance of Catholicism and the "shared" experience of rural living which bound all Irish people so neatly together into nationhood. The Irish state was established on this coercive basis and all those individuals and groups who did not fit the bucolic image did not belong. This coercive sense of nationhood took away from internal social conflicts and the grounds of social, ideological and political debate were effectively narrowed to issues of national self-determination. (1994: 85–6)

McLoughlin says that Travellers were viewed both as derivative and deviant from the mainstream in an Irish society whose homogeneity was often stifling. She links the assignation of Travellers as "other" to similar depictions of other minority groups:

Joining them in their "problem" status were various religious groups of Protestant and Jew, as well as separated individuals, deserted wives, single parents (mostly women), homosexuals and even writers and artists. Ireland from the 1920s to the 1980s had no room for diversity, pluralism and heterogeneity. (1994: 87)

RE-GAELICISATION AND THE "TINKER QUESTIONNAIRE"

Ó Giolláin (2000) identified the Irish Folklore Commission as a central plank in the project to re-Gaelicise and re-nationalise Ireland. The Commission recorded very little material from women, the English-speakers of the cities or from "marginalised" groups like Travellers. This "new" history as promulgated by the cultural nationalists of Ireland's new Catholic bourgeoisie emphasised strongly the continuity of Gaelic society and culture, partly in an effort to downplay the role which the Anglo-Irish had played in Irish cultural development. Since Travellers were an "Other" who were perceived to have "fallen out" of this Gaelic society, they, like English-speakers and city-dwellers, were not deemed to be particularly important to the project of cultural re-Gaelicisation. McLoughlin points out that "the number of those alienated and excluded by the effects of this dominant myth have only become apparent in recent years" (1994: 86). It is also only in recent times that attention has begun to be paid to the cultural discourses concerning those groups and individuals who did not accord with the homogeneity of the national project, or those who were considered to be peripheral to it.

Representations of Travelling people as outlined in the Tinker Questionnaire highlight the complexity inherent in historical narratives. They also highlight a range of questions pertaining to the point of view and class of the respondents who answered the Questionnaire, almost all of whom belonged to the emerging Irish middle class. Bhabha (1994) refers to the importance of identifying the "institutional location" and "geopolitical locale" (1994: 1) of those who purport to narrate what is considered to be historically true. The writing of one's own story or history is affected by problems which have to do with a community's perceptions, culture, class and the vagaries of memory. History is a "construct" (Healy, 1992: 15) and the writing of personal and/or communal stories is manipulable on both the conscious and sub-conscious levels. As Ziff (1995) points out, history and history texts:

> tend to be associated with imposition from the outside — by the
> state, teachers, religious institutions — memory is associated with
> the stories of a personal/communal nature. Within the life of each
> person (especially those who are land-based), histories vie with
> grandmothers, received information vies with lived experience. . .
> . If history is associated with texts, memory is associated with a
> full panoply of the senses. (1995: 19)

The responses to this Questionnaire serve as an exemplar of the manner in which Travellers have frequently been represented in Irish popular tradition generally. Travellers are depicted as culturally "Other", a cultural "Other" who are defined in terms of secrecy, dishonesty, licentiousness, violence and a type of "society within a society". An analysis of the principal stereotypes recounted in relation to Travellers in the Questionnaire clearly shows that Travellers were subsumed within a reverse ethnocentrism, based on essentialist binaries as rigid as those which had been promulgated concerning the Irish population generally under colonialism. Traveller "Othering" as depicted in this analysis is an example of what can be termed an "alterity-within-identity". It is a constructed identity that intersignifies with the construct that is Irish identity itself. History becomes "reconstructed" again to cater to the renationalisation and re-Gaelicisation project and a selection process comes into play that omits those cultural attributes of Irishness which, it was perceived, did not adhere to the self-identity of the new nation-state.

Said (1978) identified the falsity that lay at the heart of the Orientalist enterprise, a falsity that had its roots in the essentialist nature of representation and the colonialist enterprise. The Orientalist paradigm resulted in false views of Orientals and the Orient just as the English/Irish colonial context resulted in the creation of what Kiberd (1995) (speaking of the Tudor period) referred to as "a Sacsa nua darb ainm Eire": a new England called Ireland (1995: 15). Early attempts on the part of the Irish to counteract colonialist essentialism often resulted in a new form of essentialism, whereby the picture of Ireland which was constructed was equally false. Discussing the attempts of the Irish writer Seathrún Céitinn to resist the reductionism of English stereotyping, Kiberd argues that:

> A major part of Céitinn's project was his demonstration that the Irish were not foils to the English as much as mirrors. Against the view of them as hot-headed, rude and uncivil, Céitinn offered a portrait of the ancient Irish as disciplined, slow to anger but steadfast thereafter in pursuit of their rights, urbane and spare of utterance, and so on . . . to all intents, the very model of the English knight or squire. To scant avail. In centuries to come, English colonisers in India or Africa would impute to the "Gunga Dins" and "Fuzzi-Wuzzies" those same traits already attributed to the Irish . . . their official image before the world had been created and consolidated by a far greater power. (1995: 15)

That competing interpretations of history, self and others in various essentialist forms continue to struggle within Ireland, and in Northern Ireland in particular, has been pointed out by Edna Longley (1994), who describes the ideological struggle between the Unionist and Nationalist communities in the North as "a matter of aggressively displayed credentials". These credentials are couched in terms of stereotypes, caricatures and representations whereby "Orange Lil" battles constantly with "Kathleen Ni Houlihan" for ideological dominance (1994: 175). In the essentialist discourse of what might be termed Irish "Travellerism" under review here, I would argue that the Orientalist and colonialist systems of representation were paralleled and mirrored by the counter-discourse of nationalism and nativism that accompanied the emerging Irish nation.

The temptation to align the past with the present and tradition with the contemporaneous (as in Northern Ireland to this day) was undoubtedly very tempting for Irish intellectuals in the first few decades after Irish independence. By emphasising the unbroken continuity of Gaelic culture as preserved in the Irish language and Irish folklore, it allowed post-colonial Ireland to define itself as part of a unique and indigenous tradition that stood in opposition to the de-racinating attempts of the colonialist tradition. A unitary or monologic history, be it to some degree "constructed", was particularly attractive to a new nation seeking legitimisation and a sense of national history. To have a history is to be legitimised, as outlined by Ashcroft et al. (1995):

> Clearly what it means to have a history is the same as what it means to have a legitimate existence: history and legitimation go hand in hand; history legitimates "us" and not others. (1995: 355)

Eagleton (1988) goes further and argues that in a post-colonial context such as Ireland's, history is often an adaptive strategy, one where a unitary and monologic history is posited as the antithesis of the equally unitary history constructed by the coloniser:

> If colonialism tends to deprive those it subjugates not only of their land, language and culture but of their very history . . . then it is arguable that the mythological image of Ireland . . . is itself a markedly historical phenomenon. A people robbed of their sense of agency and autonomy, unable to decipher the social institutions around them as expressions of their own life-practice, may tend quite reasonably to read their collective experience through the deterministic optic of mythology, with its sense of human life as shaped by the mighty forces of some process quite hidden to consciousness. Myth is in this sense less some regrettable, primitive irrationalism than a kind of historical truth. (1988: 17)

For a post-colonial nation such as Ireland, history is inextricably linked to identity and the notion of authenticity has assumed particular importance in the arena of political struggle. Ashcroft et al. (1995) have identified the importance of myth in the construction of historical reality to those nations that are postcolonial:

> The significance of history for post-colonial discourse lies in the modern origins of historical study itself, and the mantle by which "History" took upon itself the mantle of a discipline. For the emergence of history in European thought is coterminous with the rise of modern colonialism, which in its radical othering and violent annexation of the non-European world, found in history a prominent, if not the prominent instrument for the control of subject peoples. At base, the myth of a value free, "scientific" view of the past, the myth of the beauty of order, the myth of the story of history as a simple representation of the continuity of events, authorised nothing less than the construction of world reality. (1995: 355)

In colonial Ireland historical representation was ideologically skewed in favour of the coloniser. The post-colonial situation saw a reaction to this and a move on the part of Irish society towards a history which was teleological and aspired to narrative unity and closure. As with the Orientalist paradigm history became a univocal commentary promulgating the "truth", a truth whose drive towards homogeneity was unassailable. The push towards Gaelicisation was to some degree a form of retaliation whereby the rhetoric of history became a rhetoric of opposition, the teleological and selective view of Irish history being justified against centuries of wrongdoing. The danger inherent in such a homogeneising drive is that the subaltern, in this case Irish Travellers, are obscured in the search for racial discreteness. The subaltern, without the wherewithal to voice the requisite cultural credentials in terms of historical proof of origin or evidence of cultural continuity, is subsumed within a totalising framework, resulting in a Spivakian state of displacement or "shuttling" (Spivak, 1995: 212) between legitimacies based on colonialism or nativism. Under colonialism and Orientalism essentialist characteristics as attributed to the Irish were primarily negative. With the emergence of the Irish nation-state these essentialist attributes were transferred to the "Other" and a nationalist alter-ego was constructed, as argued by a prominent opponent of the repressive aspects of nationalism, James Joyce:

Nations have their ego, just like individuals. The case of a people who like to attribute to themselves qualities and glories foreign to other people has not been entirely unknown in history, from the time of our ancestors, who called themselves Aryans and nobles, or that of the Greeks, who called all those who lived outside the sacrosanct land of Hellas barbarians. (Joyce in Cheng, 1995: 19)

CONSTRUCTING THE TRAVELLER

When taken as a whole the responses to the Tinker Questionnaire which I examine here constitute a construct or myth of Traveller identity, a myth that replicates teleologically the notion of Ireland's colonial history that was in the ascendant in the Ireland of the first half of the twentieth century and a construct which subsumed Traveller identity within its framework. The written depiction of Travellers as outlined in the popular tradition and as transcribed in the Irish Folklore Commission's 1952 *Tinker Questionnaire* can be viewed as an example of "Othering" that evolves whereby the subaltern or "Other" is represented and "translated" through the essentialist language of the dominant culture. Essentialism, involving binary articulations and stereotypes, is inevitably reductionist as it obscures any notion of heterogeneity. Essentialism consists of opposition to difference. Its insistence on the fixed or unchanging nature of certain representations is of necessity historically inaccurate as any scope for the cultural evolution of the people "fixed" within such representations is non-existent. Cheng (1995) has outlined the manner in which nationalist movements attempting to evolve away from colonialism frequently fall into the same trap as that in which they were previously entangled. In attempting to invert the reductionist stereotypes previously attributed to them under colonialism they revert to a reverse ethnocentrism based on stereotypes which are by nature perennial and unchanging:

This binary pattern is a trap that essentialises and limits representation to precisely its own terms, terms one must play by if one accepts the binary oppositions. In other words if you are trying to prove that you aren't what "they" say you are, you are judging/arguing by the same rules/categories "they" are and so you end up reifying/ maintaining those categories in place as functional realities; for example if you try to prove that you are more

angel than ape . . . than you are only reinforcing and reinscribing
the terms of a hierarchy that places angels (and Anglos) at the top
and "Negroes" and Orientals near the bottom. . . . In needing to
prove that one is more angelic and less ape-like than the others,
one ends up buying into the very terms of a binary hierarchy of
Self and Other that needs to label and denigrate the Other
(whether "Negro", Oriental or Irish) as barbaric and subhuman in
order to assert the Self's own unquestionably civilised "culture"
and humanity by contrast. (1995: 54)

National self-definition for the Irish becomes a form of denial by virtue
of the fact that they are trapped within a discourse that was initially created by the colonisers.

One of the easiest options for the nativist tradition in such a situation
is to direct this reverse ethnocentrism towards the Other in its own society. Travellers were hitherto one of the few very identifiable "Others" or
subalterns onto whom this altered ethnocentrism could be transferred.
The analysis of the way in which Travellers have historically been represented or "imaged" by the settled community in Ireland is important as
collective representations or the attachment of particular labels or identities to a group play a large role in shaping responses to that group even
today. Today most Irish people are presented with representations of
Travellers though the media and the arts. In the earlier part of the twentieth century it was primarily through the lens of the oral tradition or folklore that people formed their collective representation of Travellers and
other communities who were considered as "Other". Mayall (2004) has
outlined how important the question of representation and image-making
is in attempting to understand the reaction of the mainstream community
to those groups considered as marginal.

Stereotypical images of groups affect how they are seen, how
they are treated and the expectations that are held of them in
terms of behaviour and abilities. Indeed, the connection between
images and responses, especially in their negative and hostile
forms, is a major theme and argument in host-immigrant studies
in general. Many commentators have linked the hostile responses
to Jews with the presence of anti-Semitic stereotypes in culture
and language, and a similar connection is made between repre-

sentations of the barbaric Irish and anti-Irish sentiment, and the crude racial imagery of blacks and other minority groups and overt racism. (2004: 15)

Ian Hancock (1992), a Roma activist and writer, goes so far as to say that this persistent and hostile imagery as created by outsiders is at the core of the often-tense societal relationship that exists between traditionally nomadic (i.e. Gypsy) and non-Gypsy communities. Not only is it the case that stereotypes give rise to hostile imagery, the reverse can happen also; and pre-existing prejudices can give rise to the further evolution of prejudice. Bohdan Zawadzki (1948) in an early analysis of the functioning of prejudice described stereotyping as a rationalisation of reductionism against the group as opposed to the individual:

> In order to rationalise one's hatred against a whole group rather than against a single individual, the prejudiced person must resort to the use of *stereotypes* in his thinking. (1948: 130) [original emphasis]

The importance of representations or images lies in the fact that they may be the only source of information about a group that people who may not have direct contact with the group ever receive. Mayall (2004) outlines the responsibility that lies with the creators of a particular representation:

> Images, created for the most part by outsiders, provide a basis for how we interpret our experience, and pre-informed information and knowledge affect our perceptions and judgement by providing a normative, or standard, picture. Images themselves are rarely value-free, and the judgements they contain are often those that will generally be accepted. There can be little doubt that negative images reinforce negative responses and that there is some connection between racial stereotyping and discriminatory treatment. . . . Because the stereotypes of a group cover every aspect of their life, behaviour, appearance and propensities, it is possible to find confirmation and justification for any action, hostile or favourable, by calling up the required image. (2004: 17)

Labelling and representation have seemingly always lain at the heart of majority–minority relations, the imperialist expansions of the nineteenth century being a prime exemplar. Said (1978) warns of the dangers in underestimating the power of representation as incorporated in the text:

> It seems a common human failing to prefer the schematic author-
> ity of a text to the disorientations of direct encounters with the
> human. (1978: 93)

Representation is a core function of every written text because "in any instance of at least a written language, there is no such thing as a delivered presence, but a re-presence, or representation" (1978: 12). Textual authority relegates reality as it really is and a textual representation is superimposed on this reality instead. The word of the stranger speaks on behalf of the subaltern or those in the subordinate position:

> ... this articulation is the prerogative, not of a puppet-master, but
> of a genuine creator, whose life-giving power represents, ani-
> mates, constitutes the otherwise silent and dangerous space be-
> yond familiar boundaries. (1978: 57)

Representations of Travellers as outlined in Irish popular tradition are therefore an element of both the Irish Self and that which is perceived as Other in Irish society. Images of Travellers as expressed in Ireland's public culture express the contradictory feelings which Irish people have towards the Other in their society and towards themselves. Since the representations of the "Other" or Travellers are by nature a constructed "re-presence" they can probably tell us a lot more about Irish society and its attitudes than they can about Travellers. Bhabha (1990) reiterates this point when he makes the observation on this narrative aspect of representation that "As narrator she is narrated as well" (1990: 301). In narrating the "other", one is inadvertently narrating the "self", including the latter's insecurities, ambivalences and contradictions.

Durkheim (1954) pointed to the *sui generis* nature of such collective imaginaries. Collective representations generate an "independent" reality that cannot be wholly explained with reference to facts about individuals. They are thus partially autonomous in nature and have the ability to "live their own lives", form syntheses of all kinds and even engender new representations. It is important to do justice to the compelling and (often) ambivalent nature of collective ideation or imagery in a globalised world where emerging technologies ensure that images and representations can be transferred at incredible speed. The significance of new forms of communication has combined with a number of developing traditions in the social and human sciences to ensure the increased significance of the question of collective representations. There is a growing acknowledgement of the necessity to study both language and meaning in terms of their status as cultural constructs as opposed to their position as "natural" aspects of a material "reality" (see Hall, 1997).

Durkheim (1954) found that the common denominator between members of a society is their collective conscience or that range of beliefs and ideas that are collectively shared by that society. These collective ideations tend to be expressed in symbols that are commonly recognised and through meanings that are collectively understood. It follows that collective ideations operating in modern society, including morality, politics, education and the mass media, ought to be seen in terms of symbolic classifications. These symbolic classifications are organised in terms of shared collective representations, "social facts" and certain shared perspectives that make up the "superstructure" of society. A wide diversity of sources combine to contribute to a society's collective understanding of things and events, sources that are independent of the particular societal conditions in which individuals find themselves. Making visible the invisible points to the role of stereotype as construct. Hall (1997) emphasises this aspect of stereotyping which he terms the "poetics" or "politics" of stereotypes:

> The important point is that stereotypes refer as much to what is imagined in fantasy as to what is perceived as "real". And what is visually produced, by the practices of representation, is only half the story. The other half — the deeper meaning — lies in what is not being said, but is being fantasised, what is implied but cannot be shown. (1997: 263)

Inherent in the symbolic process that stereotyping entails and outlined by Hall is a gross inequality of power, a power that is usually directed against the subordinate or excluded group. Binary oppositions such as

Us/Them and Self/Other involve the exercise of symbolic power through representational practices. Hall identifies this power as representing someone or something in a certain way — within a certain "regime of representation" as a form of "symbolic violence" (1997: 259). Peart (2002), commenting on the way Ireland was represented or "translated" in British colonial texts cites Cronin's succinct summary of the symbolic power inherent in representational practices, a power that frequently has a political agenda:

> The power of representation is that it can affect the way we per-
> ceive people, events, and the past as well as the present (Cronin,
> 1996: 95). Representation can make the foreign familiar but it can
> also make the foreign even more foreign. (2002: 7)

Nowadays it is the media, primarily, who filter Irish public perceptions and the "collective conscience" of Irish society. This is a relatively new vehicle for the collective ideation of Irish culture, however, and until the mid-twentieth century there is no doubt that the oral tradition played a very significant role in the formation of collective ideas and representations of Travellers and other communities who were considered as "Other". The reasons for the primarily discursive "collective ideation" of Irish Travellers as evidenced in Irish culture are not immediately obvious. Travellers today score high on all indices of poverty and exclusion, a marginalisation that is often attributed in part to the long history of prejudice against this community. Why a relatively tiny indigenous group who have lived in Ireland for centuries are "Othered" to such a degree is in many ways difficult to comprehend, as was outlined in the 1970s by S.B. Gmelch (1974), one of the few anthropologists to study Irish Travellers:

> The picture that emerges . . . is one of a deprived, misunderstood
> and powerless group living on the periphery of Irish society. Of
> special interest is the lack of any genetic basis for their persistent
> exclusion and deprivation . . . their rejection by the settled com-
> munity is not based on colour or "racial" considerations as it is
> with American Indians, native Blacks in South Africa or aborigi-
> nes in Australia. Nor is it perpetuated by notions of ritual impu-
> rity or contamination as it is with untouchables in India or the Eta

(Burakumin) in Japan. . . . The Travellers' socially and economically deprived status in Irish society is not based on or perpetuated by religious antagonisms as is the case with the Catholic minority in Northern Ireland. And lastly their rejection is not based
on economic or political competition as it is with many such
groups in Asia. . . . Irish Travellers are both poor and powerless.
In a society such as Ireland where equality is a fundamental
value, the persistent deprivation and exploitation of the Travelling People appears an anomaly. (1974: 6)

Constructions of Irish Travellers as depicted in the Irish Folklore Commission material surveyed here show the processes of reductionism and
essentialism working at their most efficient. Negative stereotypes attributed to Travellers portray them as an outsider group whose community's
traits include licentiousness, secrecy, dishonesty and violence, to name
but a few perceived shortcomings. Travellers are represented within a
discourse of difference, one which translates them as a category of cultural "Other". They are assigned the position of subaltern or "cultural
Other" and are subsumed within a reverse ethnocentrism characteristic of
the teleological efforts and historical "re-constructionism" of early twentieth-century Irish nationalism. This collective representation was reflec-
tive of the many stereotypical assumptions about Travellers that were
common amongst the Irish settled community during the midpoint of the
twentieth century, a collective "ideation" whose central tenets continue
to exert a strong influence in modern-day Ireland. This tendency towards
stereotype, reductionism and essentialism is increasingly being targeted
by Traveller activists and those who advocate Travellers' rights in an
increasingly multicultural Ireland, an Ireland where public calls for dialogue between both communities have become more vociferous on the
part of the representatives of Traveller and non-Traveller communities in
recent years.

Chapter 8

An Irish "Other"

"What is going on is not really about Travellers at all
but about the rest of us, the 'settled' people"
(Fintan O'Toole, The Irish Times, 16 June 1995)

PREJUDICE AND ITS THEORISATION

This analysis now focuses on some of the principal pathologising and
reductionist views that served to "Other" Travellers and which were
common in the Ireland of the mid-twentieth century, as elucidated in the
Irish Folklore Commission's 1952 Questionnaire on Travellers. This
analysis, it can be argued, is an effort to map the contours of a discourse
of "difference" in Irish tradition where the Traveller is depicted primarily
in a negative fashion. This discourse takes the form of a "construct" or
myth of Traveller identity as elucidated by the "settled" community
whereby Travellers are defined as a cultural "Other", in terms which are,
in the main, stereotypical and negative. To date the roots of anti-
Traveller and anti-nomadic prejudice or racism have been seriously under-theorised. Travelling people have been "othered", primarily through
a range of reductionist stereotypes, in Ireland and the western world generally. The understanding of Traveller identity has always been very
vague amongst the settled community. Many negative stereotypes which
are enumerated regarding (traditionally) migratory groups and which are
still quite openly pronounced in the public sphere today regarding Gypsies (Roma) in the former Eastern bloc continue to have a strong resonance in Ireland today. The settled or mainstream community in Ireland
commonly perceives Travellers to be a criminal subculture, a people who
are inherently dishonest and who display cultural attributes which are

simply a throwback to a primitivism associated with a former peasant society. This particular form of "othering" is in many ways a form of projection, an institutionalisation of ideas which are subsequently seldom challenged. While a small but growing canon of scholarly work exists outlining the social history of Roma Gypsies and indigenous Travelling groups on mainland Europe and the evolution of racist and repressive attitudes and policies against them (Cottaar et al., 1998; Hancock, 1987; Kenrick and Puxon, 1972; Willems, 1997; etc.), the same cannot be said regarding the history of Irish Travellers in Ireland.

The research in this area to date only comprises a small canon of work (Fay, 1992; Helleiner, 2000; MacLaughlin, 1995, McVeigh, 1992; Ní Shúinéar, 1994). Irish Travellers have largely been invisible among the Irish poor, as were those many Irish (e.g. people referred to as *bacachs*, beggars and seasonal cottiers) for whom nomadism was the norm prior to the twentieth century. As outlined earlier Travellers and other mobile Irish remained relatively invisible in the social and historical record inherited from the colonial era. Travellers were most frequently referred to as an occupational or social subgroup, if they were referred to at all. They appear under a variety of ambiguous descriptions in state-sponsored laws and documents such as the *Act for the Erection of Houses of Correction and for the punishment of Rogues and Vagabonds, Sturdy Beggars and other lewd and idle persons* (1634) and the *Poor Law Enquiry Report* (1836). As a consequence, it is the case that prior to the first half of the twentieth century prejudice against Travellers was part of an often colonially inspired discourse that encompassed prejudice against Irish people as a whole.

The study of anti-Traveller prejudice changed in the latter half of the twentieth century, however. Recent decades have seen the emergence of an increasing body of scholarly work on anti-Traveller prejudice or racism as it applies to Travellers. This literature has been produced by Traveller organisations such as Pavee Point and the Irish Traveller Movement and community-based or non-statutory organisations such as Harmony and the Campaign for Research and Documentation. Academic work on the issue of anti-Traveller racism is minimal (Fitzgerald, 1992; MacLachlan and Connell, 1999; MacLaughlin, 1995) and has in common with the work of community-based organisations that it is primarily concerned with detailing the racism which Travellers experience and proving that they do, as a group, experience prejudice. A significant gap, however, remains in the scholarship which theorises the roots of anti-Traveller prejudice or racism and its subsequent evolution. A number of reasons may be put forward to explain this, none of which can suffice as a full explanation.

It is the case that the study of Irish Travellers has, until relatively recently, remained a relatively peripheral interest for many Irish scholars. There are a number of possible reasons for this, none of which provide anything approaching a full explanation. Irish Travellers only make up a very small minority in Irish society. While estimates vary it is thought that there are approximately 28,000 people living in the Irish Republic who identify themselves as Travellers with a further 1,500 living in the north of Ireland.

Very little was ever recorded in social and historical records regarding the origins and culture of the Irish Travellers. Consequently there are real limits to what the sources can tell us about the history of the Irish Travellers. What social and historical records do exist simply highlight the relative invisibility of Travellers as a group in Irish society, the difficulty being compounded by the large mobile population travelling the Irish roads — variously termed tradesmen, beggars, healers, poets, tramps, "Knights of the Road", *bacachs*, *mangairí, shoolers* etc. prior to the twentieth century. Another major factor explaining the invisibility of Travellers in the historic record is the perception, still common in Irish society today, that Travellers are simply a group comprising the descendants of "drop-outs" from the settled community, people who most likely were the victims of colonial expulsion policies and who consequently, according to this perception, deserve little further research.

A scholarly reticence regarding the theorisation of anti-Traveller prejudice may also be understandable to a certain degree as some theorists may have been anxious to avoid lending credence to any model of prejudice or racism deemed "psychological" in nature. However, the work of Miles (1989) on the question of racism and its manifestations makes clear that it is possible to discuss the question of Otherness and difference in an enlightened manner when the issue is placed in its proper historical and materialist context. The little that we know of the historical situation of Irish Travellers and their current position in Irish society would seem to make the case for further theorisation of their role as (often negative) "Other" something which is of vital importance. It is certainly the case that in the past, and to some extent today, the Otherness of Travellers has been ascribed to their nomadism and their reluctance to settle down or integrate into the "settled" community. However, Traveller Otherness as ascribed in an Irish context, while frequently structured around the question of their nomadism, is not something that has ever remained static. It is a complex question that encompasses a range of historical contingencies and trends including periods of oppression and direct and almost coercive attempts at assimilation. While the most salient aspects of Traveller Othering may have changed relatively little during the past few hundred years, they have been subject to different emphases depending on the political and historical circumstances in which they have been invoked. Notions such as civilisation, private property, the control of nomadic workers, the threat of economic competition and the use of pseudo-religious tenets to legitimate the pathologisation and "control" of an "outsider" group are all facets which have intermeshed to different degrees in the history of anti-Traveller "Othering" in Ireland, as evidenced in the discourses invoked in both the 1952 Irish Folklore Commission's *Tinker Questionnaire*, the folk tradition generally and Irish public discourse as a whole.

One point in particular almost immediately strikes those readers who come to examine either historic or contemporary constructions of Irish Travellers and who have a relatively good understanding of Traveller history and culture. It is obvious that, historically, the understanding of Traveller identity among non-Travellers has, as today, been quite vague. As occurs today, this vagueness has often resulted in prejudice, a prejudice that has become ingrained through the institutionalisation of stereotypes and misinformation. That this institutionalised image of Travellers has "taken on a life of its own" and become the conventional wisdom regarding Travellers is as true today as it was over half a century ago.

While some non-Travellers who have written on or commented upon the Traveller community in the past have known some Travellers and engaged with the Traveller community, there are many others who have known very little about them. Yet, as with many members of the non-

Traveller population in Ireland today, there are many who would claim to be able to provide a fairly detailed picture of how they *think* Travellers look and live and what this community's history and culture consists of. This mental image — partly negative, occasionally romantic but often inaccurate — stems from a Traveller identity that has become so institutionalised in the Irish psyche as to be part of the Irish cultural heritage itself. Irish people's (comparative) ignorance of Traveller culture in past decades has encouraged the institutionalisation of ideas which, when seldom challenged, became and continue as a part of a misinformed, conventional wisdom.

A visitor to Ireland today who chanced to pick up a newspaper would see little in the non-Traveller's depiction of Travellers that would differ from the common and historical portrayals of the Traveller community as the Irish "Other". At its simplest and worst, present-day perceptions of Travellers continue to build on a collection of primarily negative constructs — e.g. disorder, nomadism, laziness, dishonesty, backwardness, dependency, etc. — most of which were at one time a mirror-image of the phenomenon that was once colonial-era anti-Irish "Othering". The discourses which I examine here endeavour to outline the historical development of the majority community's "Othering" of the Traveller community. While my analysis is based primarily on historical material elucidating the non-Traveller community (i.e. the majority's) view of the minority group, it nonetheless traces the later development and construction of an identity for the Traveller community which continues to have a strong resonance today.

While some aspects of the negative "Othering" may have changed with the passage of time it is arguable that the core intent and spirit of the "Othering" process has remained virtually the same into the present day. It is a process which has constructed an identity for Travelling people, one that situates Travellers within the non-Traveller community's own terms of reference. That this Traveller identity as constructed by the settled community was/is primarily a negative one can be attributed to a number of factors including ignorance of Traveller culture and traditions and the institutionalisation of reductionist stereotypes and views of Travellers generally. Although almost all socio-historical records give us to understand that Travellers were perennial "outsiders" it is clear that they

have always operated in a certain symbiosis with the "settled" community, primarily in the context of trade. It is very clear that Travellers inhabited their own place in the social and economic fabric of pre-
urbanised Ireland and that they were vital to an Irish economy which was
primarily rural-based and agricultural.

TRAVELLERS AND NON-TRAVELLERS:
A CHANGING RELATIONSHIP

Prior to the 1960s and the relatively rapid urbanisation of Ireland Travellers were an important (if often transient) feature of the social life of most
Irish villages. Travellers had extensive, if sometimes short-lived contact
with the settled community through the peddling and swapping of small
household items, in an era when there were no shops, through their multi-
faceted craftwork (tinwork, chimney-sweeping, *poitín*-making to name
but a few), through their soldiering, fortune-telling and herbalism and
through their begging in times of scarcity. Travellers and settled people
interacted socially at fairs, patterns, pilgrimages, sporting events and religious occasions. There was also more prolonged contact between both
groups through occasional intermarriage and the part-sedentarism of
many Travellers who owned or rented houses in towns during the winter
months when the weather was most inclement. It is generally acknowledged that Ireland in the post-partition era and until the late 1950s was
characterised by a marked conservatism in terms of its socio-economic
and cultural life, securing the newly emergent nation-state being the overriding priority of successive governments during this era. Ireland was a
primarily rural and agriculturally based society and this was the environment in which the majority of the Travellers within the Irish population
also operated. While Travellers were undoubtedly seen as Other, a question remains regarding the extent of the societal exclusion that they experienced and to what extent this exclusion was seen in terms of their apparently anachronistic and nomadic culture, as is the case today.

Despite the frequency of interaction between the Travelling and settled communities most socio-historic records that have come to light indicate that significant boundaries were maintained between both the
Traveller and settled communities, boundaries which, it is arguable, solidified even further in the later twentieth century. While both Travellers

and non-Travellers frequently traversed the boundaries delineating the two communities in contexts such as trade, healing, accommodation (in pre-caravan days), religious and sporting events, etc., it is nonetheless the case that when the lifestyle or behaviour of Travellers did not correspond with the norms of the majority (non-Traveller) community, they were often ostracised and subjected to the prejudices, stereotypes and suspicions that many other nomadic peoples have suffered and continue to suffer. What may have been only a vague understanding of Traveller identity on the part of members of the majority community could easily be twisted or misinterpreted depending on particular circumstances.

It is likely too that the nomadism and the occupational flexibility of Travellers meant that they were frequently perceived as an economic threat to other sedentary or semi-nomadic tradesmen. This is a major aspect of the often fraught Traveller/"settled" relations, hitherto unduly overlooked in the socio-anthropological analyses to date. For those who might gain economically through accusing Travellers of unfair competition, it was an easy step to impute any manner of anti-social behaviour to them. It is also noteworthy that negative stereotypes which were frequently imputed to Irish Travellers show a remarkable uniformity with those that were imputed to other indigenous Travelling groups throughout Europe, as well as to other non-indigenous groups like the Roma Gypsies. Travellers were said to be uneducated, stupid, sexually lax and prone to laziness, criminality and violence. Unfortunately, the mid-decades of the twentieth century, in particular, saw these stereotypes of Travellers and Gypsies coincide with those of the administrations of a wide range of many European countries, many of whom have continued since then to classify Travellers and other nomadic people in terms of social behaviour rather than by their "racial" or cultural distinctiveness.

Travellers were one of a number of different minorities in the Ireland of the early twentieth century, who by their position on the fringes of Irish society were frequently rendered inarticulate and powerless when confronted with the intolerance of sections of the majority community. Travellers were positioned on a subtly graded class hierarchy in Ireland, the stratification of which was to a great degree based on the possession of land. Other groups perceived to be at the "bottom" of the social hierarchy included the many urban poor, the lower working-class of the

inner-cities and in rural areas, the cottiers, their unmarried daughters or
the journeymen labourers and *spailpíns*. The list of people considered
"outsiders" in a formerly "rural" Ireland is long when one considers the
relatively small population of Ireland.

Other "outsider" groups who also experienced ostracism or who
were sometimes only barely tolerated included illegitimate children, deserted wives, single parents, and certain other "undesirables" who, as
with today's homeless, mentally ill people or drug addicts, were people
who fell outside what were regarded as the norms of the majority society. It is only in the past decade or so that Irish society has begun to ini-
tiate a meaningful debate about the manner in which the Irish Other and
those considered "strange" or outside the community were treated in
previous generations. As with many of the aforementioned groups of
people Irish Travellers themselves have had very little input into how
their identity and culture has been defined. Traveller culture, in recent
generations, has primarily been a non-literate one, a fact which has
meant that how their culture is "constructed" and defined has frequently
been beyond their control. This has meant that Travellers were increasingly disadvantaged when articulating their struggle for identity in an
Ireland which became increasingly state-oriented over the course of the
twentieth century. This fact has resulted in a situation where the very
survival of the Traveller community and their culture has been dependent
to a large degree on the attitudes and perceptions which the "non-
Traveller" community exhibit towards this small Irish minority.

THE DISCOURSE OF THE "OTHER"

For the purposes of this discussion I give a brief introduction to some
widespread "constructions" of Travellers as they were perceived historically in the Ireland of the nineteenth and twentieth centuries and outline
some general suppositions the "settled" community had/has concerning
the Traveller Community, suppositions which continue to have a strong
resonance in Irish public discourse today. This discussion draws on a
range of sources including recent ethnographic and anthropological work
undertaken amongst the Traveller community; advocacy literature as
produced by groups campaigning for Travellers' rights; older imagery of
Travellers that was nurtured within the Irish folk tradition; and the bur-

geoning area of recent Traveller autobiographical literature. My discussion focuses on three major historical and discursive "constructions" of Travellers, elements of which are prevalent amongst the non-Traveller community today.

I link this process of Othering, where possible, to the historical discourse of anti-Irish "Othering" and constructions of Travellers and Gypsies as negative "Other" within the European imaginary. The analysis culminates with a discussion of the way in which this mid-twentieth-century discourse as outlined in the Irish Folklore Commission continues to reinvigorate itself through the lens of the often-hostile media portrayal of Travellers in modern Ireland, a process whereby Travellers and Traveller culture are framed within a discourse which is considered degraded and inferior. The discussion culminates with an overview of Travellers' current position in Irish society, the aims and achievements of the various advocacy and Travellers rights initiatives which have been ongoing from the early 1980s onwards, the recent emergence of a powerful body of autobiographical literature from within the Traveller community itself, a body of work which serves to usurp many long-established and widespread constructions of that self-same community as held by non-Travellers. This discussion also attempts to pinpoint the likely direction of the future campaigning work that remains with a view to Travellers achieving parity of esteem in all areas of Ireland's economic and socio-cultural life.

The first discourse which I discuss in the subsequent chapters of this book is the concept that Travellers are "drop-outs" from the settled community, by choice, or by force of circumstance. This common belief regarding Traveller origins has had probably the most serious implications of all for the Travelling community in modern Ireland. The self-definition of Irishness that accompanied independence was to some extent "constructed" and as a consequence was unitary or monologic in nature. A history that was unitary or homogenous in nature served the demands of a postcolonial nation where history itself was both an adaptive mechanism and a form of legitimisation. In such a context the dangers for subaltern or sometimes non-literate groups who could only with great difficulty posit a historical tradition, are obvious. As outlined in Chapter 2 of this book, the "drop-out" theory continues to be the most common belief regarding Traveller origins in Ireland today and has been a major factor in the imposition of policies recommending the settlement and assimilation of Travellers.

The second discourse is one whereby Travellers are "othered" as a morally suspect group. This discourse depicts Travellers as liars who steal under the cloak of begging and who plead poverty but are lazy and unproductive. According to this discourse Travellers survive by pursuing activities that are now considered anachronistic by the settled community (e.g. begging or trickery, the former sometimes encompassing threatening behaviour).

The third discourse is one where Travellers are described in terms which imply a countercultural threat; that is that they form an exclusive and secretive society which operates both within the body of and on the margins of the settled community. These discursive tenets imply that Travellers have their own superstitions, their own coeval and morally suspect traditions concerning "rites of passage" including birth, death and sexual behaviour. The suspicious aura that surrounds them is enhanced by what is perceived to be an exclusive nature, an exclusiveness that includes marriage within the group, the use of a "secret" language and a preference for behaviour that makes them part of a suspicious or "outsider" group who operate within a separate "sphere" within Irish society. This third discourse encompasses historical suggestions that Travellers had their own leaders or kings who ruled an "internal" society which had its own organisational criteria for life's "rites of passage", criteria which did not conform to those of the majority (non-Traveller) community.

The last discourse is one which can be linked to historical processes whereby the "othering" of Travellers and other traditionally nomadic and minority groups throughout Europe has constantly re-invented itself through a sustained reductionism that is almost theologised within language itself.

THE QUESTIONNAIRE: SOME GENERAL SUPPOSITIONS

Travellers as described by many of the Questionnaire's respondents were family groups of nomadic or semi-nomadic tradesmen who travelled from one village to another and performed jobs and services for which there was an occasional or limited demand. They tended to be endogamous, inter-marrying within certain families who were known to them and within whom they had intermarried for generations. They also tended to travel fairly regular circuits usually encompassing a relatively small area. They stayed about a week on average in a particular area before moving on to a new village or town. Most families tended to travel a circuit of two or three counties and might undertake two or three circuits a year. They generally travelled from early spring to late autumn while there was still work available. In winter their services were less in demand and many Traveller families moved less often. Some of them sheltered in abandoned farmhouses while others built small houses or rented cheap accommodation, often in the poorer sections of provincial towns. After the acquisition of tents and wagons, however, the majority of Travellers stayed living on the road all year around.

As implied by the term "tinker", many Travellers were tradesmen who worked in tin. However, they also combined tinsmithing with a range of other tasks, both skilled and unskilled, to meet their subsistence needs. Traveller occupations as described by the Questionnaire respondents were of a general and varied nature, occasionally mixing the skilled with the unskilled and the legal with that which was semi-legal. The majority of Travellers seemed to have lived independently of the wage-labour system and survived on a subsistence basis. Families supplemented the small earnings of the men with the begging and hawking activities of the women. Their work was temporary, insecure and subject to seasonal variations. Most Travellers were self-employed niche-workers who changed the work they did according to the opportunities that presented themselves in different situations. In addition to tinsmithing, they were known for peddling, hawking, fortune-telling, horse-trading, playing music and begging.

> *Déanann na fir cannaí agus sáspain agus buicéid. Na mná agus na páistí is iondúla théas timpeall dá ndíol sin, ag díol mion-earraí eile igciseán scaití (bioráin, pictiúir) nó ag iarra déirce. Bia is mó a bhíos uathu. . . . Barail ag daoine gur fearr as iad ná cuid aca féin ó tharla iad ag plé le ceannach capall freisin go minic.*[1]

---

[1] Iml. 1255: 220

(The men make cans and saucepans and buckets. The women and children normally go around selling these and selling other small items in baskets (pins, holy pictures) or begging. They usually ask for food. . . . People are of the opinion that they are better off than some of ourselves since they also often deal in horses.)

One respondent mentioned the wide range of metalwork undertaken by tinkers and also mentioned umbrella-mending, another trade that was traditionally associated with certain Travelling families:

Tinkers generally are tin-smiths. They make all sorts of household utensils, pans, cookers, mugs etc. They repair tin also and are adept at their trade. It is amazing what they can do in a few minutes on the side of the road with a sheet of tin and a hammer — just that. I have seen them turn out expert work with a piece of galvanized iron, which they first hammered out to take away the corrugation. They mend umbrellas and do all sorts of welding and soldering.[2]

They mend kitchen stoves and ranges — they sweep chimneys and clean out closets of public buildings.[3]

A respondent from County Clare, speaking of Travellers known as the MacMahons, outlined the fact that Travellers' skills extended beyond metalwork into the crafts of woodturning and woodcarving:

The gipsy men spend part of their time in making little tables and ornaments of wood or reeds. They also mend cans and tins and kettles, and in the autumn some of them take a turn gathering potatoes for the local farmers.[4]

Two respondents from the north of Ireland described those Travellers who were sometimes known as "show people" and who entertained at fairs:

One group which I know has several branches under the surname of Hunter. One family of this group has a winter residence two

---

[2] Iml. 1255: 245

[3] Iml. 1255: 245

[4] Iml. 1256: 218

miles inland from Glynn and itinerate around Ballycastle district in North Antrim in the summer. Another family of this group used to visit fairs at which the man invited others to bind him; he undertook to untie himself, however this was done. He was usually called "Tie-the-boy". He also "ate glass" and ate fire. He died two years ago. I think the other members of his family then settled down in Camlough . . .[5]

The tinkers make tins, cans and would sometimes mend tinware by soldering holes in saucepans and buckets, etc. . . . and go around from house to house selling lace and telling fortunes or selling made-up flowers of paper and wire. Some have amusements such as "Swing Boats" and "Hobby Horses" and people are glad to see them away as they take up all the people's earnings.[6]

A man from Kilfinane, County Limerick gave a good description of Travellers who worked as showpeople. Travellers who were sometimes referred to as "trick-of the-loop" men by members of the "settled" community.

Yet another departure: some have a stock of gambling games, which they set up near the town or at sports and races. A table with squares, marked: feather, cross, star, diamond and anchor is produced. A dice cube is similarly marked. You bet on the squares by putting a penny down on what you fancy. Even if all the squares are covered the odds are such that a penny remains, as the operator says, for the "use of the board". There are wheels, with numbers and cards to correspond at so much each etc. Often some produce the "old pack of cards" In the old "forty-five" game played around this district it is sometimes said when a man throws the five of trumps (best trump) rather cheaply or untimely away, "You'd get that in Cahirmee". [This is an allusion to the great fair of Cahirmee, the biggest horse fair in the south, and at one time the biggest in Ireland.] Numbers of cardsharpers or trick o' the loop men frequent that fair, not all of them tinkers either.[7]

---

[5] Iml. 1256: 211

[6] Iml. 1256: 215

[7] Iml. 1255: 201

Some respondents from the midlands described the trading in "seconds" which Travellers undertook and for which they are still known today, a respondent from County Westmeath describing the internal trading within the Traveller community itself which also contributed to the Traveller economy generally:

> During camping time they travel the roads around selling house-hold articles, usually "seconds", at prices similar to that ruling in shops. Linoleum and delph are their special lines. The men-folk trade in horses and donkeys. They favour "piebald" in horses. Have fine strong well-fed animals and good harness.[8] *(Respondent from Carlow speaking of the Berry family)*

> There is truck from one to another. They swap goods among each other. They sell tinware around their "area", sometimes artificial flowers, or peddle holy pictures, combs, hair clips. Of later years these gangs deal in goats, asses, and now and then rolls of lino-leum.[9] *(Respondent from Westmeath)*

A respondent from Clare implied that certain Traveller families were associated with a specialisation in particular trades:

> The Delaneys trade in donkeys, ponies and goats. I have never seen them do any tin-smith work. The McDonaghs come from Galway. They are good tin-smiths — repair household utensils and umbrellas, clean chimneys and school closets.[10]

A Mayo respondent outlined the subsistence strategies which were both semi-legal and indicative of an ability to adapt to the needs of the local mainstream population with whom Travellers had a symbiotic economic relationship:

> They make false coinage. They sweep chimneys. During lean pe-riods in the tin trade they interview local schoolmasters and empty the privies. . . . The main stock dealt in is asses. . . . They

---

[8] Iml. 1255: 453
[9] Iml. 1255: 454
[10] Iml. 1255: 243

used to sell soot during the war years to allotment holders. Make worms for poteen distillers. Also gadgets for fishing with.[11]

Although used as a pejorative today the term "tinker" described an important aspect of the Traveller economy. Tinsmithing is one of the crafts as practised by nomadic people to which some of the earliest references have been made in Irish literature. Hughes (1967) points out that the sparsely populated nature of early Ireland entailed a nomadic lifestyle for these craftsmen who travelled the countryside making weapons, personal ornaments and "horse trappings out of bronze, gold and silver in exchange for food and lodgings (1967: 86). Hughes posits that many of these travelling metalworkers had become more sedentary by the eight century as a consequence of the development of large monastic communities for whom they exclusively worked, but that nomadism reasserted itself with the decline of the monastic settlements between the twelfth and the fourteenth centuries. Tinkers travelled extensively throughout Britain and Ireland and probably further afield and Pound (1971) mentions sixteenth-century sources which noted the stiff competition which they provided for immigrating Roma Gypsies in the mid-1500s. Specific mention of tinkers was made in the large volume of statutes that were issued by the English government between the sixteenth and nineteenth centuries, concerned as they were about the expanding nature of the vagrancy problem that accompanied the end of the feudal way of life. Mayall (2004) links the vagrancy "problem" in England to a much wider phenomenon that became a major course of concern throughout Europe:

> . . . the increase in migrancy was not a peculiarly English feature and should be understood as part of a much wider European phenomenon associated with the transition from feudalism to capitalism. This is to locate nomadism within the longer-term economic and demographic changes which contributed to increasing landlessness and the insecurity of wage labour. . . .This, accompanied by the shift in agrarian society from demesne farming to enclosure, the dissolution of the monasteries, the break-up of feudal households, inflation and the immigration of pauper vagrants

---

[11] Iml. 1256: 95–6

> from Ireland, further contributed to the sixteenth-century increase
> in landlessness, migrancy, poverty and vagrancy. (2004: 58)

Historians have identified the period between 1560 and 1640 as the time
when concern with vagrancy became "one of the most pressing social
problems of the age" (Beier, 1985: 19). In Europe as a whole, vagrancy
or migrancy began for the first time to assume a particularly stigmatised
status, which needs:

> to be located within the structural economic developments occur-
> ring from the Middle Ages onwards and related to the move from
> bound to free labour, and from a feudal to a market-oriented capi-
> talist economy. Repression, by means of Vagrancy and Poor Law
> statutes, was a means of controlling the labour migration of so-
> called "masterless men" and of ultimately binding them to capi-
> tal. (Mayall, 2004: 59)

The reign of Edward VI (1551–2), for example, saw the issuance of the
following statute targeting tinkers and other nomads:

> For as much as it is evident that tynkers, peddlers and suche like
> vagrant persones are more hurtful than necessarie to the Common
> Wealth of this realm. Be it therefore ordeyned . . . that . . . no per-
> son or persons commonly called tynker, pedler or pety chapman
> shall wander or go from one towne, parishe or village where such
> person shall dwell, and sell punnes, topes or any suche kynde of
> wares whatsoever, or gather conne skynns or suche like things or
> use or exercise the trade or occupation of a tynker. (Cited in
> Jusserand, 1889: 155).

Travellers made a wide variety of tinware including kettles, lanterns,
buckets, milk cans and cups. Many tinsmiths were so adept that they
could make tin articles on request including worms, filters and other dis-
tilling equipment for whiskey, sand buckets for holiday-makers, horse
reins and harnesses for horse merchants and fishing rods. Tinkers who
were known as musicians, such as the Dohertys in Donegal and the Dun-
nes in Limerick, also made fiddles, whistles and parts of uilleann pipes
from tin. Travellers also spent a significant proportion of their time "job-
bing" or mending used tinware, while tinkers who were known as "metal-

runners" specialised in melting bits of metal and casting metal parts such as a new handle for a kettle or a leg for a pot. Tinsmiths sometimes came to a particular house in the neighbourhood and worked from a farmer's yard where customers came to him, echoing the older pattern of the journeyman tinker or tailor in the era prior to separate accommodation in the form of tents and wagons. In addition to tinware some Travellers specialised in the mending of clocks, crockery, earthenware milk containers and umbrellas. Interestingly, some Travellers specialised almost entirely in umbrella-making and mending to the extent that they almost formed a separate "sub-group" within the Travelling population. A Limerick Traveller named Willy Cauley gives a short description of the work of travelling umbrella-menders in Limerick city as follows:

> There were Travelling men who were experts at fixing umbrellas at one time too. I remember a lovely man named John-Joe Criggs. He died about twenty years ago, may he rest in peace. He was a Travelling man from Limerick who got a house eventually in Kileely, in Limerick city where he decided to settle down for the rest of his days. He used to go around the outskirts of Limerick city and all over the inner-city and he would get young fellas to collect little bits of copper wire for him. And he would fix broken umbrellas, a trade for which there was a big demand one time. God knows umbrellas are always needed in this country seeing as we get the odd drop of rain! Umbrella-fixing was John-Joe Criggs's gift, his own trade. He didn't go around with a horse and cart. He walked instead and he was well-known all over Limerick city. (Cited in Cauley and Ó hAodha, 2004: 20).

Tinkering was a process that gave rise to a number of interesting descriptions of the tinsmithing process as practised at the time of the Questionnaire:

> The earliest recollection I have of a local tinker was of one James McInerney. He was known locally as "Jimmy the tinker", an appellation he very much resented. He called himself a whitesmith. He dressed in typical Irish style. He wore a tall hat, knee-breeches with brass buttons, long stockings and brogues. He was a perfect tradesman — made tin-cans, tin mugs which he supplied

to the local Workhouse as well as to local shop-keepers. He used to fuse metal for which he used a bellows, coal and a ladle. This fused metal he used in the mending of pots. It was usual at the time, when a pot had a piece knocked out or had a leg broken off, to bring it to "Jimmy". When he had a number of those pots he proceeded with the work of mending. He filled each pot with clay and turned it mouth downwards. The piece was then fitted in and around it he put a "dam" of *dóibh bhuidhe* (lit: "yellow clay") (or a "tinker's dam") to confine the molten metal. This molten or fused metal he poured in over the broken piece and allowed it to cool and solidify when the job was completed. There was such another in Feakle who did the same work but used soft cow dung for the "dam". His name was O'Brien . . .[12] *(IFC respondent from Tulla, County Clare)*

---

[12] Iml. 1255: 129

Chapter 9

Constructing Irishness and the "Drop-Out" Hypothesis

Cottaar et al (1998) have outlined the fact that ethnographic portrayals of Travelling people throughout Europe have generally been conducted only within the context of marginality, criminality and poverty. They acknowledge that the social history of those groups referred to as Travellers, vagrants and Gypsies remains very clouded and implicate the pre-determined frameworks within which these studies have been conducted as part of the problem. The "poverty" framework within which a wide range of indigenous travelling groups have been studied has determined to a large extent the outcomes of the various analyses and contributed to an increasingly reductionist view of the group in question:

> . . . the framework chosen by studies on poverty already determines the outcome of the analysis. Ambulatory professions, seasonal labour and migration have often been considered as signs of social decline. The opinion dominated that only when there were no possibilities of making a living left did people start to wander and become vagrants. (1998: 4)

The poverty framework has strong analogies with the way in which Irish Travellers have been viewed by mainstream Irish society, a view echoed by the respondents to the Irish Folklore Commission. The belief that the ancestors of today's Travellers are drop-outs from the settled community continues to be the most common belief regarding Traveller origins in Ireland today and has been a major factor in the imposition of policies recommending the settlement and assimilation of Travellers. Traveller origins as recounted by the Questionnaire respondents were attributed to a range of possibilities, all of which implied a previous existence where Travellers were more respected, one where their outcast status was not apparent. That Travellers were outcasts or "drop-outs" from a previously harmonious existence with and as part of the settled community was the view expressed by the overwhelming majority of respondents to the Questionnaire. What is significant about this form of "othering" is the fact that it absolved the "settled" community from any responsibility for the difficult circumstances in which Travellers found themselves. The "blame" for Travellers' marginal status was frequently and conveniently attributed to the consequences of British rule, the tragic history of Ireland or the Travellers' own inadequacies in adapting to changing circumstances. A respondent from Omagh, County Tyrone attributed the lack of respect for Travellers prevalent in the settled community to measures instigated as part of Britain's colonisation process:

> Inquiries among many old people concur in the statement that no tinkers or travellers, in tribes or family groups, were known in this district in their youth and early days . . . The following data was mainly given me by Patrick McCullagh of Currinalt. . . . Tinkers, according to him, were originally a respected sect of local society (I have recorded this data I believe: he had new detail herewith) until "the British Government levied five pounds on their smelting pot and reduced them to beggary". Tinkers used haul this pot and other gear around in a cart or car; "they could put new legs in a pot — any job at all. The tinkers could keep a pot living a lifetime" (by repeated repair). They also mended umbrellas, as well as pots and cans, and often made stills and worms for poteen making.[1]

Other elderly respondents who would have been born in the late 1800s made even stronger links between British oppression and the origins and nomadism of Travellers:

> The tinkers, as I have stated, are believed to have descended from some of the noble clans in Ireland long ago, who were banished from all their possessions by cruel laws.[2]

---

[1] Iml. 1256: 258
[2] Iml. 1255: 282

It is thought they are the remnants of tribes who defied transplantation and absorption, but not confiscation. They have been residing in this district for centuries.[3]

Some of the tinker groups were supposed to hail from the North, and left it after the Flight of the Earls, as they were dispossessed of their lands.[4]

Are they not the displaced persons or evicted tenants of the Land War?[5]

Interestingly, few respondents mentioned the "drop-outs from the Famine" theory which is probably the most common view regarding Traveller origins in Ireland today, a fact which may indicate that the "Famine" theory has conveniently seeped into the public consciousness, the more that tensions over land accompanying urbanisation have encouraged assimilationist pressures on the part of the state. One respondent who believed the "Famine drop-out theory" assumed that a culture had built up amongst the people who "fell out" of the community through intermarriage:

> *Fadó sa drochshaol bhíodh said ag imtheacht ag cruinniú agus phós said féin a chéile agus thugadar na bóithre orthu féin.*[6]

(Long ago at that time of the Famine they used to go around begging and they married amongst one another and took to the roads permanently.)

A respondent from Northern Ireland alleged moral transgression on the part of the Travellers' ancestors when he summarised the "Nail Myth",[7] an international folktale (and folk-anecdote) of wide currency which is

---

[3] Iml. 1256: 139

[4] Iml. 1255: 148

[5] Iml. 1256: 247

[6] Iml. 1256: 29

[7] This folktale, which was well known in Ireland until recent decades, describes the traditionally nomadic lifestyle of many Traveller or Gypsy groups as a punishment for an alleged indiscretion perpetrated against a holy figure such as one of the saints, Christ or the Virgin Mary. One of the most common versions of the folktale describes the Travellers/Gypsies as a people who are forever cursed to a life of "insecurity" and wandering because they were complicit in deicide by agreeing to make the nails which crucified Christ on the Cross. See Kenrick and Puxon (1972) and Ó Héalaí (1985) for further discussion of the significance of these folktales.

alleged to provide an explanation for the "degraded" origins of Travellers
and Gypsies worldwide. Of interest is the fact that the man says he heard
a version of the "Nail Myth" from a local smith, a tradesman who would
of course have been in direct competition for business with the tinkers.

> Tradition is that the tinkers and the blacksmiths are the two oldest
> trades known or extant. Story heard locally, but not now clearly
> remembered (I recorded a version from a smith in Beragh, in
> Omagh) that tinkers made nails for the Crucifixion when black-
> smith refused; were cursed and have to keep travelling since.[8]

Cairns and Richards (1990), discussing the inequalities of binary discursive practices as relating to representations of Ireland discuss the way in
which writers such as Ashis Nandy (1983) and Homi Bhabha (1990)
foregrounded "the reciprocity between coloniser and colonised"
(Bhabha, 1990: 8). Said speaking of similarly discursive representational
practices spoke of the concept of "overlapping territories" between the
"us" and "them" or the dominant power and the subordinate. Nandy suggested that discursive assumptions and stereotypes could be used as a
protection by the subaltern as a form of self-defence. Nandy (1983),
commenting specifically on the position of the subaltern in colonised
India referred to this survival strategy as the manipulation of stereotype
on the part of the subordinate or "the psychopathology of colonisation"
(1983: 85). A similar "overlapping" process is evident in those few accounts concerning Traveller origins which the Questionnaire respondents
alleged to have garnered from Travellers themselves. In the following
account a female respondent outlines how a County Limerick Traveller
woman who called to the door of her daughter's home echoed the "settled" community version of Traveller history as a "dropping out" process
as a consequence of colonial-induced dispossession. The comments of
the same woman can also be seen as buying into the mainstream Irish
community's notion of fixity or a "sense of place" so as to enhance their
"respectability" in the eyes of the settled community:

> My daughter Lizzie lives within four miles of Rathkeale in the
> parish of Clouncagh. She has obtained some information from the

---

[8] Iml. 1256: 258

tinker families which call at her house from time to time. Rath-keale is the centre for the Sheridan and Quilligan clans. The Sheridans according to her informant, a Quilligan (an old woman) came from some place "up" in Tipperary where owing to trouble with landlords they had to leave. They stayed for some time in Tipperary town but rents being excessive they moved on and finally settled in Rathkeale, Co. Limerick.[9]

Another Limerick respondent, reporting the comments of another Traveller caller, echoed the Traveller equation of house ownership with respectability, a sentiment which continues to be replicated in Traveller/mainstream interactions even today:

> The Hegarty lady said to Lizzie that she came from Doneraile Co. Cork and belonged to the "housepeople". She took a bit of pride in this fact, but the old lady also shook her head and said she'd never leave the "van" for any house no matter how fine. They paid one shilling a week to the King Sheridan for their house. I saw where some houses of his were sold to the County Council, I think, but these were occupied by ordinary folk . . .[10]

A number of Questionnaire respondents also reiterated the "drop-out" view of Traveller origins because of their belief that some Traveller families were the descendants of people who had left a previously sedentary existence and whose surnames were still associated with the areas from where they had allegedly originated. One respondent from the Kerry Gaeltacht described the origins of the Kerry Travellers known as the Coffeys in the following manner:

> *Bhí Gaedilg mhaith ag an sean dhream de mhuintir Cathbhuaidh ach níl sí ag an dream óg. Deiridís gur i bparóiste na Tuatha idir Cillorglan is Corán Tuathail a bhí a sinnsir fadó. Tá an cine flúirseach go fóill ann.*[11]

---

[9] Iml. 1255: 331

[10] Iml. 1255: 334

[11] Iml. 1255: 19

(The old people amongst the Coffeys had good Irish but the young people don't have much Irish. It is said that their ancestors came from a parish called Tuatha between Killorglin and Carrantoohil. That family is still plentiful around that area.)

Another Munster respondent also reiterated the view that some local Travellers' origins lay in the local settled community, a fact which is significant in view of the longevity of "genealogical memory" that is typical of many rural Irish communities:

> *Is ó Chill a'Dísirt a tháinig na Faulkners i dtosach. Bhí an t-athair is an máthair ina gcomhnaidhe ann. Céardaidhe stáin a b'eadh eisean agus phós sé bean de na Cárthaigh. Deirtear go raibh braon éigin d'fhuil na dtinncéar inte siúd.*[12]

(The Faulkners were from Kildysart originally. The father and mother were living there. He was a tinsmith and he married one of the Carthys. It was said that there was a drop of the tinker blood in her.)

That Travellers exoticised their origins so as to both appear more "respectable" in the eyes of the "settled" community and in an effort to fit into the logocentric or univocal early twentieth-century view of Irish history incorporating the colonisation and dispossession of a once-unified and noble Gaelic people is probable. A respondent from County Cork said that Travellers had described for him a lineage that incorporated nobility, a concept encapsulated in the common Irish phrase whereby Travellers were described as "knights of the road":

> Some tinkers claim to belong to Irish septs and the names Driscolls, Learys, McCarthys, etc. would seem to support this claim. The want of a home of their own may have constrained them to use disused houses for the purposes of a home.[13]

---

[12] Iml. 1255: 272
[13] Iml. 1255: 142

The view that their origins lie in the infliction of a historical "wrong" is echoed by certain Travellers. An anonymous Traveller quoted in *Irish Tinkers* (1976) described Traveller origins like this:

> Well it happened in Scotland during the Clearances, it happened in Ireland with Cromwell. We are born into times of persecution when countrymen were dividing the lands. That's what has us blackguarded that we don't know our names rightly and the right way of saying what happened to the lands and all belonging to us ... (Ó Fearadhaigh and Wiedel, 1976: 9)

Another also echoed a history of origin that encapsulated the notion of "fallen nobility":

> There are no more tinkers, Daughter, no more. If there was, you'd have to go and make a spleen over it. Some say we took to the road with a curse that hung over us since Cromwell. Some say we're the old from before the Famine and we have the old family names of the old Celtic lords. But there's no more tinkers. Not since the time of the Black Stranger and ever since we're eking out our history on the old dole money. (Anonymous Traveller in Ó Fearadhaigh and Wiedel, 1976: 27)

The notion that the Travellers are the "true" Irish people who lost their true status through adversity is also a sentiment that pervades the discourse of Travellers themselves when discussing their origins and their currently marginalised position in Irish society: "We are the real Irish, the true original Irish (Mongan, 2000: 125). This concept of the "true" Irish can also be seen as a defence mechanism against two discourses which served to exclude Travellers. These were the discourses of Gypsiology which defined Travellers as less "true" or less "culturally pure" than other more "exotic" Travelling groups such as the Gypsies; and the discourse of the emergent Irish nation-state where Travellers were virtually excluded from the historical story of the nation by virtue of their perceived "drop-out" status. Traveller activists like Margeret Sweeney have incorporated this notion in their struggle for Travellers rights and the societal acknowledgement of Traveller identity. In a speech given in University College Galway in 1986, Sweeney said that Travellers were

entitled to live in caravans and on serviced sites because of their distinctive way of life, culture and tradition, a tradition which represented the
essence of Irishness:

> I think that the Travelling people are the true Irish people of Ire-
> land and no Travelling person should be ashamed of what we are.
> We should be proud of it because we came from real Irish people.
> Our ancestors fought for this country and they had to leave their
> homes just the same as I'm sure some of yours had to years ago. .
> . . Now is the time for the politicians to stand up and realise that
> we are Irish people. We have a right to be in this country. We
> have a right to say where we want to live. We have a right to live
> the way we want to live and it's not up to anybody else to plan
> how we should live. (Sweeney in Helleiner, 2000: 127)

Helleiner (1998) has suggested that the endogamous marriage patterns
characteristic of Irish Traveller marriages and the importance of kinship
to Traveller identity may also have been a factor in the dissemination of
this notion of Travellers as the "true" Irish, a notion which may para-
doxically have obscured the heterogeneity of the Traveller population:

> The significance of kinship to Traveller identity was apparent in
> the assertion that all Travellers were related to one another, and
> could claim pure Irish ancestry. Travellers' claims to be the
> "pure" or "true" Irish challenged the dominant non-Traveller
> stigmatization of them as a collectivity, but also obscured internal
> divisions among the Travellers themselves. (1998: 28)

Traveller declarations of their "true" status may also have been a response to the Gipsilorist discourse of the "true" Romany and attendant
hierarchisation of Travelling groups which had also entered the scholarly
discourse in Ireland as evidenced by the theories of folklorist Séan
McGrath (discussed in Chapter 2). That this concept of the "true" Gypsy
or Traveller with a particular link to occupational status had entered the
Irish public imaginary is clear from quite a few responses to the IFC
Tinker Questionnaire. The demise of the tinsmithing trade from as early
as the first decades of the twentieth century and the disappearance of the
"true" tinker meant that many respondents saw Travellers who were not

tinsmiths as less "true", or as a motley collection of misfits and drop-outs who were economically redundant. The testimony of a 66-year-old fisherman from Clear Island in County Cork indicates as much:

> *Ba chuimhin liom agus mé óg go bhfeaca tincéirí siubhail, go raibh ceard an stáin aca, ag dul ó tig go tig, ag deisiú is a miúndáil áiristí stain agus ag díol áiristí nuadh. Ní rabhadar ag baint leis an ndrom so "drom tincéirí". Do bhídís ag imeacht na naonar ag obair go neamhspléach dóibh péinn. Ba chuimin liom duine aca d'fiscint ag teacht chuin an tighe seo, a mhála lúbana tuighe caithte air a drom, thuas idir a dhá shlineán aige agus a sámhthfach an chasúra sáighte isteach thrí stropaí a bhí a mbéal an mhála, ceann na sámhthfaí de dhruim a ghualann aige, agus greim an phartáin aige ar.*

> (I remember when I was young that I saw walking tinkers that had the tin trade, going from house to house, fixing tin items and selling new items. They didn't belong to this crowd "the crowd (tribe) of tinkers". They would go around on their own working independently for themselves. I remember seeing one of them coming to this house, his bag of loops thrown on his back, right up between his shoulder blades. His hammer would be stuck in between the straps that were on his bag, the head of the hammer jutting out over the back of his shoulder and he holding onto it with the grip of a crab (i.e. a good grip).)

The possibility of a real historical link between the ancestors of today's Travellers and Irish "noble" families who may have lost their ancestral lands was given some credence by the late Bryan MacMahon. An American student named Electa Bachmann O'Toole who interviewed MacMahon in the early 1970s repeated MacMahon's opinion that some of today's Traveller families may be descendants of some of the most poweful Irish septs who lost status with colonisation:

> He explained that, traditionally, the various tribes have travelled in a small area and that they refer to this area as their "cut". This term comes from an Irish Gaelic word, meaning share. Formerly, no tribe could safely invade the cut of another. . . . Mr MacMahon found it interesting that the cut of some families is the same area

which, in ancient times, belonged to the clans of the same name, such as the O'Briens in the Kerry area. (O'Toole, 1972: 10)

The fact that Irish tinkers allegedly elected "kings" at horse fairs such as Ballinasloe in County Galway helped to perpetuate the image of "tarnished nobility": although in fact, a "king" had no more authority by virtue of his title than he would have had because of his position as the senior male parent of his immediate family:

> . . . in Ballinasloe in October I saw hundreds of gipsies or tinkers there . . . eligibles from each family fought for the kingship. The champion who was successful in overcoming all his rivals was declared "King of the Gipsies" as long as he lived.[14]

Another view of Traveller history incorporating both "dispossession" and a previously more "noble" and "respected" existence was the possibility that the Travellers were descended from the bards or hereditary musicians who played a leading role in the fosterage and maintenance of the purity of Gaelic culture:

> I knew tinkers in County Leitrim in about 1912 named McDonaghs. They camped on our road every winter. . . . They were the soul of honour and decency. . . . There were seven children and the father and mother. . . . The father (Martin) told us they were descended from the bards and they were very proud of the fact.[15]

Historical evidence for "bardic" influence in the evolution of Traveller identity is increasingly cited by Travellers themselves:

> Ward is one of the most common names in the Traveller community. This comes from the Irish Mac an Bháird meaning "son of the bard" and in past times the Travellers were the bards. (McDonagh, 2000: 22)

Possible links between the Travellers and the bards were mooted by the early gypsilorists based on linguistic evidence. Charles Leland, one of

---

[14] Iml. 1256: 227

[15] Iml. 1255: 381

the first scholars to have discovered the existence of the Travellers' "secret" language Shelta surmised that the Travellers' language was:

> an artificial, secret, or Ogam tongue, used by the bards, and transferred by them, in all probability, to the bronze workers and jewellers — a learned and important body — from whom it descended to the tinkers. (Leland, 1892: 195)

Recent analysis of Shelta by Ó Baoill (1994) and Ó hAodha (2002a, 2002c) points to the existence of "disguise" processes like metathesis and the interchange of consonants and hints at possible cross-fertilisation between tinkers and other Travellers and/or the existence of a more diverse or "amorphous" population of Travelling people in earlier times, including highly literate Travelling people such as Travelling bards and monks. The oral history of the Travellers themselves also provides clues in this regard, the link between "fallen" nobility and the "travelling scholar" or poet serving as a bolstering factor for Traveller self-identity as outlined by the Traveller and writer Seán Maher (1972):

> Make no mistake son, we on the road are descended — not from the famine era or the Cromwellian era — but from the days of the kings of Ireland and their clans. . . . Another thing son . . . a lot, if not all, of the writing that has survived from early Irish history was written by travellers. . . .These are things that historians have overlooked, or is it they want to overlook? These men overlook too our great scholars of the past. They skip or gloss over the wanderlust of such people as the monks in the early Christian days; St Patrick himself was a great *pavvy* (lit: Traveller). Then there were the Irish minstrels who travelled the country to entertain. All these men — your ancestors and mine that is . . . you must realise that being born to the road is no disgrace, for behind you is a unique culture, language and way of life that has survived for many centuries. (1972: 97–101)

Factual historical evidence exists linking at least one well-known Traveller family with bardic antecedents. The tinsmith and musician John Doherty, one of the "Simey" Dohertys, who was born in 1895, is generally acknowledged as the most famous fiddler ever to have come from County Donegal, a county which has specialised in producing talented fiddlers from one generation to the next. His nomadism, amongst other factors, led to him having such a huge influence on the musical tradition of his native county. His family like many other families were said to be descended from "bardic aristocracy" and genealogical records show that his great-grandaunt Neansaí Rua Nic Shuibhne (Red Nancy Mac-Sweeney) was an aunt of Tarlach MacSuibhne (Turlough MacSweeney) the man known as the Píobaire Mór (the Big Piper) and a hereditary piper to the Sweeneys, aristocratic Gaelic princes and landowners who controlled significant swathes of County Donegal in the era prior to colonisation. An aristocratic aura was said to be part of the Donegal Dohertys' nature according to this "picturesque" description:

> *Tig bean tincleora isteach agus dhá pháiste léithi agus mála líonta d'áráistí stain. . . .Mar is gnách lena leithéid labhrann sí go deas séimh le bunaidh an toighe. De threibh na nDochartach í. Sin na "Simeys" nó tá Simon mar ainm coitianta sa teaghlach i gcónaí. Bhí said i gcónaí ag obair ar an stán agus bíonn said uilig go maith ag seinm ar an bhfideal agus an seancheol ar fad acu. Siúlann said go státiúil ar an mbóthar agus deirtear go bhfuil said síolraithe ó na ríthe.*[16]

(A tinker woman comes in accompanied by two children, her bag filled with tin items. As is usual for her type she speaks in a nice gentle voice to the occupants of the house. She is one of the Doherty clan. One of the "Simeys" as they are called, because Simon has always been a common name in the family. They were always tin-workers and they are all good at playing the fiddle, many of them being experts on the older tunes. They walk along the road in a stately fashion and it is said that they are descended from the kings.)

That Travellers "exoticised" their origins in order that they might be treated more humanely and viewed with less suspicion is further indicated by the association of Travellers with the more romantic and thereby "acceptable" tradition of the romantic "Gypsy" as outlined in the Victorian discourse of gypsiology and in literature and film:

---

[16] Iml. 1256: 35

> Many of these gypsies, especially the females, have lovely brown
> eyes, a nice gait and to a great extent a resemblance to the people
> of eastern lands from which it is thought that they came to Europe
> and after many years later to Ireland. Some of them maintained
> that they are natives of Spain and that their descendants left the
> poor land long ago to settle in some more suitable country where
> life would not be poor.[17] *(Respondent from Kildare)*

Traveller "Othering" in terms of origin was given a more exotic slant
incorporating romanticism and the mysterious by being telescoped
within the history of the Gypsies who were associated with England and
continental Europe.

> Nothing is known of their origin locally but Mr. O'Neill is of the
> opinion that they are an off-shoot of the gipsies. They have been
> coming to this district longer than he can remember and his
> memory goes back 70 years.[18] *(Respondent from Clare)*

> Frank Corduff, to whom I am indebted for much of my material,
> says the tinkers are of alien origin who in the course of their
> wanderings settled down in this country in the dim past, adopted
> Irish names, and to this day have preserved their distinctiveness
> and individuality.[19] *(Respondent from Ballina, County Mayo)*

When one examines the nature of social upheaval experienced by the
Irish peasantry between the eighteenth and nineteenth centuries it is not
so surprising that the most current and commonly held explanation for
the existence of Irish Travelling people situates their emergence within
the context of dispossession and eviction, particularly the last great "dispossession" engendered by the Great Famine of 1845. It will never be
possible to know how many spailpíní and dispossessed labourers joined
those Travelling craftsmen/dealers already on the road at the time of the
Famine. S.B. Gmelch (1974) suggests that the nomenclature of present-
day Irish Travellers indicates that at least some Travellers are descendants of dispossessed peasants. The fact that 11 of the 15 most common

---

[17] Iml.. 1256: 285

[18] Iml. 1255: 239

[19] Iml. 1256: 120

surnames found amongst Travelling families today (e.g. Ward, McDonagh, McGinley, etc.) are unmistakably west of Ireland in origin — the area where the greatest number of evictions occurred and where the peasantry found themselves most destitute — she says, is indicative of possible origins in dispossession. Given the oral nature of Traveller culture and their virtual invisibility in Irish public records it is likely that the exact origins of the Traveller community will remain a matter of conjecture. What remains most pertinent to the Traveller fight for self-recognition in the modern era is that the belief that their ancestors were drop-outs from the settled community is the most commonly-held belief amongst the settled community in Ireland today.

That Travellers may be fairly recent "drop-outs" as a consequence of the last great societal calamity in Ireland — the Great Famine of the late 1840s — is often mooted as a source of origin in Irish public discourse. This view is prevalent despite the existence of large communities of Irish-American Travellers in the southern United States, communities who continue to exhibit cultural traits associated with the Irish Travelling community — e.g. language, economic strategies of self-employment, endogamy, etc. — and whose ancestors left Ireland at the time of the Great Famine. That it is a culture that pre-dates the Famine is irrelevant to popular perceptions of Travellers as drop-outs who hit the road at a period of widespread social upheaval and poverty. Traveller activists in Ireland are today increasingly challenging the "drop-out" notion because of its ideological significance in the imposition of state-led assimilation-ist polices in Ireland and because of its negative implications for Travel-ler self-identity. Traveller and Traveller activist Michael McDonagh (2000) summarises the historical evidence for the existence of Travellers which predates the Great Famine and which indicates the presence of a distinct Traveller identity. He also instances the existence of the word "Tincéard" (meaning "Tin trade") in Irish language sources which date as far back as the twelfth century as indicating the existence of a group of distinct craftspeople who practised tinkering. He also refers to the six-teenth-century Irish and British laws enacted to repress those Travelling people then referred to as "Egyptians". McDonagh (2000) acknowledges the difficulties in pinpointing an exact historical moment when Travel-lers came into existence. He challenges the "drop-out" image as applied to Travellers in Irish public discourse, a discourse that serves to legitimate attempts at their assimilation.

> I am not trying to prove the exact origins of Travellers in Irish society, but to disprove any theories that suggest that we only came about as a result of some disaster in Irish history. The perception that we are drop-outs or misfits, because either ourselves or our ancestors couldn't cope, is wrong . . . No longer is it acceptable to say that Travellers were settled people and therefore it's perfectly alright to resettle or reassimilate them. Now you must look at Travellers as having an identity and culture to be celebrated and resourced. (2000: 21)

Nan Joyce (1985), another Traveller spokesperson and the first Irish Traveller ever to campaign for a seat in the Dáil (Irish Parliament) points to the oral tradition as a buffer to the drop-out theory:

> Some of my ancestors went on the road in the Famine but more of them have been travelling for hundreds of years — we're not drop-outs like some people think. The Travellers have been in Ireland since St. Patrick's time, there's a lot of history behind them though there's not much written down — it's what you get from your grandfather and what he got from his grandfather. (1985: 1)

The advent of increased levels of literacy within the Traveller community has meant that Travellers have begun to challenge "exotic" notions of their origins and highlight instead the diverse make-up of the Irish Travelling population:

> The original travellers were tinsmiths and musicians and they were great carpenters, they made all their own musical instruments and the wagons and carts. Over the years they mixed in with Travellers from other countries, like the Spanish who came to Ireland four or five hundred years ago. You can see the Spanish blood coming out today in our family; my mother and her brothers were completely dark. . . . My other granny's name was Power, that's a Norman name. Her people would have been English travellers who came here years and years ago and married in with Irish travellers. Then there were settled who took to the road for various

reasons and mixed in with the travellers. One of my great-grandfathers, going back six or seven grannies, was a Protestant minister. His son married in with the Joyces, a tribe from Galway. Other people were burned out during the Cromwell evictions or they were made homeless during the Famine. (Joyce, 1985: 2)

Perhaps the last word can be left to the Travellers themselves as narrated in the folktales recorded by Tong (1989):

This happened long ago. A gypsy and his family were travelling along. His horse was skinny and none too steady on his legs, and as the Gypsy's family grew he found it harder to pull the weighty wagon. Soon the wagon was so full of children tumbling over one another that the poor horse could barely stumble along the rutted track. As the wagon rumbled on, veering first to the left, then rocking to the right, pots and pans would go tumbling out, and now and then a barefoot child was pitched headlong onto the ground. It was not so bad in daylight — then you could pick up your pots and tiny children — but you could not see them in the dark. In any case, who could keep count of such a tribe? And the horse plodded on its way. The Gypsy travelled right around the earth, and everywhere he went he left a child behind: more and more and more. And that you see is how Gypsies came to be scattered about the earth. (1989: 39)

Chapter 10

Parasite and Pariah:
Some Traveller Stereotypes

A MORALLY SUSPECT "OTHER"

The second significant discursive "Othering" evident in the construction of Irish Travellers as defined by the settled community respondents to the Irish Folklore Commission concerns the representation of Travellers as a morally degenerate group whose socially exclusive mode of life was a cover for suspicious behaviour and crime. A wide range of reductionist stereotypes were applied to Travellers, many of which were analogous to discursive descriptions of archetypal Travellers/Gypsies in other countries. Cottaar et al. (1998) have described the pervasive institutionalisation of such ideas in Europe, even within socio-economic and socio-historical scholarship:

> During the last few decades the negative image of travelling groups among professional historians has only changed slowly. It is not strange to see that in more general overviews of the socio-economic history of Europe the image is repeated time and again. A good example is the recent book by Henri Kamen (1986) on Western European history in the sixteenth and seventeenth centuries, in which "poverty", "beggary", "vagrancy", "seasonal migration" and criminality are lumped together point blank. More or less the same mixture can be found in Wehler's (1987) overview of German social history. Travelling people are depicted as aimless wanderers, whose criminal behaviour forced authorities to adopt cruel repression. (Cottaar et al., 1998: 135)

Travellers in Ireland were accused of a wide range of vices including depravity, sexual immorality, dishonesty, filth and violence. In short, they were constructed as the archetypal embodiments of deviance and anti-social behaviour. The discursive construction of Irish Travellers as defined in Ireland was able to draw on two principal well-springs of stereotypical reductionism. These were the negative constructions of Gypsies and Travellers in the European imaginary generally and the long discourse of anti-Irish "Othering" that had existed in Ireland associated with colonisation, a discourse where the words Irish and Ireland were indelibly linked with immorality, violence, parasitism and deception. To see how sweepingly dismissive attitudes towards the "archetypal" Gypsy or Traveller as defined by writers such as Grellmann (1787) have infiltrated the European imaginary so as to achieve the full sanction of scholars and the intelligentsia it is necessary only to examine the comments of a professor of psychiatry and criminology at the University of Turin in the early years of the twentieth century. His opinion concerning Gypsies was published by the American Institute of Criminal Law and Criminology in 1918 and it bears striking analogies with the construction of Irish Travellers:

> They are the living example of a whole race of criminals, and have all the passions and all the vices of criminals. They have a horror of anything that requires the slightest application; they will endure hunger and misery rather than submit to any continuous labour whatever; they work just enough to keep from dying of hunger . . . they are vain, like all delinquents, but they have no fear or shame. Everything they earn, they spend for drink or ornaments. They may be seen barefooted, but with bright coloured or lace-bedecked clothing, without stockings, but with yellow shoes. They have the improvidence of the savage and that of the criminal as well . . . they devour half-putrified carrion. They are given to orgies, love a noise, and make a great outcry in the markets, they murder in cold blood in order to rob, and were formerly suspected of cannibalism . . . this race, so low morally, and so incapable of cultural and intellectual development, is a race that can never carry on any industry, and which in poetry has not got beyond the poorest lyrics. (Lombroso, 1918: 40)

Stealing is a stereotype which has been associated with Travellers and Gypsies for centuries. Some of the earliest descriptions of "Egyptians" (Travellers/Gypsies) in Britain linked the survival of nomadic people with stealing. An *Acte concyng Egypsyans (*1530–31), issued by Henry VIII, maintained that "Egyptians" survived by "using deep, deceitful practises" and by the use of "greate subtyll and craftye meanes to deceyve the people" including palmistry, robbery and pickpocketing (cited in Mayall, 2004: 68). A woman from County Galway gave sustenance to this stereotypical denunciation of the Travellers:

> *An fhaid is a bhíonn siad sa gceanntar bíonn siad ag goid agus ag fuadach. Is fada leis na daoine nó go mbíonn said ag imtheacht.*[1]

> (So long as they are in the locality they are stealing and plundering. The people can't wait until they are leaving.)

A respondent from the Kerry Gaeltacht implied that stealing was a hereditary part of the Travellers' nature:

> *Táid tugtha do ghoid, tugtha do bhruid, tugtha do throid is tugtha d'innsint bréag, mar is dual sinnsear dóibh.*[2]

> (They are given to stealing and brutality, they are given to fighting and to telling lies as was natural for their ancestors.)

This echoes the Traveller/Gypsy archetype that was created by Grellmann (1787) at the end of the eighteenth century. Grellmann theorised that idleness and laziness were inherent to the Gypsy lifestyle and that it was only through begging and stealing that the majority of Gypsies survived. Concepts such as honour or shame were anathema to them in his view except for the handful of Gypsies who practised vaguely respectable professions such as the Transylvanian gold-panners and some musicians. From the rest of the Gypsy population no-one was safe:

---

[1] Iml. 1256: 27

[2] Iml. 1255: 272

He considered their work to be a smokescreen that made it easier for them to be able to steal things. Gypsy women especially knew precisely how to go about their business: sales talk at the front door and children breaking in at the back. That was why, he insists, they were so eager to visit annual markets. They joined forces then in gangs; men and women began to disport themselves scandalously to divert tradespeople while others meanwhile picked unattended stalls clean. (Willems, 1997: 54)

Hancock has pointed to the longevity of this stereotype as evidenced by its endurance in police department descriptions of Gypsy society in the US, where the innocent personage of the Gypsy woman continues to be seen as a "cover" for more elaborate scams:

The label of "Gypsy" refers to any family-oriented band of nomads who may be from any country in the world. . . . The only measure of respect a Gypsy woman can get is based on her abilities as a thief. (Schroeder in Hancock, 1987: 112)

It is likely that there is some truth in some of the allegations regarding stealing and trickery on the part of Travellers, although the stereotype has no doubt magnified the extent of the problem beyond all realistic proportions. As Hancock (1987) has argued, survival in times of poverty has provided justification for petty stealing on the part of many social groups including Travellers and Gypsies:

Problems which exist today are the result of a continuum of circumstances going back for centuries. Few could argue that there has not been moral justification for subsistence stealing in the past, or that in some places it continues to be necessary, although this is not likely to be taken into consideration in a court of law. Historically, stealing has meant survival, and there are many shopkeepers throughout Europe, even today, who will not serve Gypsies. There are homeowners, too, who will refuse to give Gypsies as much as a glass of water. (1987: 121)

Travellers who pilfered petty items such as a few turnips or potatoes from a field were normally only doing so to meet their subsistence needs. Cottaar et al. (1998), citing the German context, have pointed out that the scholarly tendency to use criminal records to construct a picture of the past has given credence to the stereotype that nomadic groups and crime were inextricably linked. They refer to recent socio-historical studies on migratory groups in Germany and Austria (e.g. Schubert and Schubert, 1983) which conclude that migratory groups in general were criminal and poor by virtue of the fact that so many ambulant professions are mentioned in the lists of "wanted" people. Scholars such as Schubert acknowledge at the same time, however, the nature of criminalising processes and the likelihood that the historical picture is skewed:

> He shows how distrustful central authorities were, trying therefore to forbid and criminalise ambulant professions. The people involved were regarded to be of a low moral standard and their professions as a cloak for begging "and criminal behaviour". Schubert shows that in practice many local authorities were tolerant because they knew that this image did not completely hold true. (Cottaar et al., 1998: 138)

The association of Travellers with stealing was central to one of the most frightening images inculcated in some "settled" children from an early age. This was the image of the Traveller as a child-stealer. G. Gmelch (1977), commenting on the very early development of anti-Traveller prejudice on the part of the "settled" population links the fear of the Traveller "other" with the notion that Travellers are child-stealers:

> Parents often discourage misbehaviour in their children by threatening to let the tinkers "steal" them if they are bad. One elderly Traveller recalls the alarm her family's presence created in some settled children:

> "Sometimes we'd be goin' along in our pony and car [cart] when we'd come across a bunch of school children. Well, they'd drop their things and run off like they'd seen the devil himself. I'd get a terrible fright thinkin' one of them might fall and get hurt and we'd get the blame. Somebody must be tellin' them terrible stories about Travellin' People." (Biddy Brien in Gmelch, 1977: 203)

Timoty Neat's book *The Summer Walkers* (1996) is the most comprehensive ethnographic work on the Scottish Travellers written to date. It links the image of child-stealing with Traveller adoption, a practice that was quite common amongst the Scottish Travellers, a group who have inter-married heavily with Irish Travellers over the past few hundred years:

> . . . adoption became . . . a common fact of life. It was used by the Travellers as a deliberate mechanism to preserve families and to bolster the group's minority status. It did not perpetuate the north Highland Traveller way of life but it is a phenomenon of great hu-man interest because, for centuries, across Europe, the Gypsies have been feared and demonised as "child stealers", and in Scot-land, stories about Tinker theft, abduction and purchase of children have been an integral part of popular folklore . . . it is certainly true that some children/lovers have run away with the Gypsies —but the vast bulk of these stories are fabricated myths, reflecting fears not reality. . . . Unwanted children have, almost by tradition, been given to the Travellers and Gypsies. . . . Circumstance and need have encouraged Travellers to "adopt" unwanted youngsters. It was a natural consequence of their nomadism, their numerical vulner-ability, their traditional humanity and family-centredness. Over the years, guilt-twisted remembrance has turned "giving" into "tak-ing", agreed "deals" into "theft" . . . (Neat, 1996: 225)

A similar allegation of child kidnap incorporating ritual murder has been a stock trait of anti-Semitic discourse in the European imaginary for cen-turies and it is interesting that this stereotype was prevalent in the dis-course of the Jew as "Other" in many European countries prior to the Second World War. If ever proof were needed of the discursive power of the stereotype, even amongst the intellectual class, then this stereotype of the Jew as "Other" is an excellent example. For instance, Charles Bew-ley, the Irish envoy in Germany during the Second World War and a prominent Nazi supporter, raised the allegation of child kidnap and mur-der when defending Germany's policy of dismissing Jews from their jobs. Reporting to the Irish government in Dublin he sent literature out-lining the allegation that the Jews engaged in ritual child murder, an al-legation which had also earlier been directed at Jews in Limerick city in the early 1900s, and a premise which was used in Germany to support claims for the eradication of Jewish influence in German society. Bewley reported that while the question of ritual murder was not essential to the theory that Jewish society influence needed to be curtailed it was nevertheless the case that "This belief is held, to my own knowledge, by many well-educated and intelligent people". Bewley also questioned Jewish denials of the stereotype, thereby implying the possibility that there was some truth to them. He wondered why:

> . . . in the circumstances, on the assumption that ritual murders do not in fact take place, it seems regrettable that the Jewish authorites do not deal more circumstantially with the very detailed charges made. A general denial or denunciation of "medieval superstition" is an unsatisfactory method of meeting accusations which give dates and names, nor does it explain why at all periods and in all countries this particular charge should have been fastened to the Jewish race alone. (Bewley cited in Keogh, 1998: 102)

A Scottish Traveller named Essie Stewart providing refutation of the child-stealing stereotype by describing her own adoption and the tradition of Traveller adoption generally:

> At that time I didn't know about my own adoption — but looking back, giving children away must have been common in the Highlands, right up until the 1950s. I know myself, five people, alive today, who were given away as children to the Travellers. There were so few of us, we needed new people, and for the country folk there was nothing easier, nothing better, than giving unwanted children to Travellers. My step-brother, Gordon Stewart, he was adopted. He says if the Stewarts hadn't taken him in, he wouldn't have ended up on the dunghill! They say the Gypsies steal children! It was not stealing — but like us, the Gypsies must have been children. We gave lives and homes to many an unwanted child who might have died, been killed, put into institutions — or today, of course, not seen the light of day. (Essie Stewart in Neat, 1996: 9).

Her views are echoed by an Irish Traveller who describes the "adoption" of a local settled child by his family:

> . . . the other fella was named Simon Connor. He wasn't a Traveller by birth but my Mam reared him as if he was one of our own. He

travelled with us whenever we hit the road. I remember the morn-
ing Simon Connor arrived in our house very well. We were living
in Crumlin and the rain was lashing down outside the *glazier* (win-
dow). My mother saw him outside and he drenched in the *pani*
(rain) and she asked him in for a cup of tea. He came into the house
and he never went home after that. He stayed with us and went to
school from our *cén* (house) like the rest of us. When we would go
away travelling during the summer he would go away with us. And
he became as good a Traveller as any of us. He was like a brother
to us. (Dunne and Ó hAodha, 2004: 4)

The irony of the stereotype associating Travellers with child-stealing is
not lost on Irish Travellers who saw the state's attempts at assimilation
often framed in terms of the threat to "institutionalise" or take away their
children because they were allegedly "at risk" from the Traveller lifestyle (see Helleiner, 2000, for a more in-depth discussion of the nature of
these assimilationist policies). Nan Donahue, whose autobiography *Nan*
(1986) is one of the few firsthand accounts of Traveller life written in
Ireland, described the dangers of turning to "outside" help for assistance
in the pre-social welfare era. Aside from the convents who supplied food
to Traveller children, the only other source for food was "the 'cruelty'
[National Society for Prevention of Cruelty to Children], and if you went
and complained or said you had no way to keep yourself, the kids was
taken from you" (Donahue and Gmelch, 1986: 81). The threat to "take
away the children" was also used by some of the authorities in Ireland in
attempts to evict Travellers from certain localities until relatively recently. The notion of child "abduction" was consequently inverted by
Travellers who saw the threat as an example of the inhumanity of the
settled community, as noted by Canadian anthropologist Jane Helleiner
(2000) when living on a Traveller site in Galway in the 1980s:

Another woman living in a different camp expressed outrage
when city officials, in an attempt to evict Travellers from the
camp, threatened to imprison her neighbour and institutionalise
her children if she did not leave . . . children were central to constructions of Traveller identity and Traveller/non-Traveller
boundary making. An allegedly greater love for children was part
of a Traveller identity defined in opposition to the alleged anti-

> child character of non-Travellers. Travellers often pointed to their
> larger families in support of this claim and cited news reports of
> crimes against children such as abuse and abandonment as con-
> firmation of the hostility and cruelty of settled people towards
> children. I was frequently told that Travellers would never engage
> in such behaviour. (2000: 121)

It is known that some Traveller children were institutionalised in orphan-
ages and industrial schools in Ireland prior to the 1960s and that others
were continually fearful of this possibility (see Joyce, 1985: 48; and
Pavee Point, 1992: 26). It has also been suggested that some Traveller
children were forcibly removed from their parents and placed in residen-
tial care because they were classed as being of "no fixed abode" (see
McDonagh and McDonagh, 1993: 39) although this claim requires more
extensive research. The mirror-stereotype of the child-stealing state on the
part of Travellers or Gypsies has a very strong resonance in the Traveller
and Gypsy communities of many countries, which has been highlighted
by Roma activists like Hancock (1987) who have pointed to the deliberate
removal, in countries such as Austria, of Roma children from their families and their institutionalisation, as parts of larger governmental attempts
to assimilate Travellers and Gypsies. The stereotype of child kidnap or
adoption has also recently resurfaced in Europe (including Ireland) with
new waves of Roma (Gypsy) emigration from Eastern Europe. Sensational media reporting has contributed to the image of the Gypsy "Other"
as a group who practise "coeval" customs in the form of child-bride and
arranged/dowry marriages. A number of cases of this form of arranged
marriage as practised in the Roma community have received media attention in Ireland in recent times, with the Irish police instigating "searches"
for Roma girls who have allegedly been "kidnapped" into marriage.

Irish Travellers and stealing were also interlinked in the imagination
by a practice which both Travellers and settled people agree was a cause
of tension between communities. This was the property damage caused by
trespassing horses. A respondent to the IFC Questionnaire from Navan,
County Meath, had this description:

> The animals graze on the roadsides. Some of the gipsies with a
> number of caravans seek to turn horses from the roadside into

fields during the night, unknown to the owner. This creates friction and the Gardaí are usually brought on the scene. Their removal from the district follows.[3]

Ireland was so poor in the early part of the twentieth century that even the Traveller practice of grazing their horses along the "long acre" — the strip of grass along the verge of the road — was resented by farmers, especially those in areas where the land was less fertile, as pointed out by G. Gmelch (1977):

> Conditions were so poor that many farmers were forced to utilise some of the same marginal resources as itinerants. Because pasturage was scarce they grazed their animals on the roadside, in direct competition with the Tinkers' horses and donkeys. Many farmers also snared rabbits; they greatly resented Tinkers doing the same, especially on private land. (1977: 22)

A respondent from the Gaeltacht highlighted the extent of the tension between the Travelling and settled Irish over the question of horses and grazing:

> *San oidhche cuirid na capaill is na h-asail isteach ins na páirceanna agus bíonn gardaí is feirmeoirí ar a dtóir annsan. Is maith leo móinfhéar i gcóir na h-oidhche. Cúpla blian ó shoin bhí feirmeóir ar an dtaobh theas d'Inis, agus bhí sé cráidhte ag na capaill céadna. Oíche amháin tháinig sé ortha agus iad istigh sa choirce — chaith sé leo len a ghunna agus chuir sé pileár tré dhíon na cairte mar a raibh na tincéirí. Thugadar an feirmeóir chun na cúirte ach is beag sásamh a fuaireadar mar bhí fhios ag an ngiúistís gurbh iad na tincéirí bhí ciontach.[4]*

(In the night they put the horses and the donkeys into the fields and the guards and the farmers are after them then. They like the meadow grass for the night. A few years ago there was a farmer on the south side of Inch, and he was tormented by the same horses. One night he found them inside in his oats — and he shot at them and he put a bullet through the roof of one of the tinker's

---

[3] Iml. 1255: 379

[4] Iml. 1255: 58

wagons. They brought the farmer to the court but they got very little satisfaction from the court because the judge knew that it was the tinkers were guilty.)

A Traveller from Limerick city described the fear he felt as a child after being "burnt out" of an area because of an incident concerning horses and linked with the repression of another "Other" group, in this case the Afro-American community:

> I will never forget one incident that took place near the village of Oranmore, about seven miles from Galway city, when I was only four years of age. We had no wagon at that time and we were camped in our *lúbáns* (tents) in against the side of a ditch . . . we made camp for the night. My father left the horse into some farmer's field without asking permission. He should not have done that of course but the next thing we knew there were shouts outside our tents and we came out in the darkness to find a bunch of angry farmers standing around the camp with huge torches that were on fire. They told us to get out of the area or they would burn us out. I remember being very frightened. When you are a child and you are standing there in the darkness and all these angry faces around you roaring and shouting. It was like a scene from one of those films you see about the Ku Klux Klan and the way that they used to attack the black people in America in times gone by. (Cauley and Ó hAodha, 2004: 53)

The Traveller tradition of begging when calling to the houses of the settled community was also seen as a "cover" for stealing and deception and Traveller begging was associated with fear and suspicion in the public imagination:

> The people don't trust them and many women are afraid of them particularly if there is no man about. If there is only one person about the house they sometimes ask for something, e.g. potatoes, to get the person out of the house for a time. Things have been stolen in this way. Children often steal eggs from the outhouse while the mother is begging inside.[5]

---

[5] Iml. 1256: 235

Even those Travellers who were well known to the people because they travelled alone and stayed in settled people's houses were not immune from the stereotype as indicated by the following IFC respondent from County Tyrone:

> *The Connacht Woman*: Her name was Mary McGlinn and she was a great dancer. She would often avow: "I'm from the free estate." meaning the Free State (26 counties). One time in Annie McCrea's, when Annie's son James was alive, he played the mixed melodeon for her while she danced. Annie was washing clothes and had the tub on the floor. "The Connacht Woman" was addicted now and then to a drop "of the cordial" and "she could spin like a top, but she spun into the tub. It's no matter — It's only Mary McGlinn"[6] . . . The Connacht Woman (i.e. Mary McGlinn) . . . was said to be a thief. One time she stole a good stick from Peter Nellie's or Neilly's in Carnanrancy, and was stealing something else from Morris' when he collared her. "No wonder you stole St Patrick's goat", he said.[7]

Begging by Traveller women and children was an important subsistence activity for many Traveller families and was generally combined with the peddling of small items such as Holy Medals, Holy Pictures, pins, paper flowers, etc. Peddling was often accompanied by appeals for "a bit of help". Gratitude for generosity on the part of the settled community was often expressed in spiritual terms through the use of prayer. It is noteworthy that the Traveller Cant/Gammon word for "beg" is géig which comes from the Irish word *"guí", "guigh"* meaning "pray", "wish for", "imprecate", "entreat" (see dictionary definition in Ó Donaill, 1977).

A number of IFC respondents described the Travellers' use of prayers when begging:

> The blessing of God on you; May the Lord have mercy on all the souls that left you. May God reward you.[8]

---

[6] Iml. 1255: 408

[7] Iml. 1255: 404

[8] Iml. 1256: 124

> Sweet Anne (McCaffrey) — She come to your house cutting the
> Sign of the Cross and praying all the blessings of the day: "God
> bless all I see, and the Blessed light of Heaven fall about you and
> yours. Oh, Jesus, Mary and Joseph bless you." Cutting the sign of
> the Cross with her stick. That's why she was called "Sweet
> Anne". She begged. "God and the Virgin bless all I see. May the
> blessing of the Virgin Mary light about your door."[9]

G. Gmelch (1977) quotes a Traveller woman who described the interdependent relationship between peddling and begging:

> Once I'd sold some little thing, then I'd start to mooch (beg): "In
> the name of God, have you e'er a bit of bread or a cup of milk for
> me poor childer? God comfort you and may he have mercy on
> your dead." (Maggie McDonagh in Gmelch, 1977: 19)

Begging was a source of tension between the Travelling and settled communities, however, a situation which was exacerbated by the fact that for
many settled people it might be one of the primary contexts in which they
had communication with Travellers. This tension gave rise to other stereotypes including the image of the haranguing Traveller woman who was
never satisfied. Competition for limited resources in an impoverished
country was probably a major factor in the proliferation of this stereotype.
A Clare respondent implied that Traveller haranguing was actually a form
of deceit since they could produce "ready money" when necessary:

> Tinkers generally are regarded as well-to-do. They can always
> produce ready money when buying an animal. They buy nothing
> in the line of clothes, boots, food. The women beg all their needs
> from house to house. They ask a hundred things, and will scarely
> ever go for a copper. They always make a very "poor mouth" but
> it is known that this is deceit.[10]

The stereotype of the Travellers who "force" their way in the door when
the "man of the house" was gone out was a common one and is mentioned often by the IFC respondents:

---

[9] Iml. 1255: 403

[10] Iml. 1255: 256

They have infinite cheek and once they get inside the door they won't go till the good man of the house comes in and threathens to throw them out. They generally go when he appears. But if there happens to be no men about they sit and sit and beg and beg till the women of the house are ready to give them almost anything to get them out.[11]

Beirt dhriotháir den ainm Hiarfhlaithe a bhíodh ag siúl ó bhaile go baile sa taobh so dúthaigh . . . Bhíodh na bacaigh seo ana shiúlach ar Chinn-Áird agus ar an dTobar thíos agus ar chuid eile des na bailte timpeall agus is minic a ráinníodh leo teacht nuair a bhíodh na fearra amuich (as baile), lá aonaigh sa Daingean nú lá meithile nú a leithéid. Bhíodh na mná scannruithe rómpa — cuid acu go mórmhór. Nuair ná braithidís na feara timpeall churidís iachall ar na mná corcán ubh — uibhe cearc — a chur síos agus a bheirbhiú dhóibh . . .[12]

(Two brothers by the name of Herlihy who walked from town to town in this part of the country. These beggars would circulate a lot around Cinn Áird and An Tobar and some of the other villages here and they would often arrive when the men were away, a fair day or a day of a meitheal etc. The women were scared of them — some of them very scared. When they would know that the men were gone they would try to pressurise the women into boiling a pot of eggs — hens' eggs for them . . .)

It is noteworthy that a similar stereotype incorporating the "intimidation" of the "defenceless" housewife was alleged towards the Jewish pedlars, another "Other" group who travelled throughout Ireland in the early half of the twentieth century, as indicated by these comments by a Limerick priest:

We may notice him traversing the lanes of our cities, or visiting our country farm-houses when the "good man" is abroad and only the woman of the household has to be dealt with. He carries bundles of cheap wares or he is laden with pious pictures, or statues

---

[11] Iml. 1256: 218

[12] Iml: 1255: 33

of the Christian Redeemer whose name and following he abhors
. . . (Finlay in Keogh, 1998: 21).

A housewife from Crossmolina, County Mayo linked stealing with the
absence of the "man of the house":

> If there are no men in when they arrive — they make very bold in
> the demands. Only about four months ago one of the tinker women
> grabbed a piece of bacon which was hanging from the roof; and
> was away with it, but she just met the man of the house coming in
> and he deprived her of it.[13]

The association of Travellers with intimidation still survives in the public imagination in Ireland today, albeit in a slightly altered form. It is often rumoured that those nomadic Travellers who travel between Ireland
and England during the summer months in particular are "paid off" by
the settled community who do not wish them to park on nearby waste
land or land that has been zoned for development, as indicated by the
following newspaper headlines:

> "Boss held to Ransom" (D. Lane, *Sunday World*, 2001)

> "Visitors Intimidated by Travellers" (M. Minihan, *The Irish
> Times*, 2000)

---

[13] Iml. 1256:124

Chapter 11

Mendacity and the "Whining Irish"

A constant and as yet little-acknowledged source of tension between the Traveller and settled communities related to begging requests on the part of Travellers, a resentment that had its roots in fearful beliefs including that of the "evil eye" in relation to Travellers and their alleged "magico-religious" powers:

> People believed — some still do so — that it was unlucky not to give the tinkers something asked for . . . unlucky to have their curses. . . . I heard that the old tinkers were great prayers. I've heard of them begrudging a man a beast.[1]

> Many would not care to buy from the tinker or refuse alms fearing their curse . . .[2]

A man from the west of Ireland similarly hinted at a fear of "denying" the Travellers:

> The country people never regarded tinkers as objects of charity as they did the poor old beggarmen and women of the old workhouse days. These poor creatures begged. The tinkers just demanded and God help anyone who let one of them leave their door empty-handed. This obtains in the case of the tinkers up to the present day. They wish all kinds of ill-luck to the house — to the crops and to cattle if they are refused their demands — and people are sometimes afraid of their curses. If they are refused milk "that she may never again have a calf" — for often a

---

[1] Iml. 1256: 232

[2] Iml. 1255: 130

farmer's wife might say that she had only enough milk for the household, that she was "expecting a cow to calf".

A female respondent from County Cork described the flipside of a Travellers' blessing:

> If they get anything they say "God spare you" or "The Lord keep sickness and trouble away from you" but if they are refused they curse, "The curse of God may melt you". The women carry babies to excite sympathy. They are generally brought on their backs and sometimes two together one in their arms and one strapped on the back.[3]

It was sometimes alleged that Travellers combined the fear of their curse with their prowess as fortune-tellers as a rejoinder to those who insulted them. The following anecdote describes an apocryphal story which extols the virtue of charity and which was well known amongst the settled community:

> The women sometimes claim to be a "seventh daughter" and so privileged to be able to see into the future and fortell the happenings. Sometimes, if crossed, they use profane language and country people used to be genuinely afraid of being cursed by them, but this, I think, is dying out. There is a story told of a gypsy woman who had a large family, around 12 or 13, who came begging to a house near Drum (County Monaghan). The woman of the house (I should have mentioned that this was supposed to have happened almost a hundred years ago) was very hard and proud said something to the gypsy comparing her "to a sow and her bonhams". When leaving the woman knelt at the foot of the lane and prayed that the voice of a child would not be heard in that house for a hundred years. True enough, the people of the locality claim that altho' the house changed hands many times in all those years no child was ever born in it. The spell however was broken a year or more ago when a young married couple had a

---

[3] Iml. 1255: 47

baby born but after their marriage all the people were wondering if the curse would remain.[4]

Gypsy activist and writer Ian Hancock (1987) explains the utilisation of fear as the response-mechanism of a marginalised group who have no other means with which to defend themselves:

> When a group lacks the conventional means of redressing wrongs done to it, it will make the most of what is available; the fear of Gypsy magic was called upon as a means of reprisal some years ago in Florida, for example: a mother whose child was the victim of a hit-and-run accident vowed to cast a Gypsy curse extending over three generations on the driver and his family if he does not come forward and pay the child's hospital bill. (1987: 115)

Traveller activist Nan Joyce has described the necessity for some Travellers to exaggerate how poor and miserable they were since they were often begging from people who were equally poor:

> We stayed in Dublin and it was awful. The travellers were so poor they were reduced to begging but some of the Dubin settled people were very poor too. . . . Ever since I was little I hated begging; we never could beg in the street, we were always ashamed and sometimes when we'd go to a door the people would be as poor as ourselves. Travellers begging had to make themselves look all miserable looking before they'd be given anything but when you were selling something it was different; you felt better. (Joyce, 1985: 32–3)

An IFC respondent from County Wexford implied similar methods for arousing sympathy:

> Those tribes which continually reach our locality beg loudly, vocally and persistently but don't steal. Usually they send a child to beg or often a young woman calls with a baby on her arm. People say that sometimes she "gets the loan of the child" to go beg. I have heard of cases of boys and girls (tinkers) taking off their boots to go to a farm and to beg, and putting on their boots when

---

[4] Iml. 1256: 240

they come back out on the road. . . . Their children seem reasona-
bly well-nourished and though often dressed poorly (sometimes
this is a device to excite charity in the breasts of the local people)
seem quite healthy.[5]

A recurring stereotype concerning Travellers was their alleged dishonesty, a trait which was inherent according to many respondents to the
Tinker Questionnaire. Dishonesty in the form of "tall tales" or exaggerated behaviour was alleged to be "normal practice" for the Travellers:

> Any illness or disability is freely broadcast and used to arouse
> practical sympathy in the locality and there are many subterfuges
> for a similar purpose — bared breasts, crying child, injured hand,
> dead horse or donkey, broken cart, etc., husband in gaol or hospi-
> tal.[6]

Travellers were said to bewail their lot in life so often as part of the deception associated with begging that their voices had developed a peculiar whining and "sing-song" quality, according to a number of IFC respondents:

> . . . the women and children go around the houses begging. This
> they do in a peculiar singsong voice and if you give them twenty
> things they still want "an oul skirt for God's sake or a pair of
> pants belonging to himself".[7]

The stereotype of the whining and imprecating manner draws on a reductionist image that was applied to Irish people generally in many written
commentaries concerning the Irish character written during the colonial
period. A good example is the following description, outlined in the travel
memoirs of Fynes Moryson (1617), a senior English government official
who worked and travelled through Ireland in the late sixteenth century:

> They are by nature very Clamorous, upon every small occasion
> raising the houbou (that is a dolefull outcrye) which they take one

---

[5] Iml. 1255: 371

[6] Iml. 1256: 37

[7] Iml. 1255: 379

from anothers mouthe till they putt the whole towne in tumult. And theyr complaints to magistrates are commonly strayned to the highest points of Calamity, sometyes [sic] in hyberbolicall tearmes, as many upon small violences offered them, have Petitioned the Lord Deputy for Justice against me for murthering them while they stoode before him sounde and not so much as wounded. (Moryson in Leersen, 1996: 53)

Allegations of mendacity have been a core stereotype in the anti-Irish "othering" tradition for centuries. Giraldus Cambrensis, one of the very first writers to describe Ireland and the Irish, discussed the Irish character in terms of mendacity and dishonesty in his *Topographia Hibernia*. He described the Irish as a treacherous people, a people who always broke their pledges. The Irish were:

a wicked and perverse generation, constant always in that they be always inconstant, faithful in that they be always unfaithful, and trusty in that they be always treacherous and untrusty. (Cambrensis in Quinn, 1966: 13)

Allegations of mendacity on the part of Travellers were widespread in the responses to the IFC Questionnaire. Two respondents from County Kerry reinforced the stereotype of Travellers as adept liars and tricksters, trickery that was analogous with the satirical word-play of the *Filí Taistil* (Travelling Poets) who once had such a prominent role in Gaelic society:

Ní bhfaighfeá puinn den bhfírinne ó chuid mhór aca 'á n'oirfead an t-éitheach don ócáid.

(You wouldn't get a word of the truth from most of them, just whatever lie suited the occasion).[8]

Tinkers are fond of family life when their day's rambling or work is over. They are affectionate to both man and beast. Their greatest failing is scheming or trickery, also having a taste for alcohol . . . [9]

---

[8] Iml. 1255: 20
[9] Iml. 1255: 30

They are the greatest white liars in existence. But they enjoy being tripped up and caught out in their lies — and it's remarkable
the respect they have for one who can assess their veracity. They
approach you differently next time.[10]

The latter-mentioned quote hints at the use of mendacity as a game or a
tactic rather than as a wilful form of deception for criminal reasons. It is
likely that Travellers, like the Irish people generally, may have used mendacity as a method of self-defence. Historian Robert Bartlett (1982), who
analysed the anti-Irish stereotype tradition as first promulgated by Ger-
aldus Cambrensis in the twelfth century, situated the alleged Irish (and
Welsh) propensities for mendacity within a colonial framework. Bartlett
argued that native peoples sometimes found it expedient to make temporary surrenders or peace agreements only to renege on them in a renewed
drive for independence when they felt the enemy's position might have
weakened (1982: 13). Robert Welch (1993) also analysed the stereotype
of the untrustworthy Irish. He, too, located its roots within the self-
defence mechanisms of oppression:

It was often said that you could not trust what the Irish will tell
you because they will make sure that they tell you what you want
to hear. At its worst the racial slur here is that the Irish cannot tell
truth from falsehood. But in another sense there is a vital cultural
manoeuvre going on: it is most important that strangers feel at
home, that they be accommodated within the structure, and that
means adapting elements of the structure to take account of the
new presence. . . . They (strangers) must be told what they want
to hear; not to do so leaves them outside and therefore dangerous.
(1993: 279)

Fortune-telling was another Traveller subsistence activity which served to
"other" Travellers, an "othering" that was two-sided. For the settled
community fortune-telling incorporated notions of fear, trickery and deceit on the one hand, and romanticism and exoticism on the other. Fortune-telling is the one activity which has probably been most associated
with Travellers and Gypsies in the European imaginary and in the artistic

---

[10] Iml. 1256: 96

and cultural spheres generally. Fraser (1995) describes the early evolution of the image of the Gypsy fortune-teller and says that it has been associated with Travellers and Gypsies since the fourteenth century. The image became so engrained in the European imaginary that eighteenth-century French encyclopaedias even included the category of fortune-teller as part of the definition of a "bohemian", despite the fact that fortune-telling has never been a Traveller or Gypsy monopoly but has been practised by many sedentary practitioners throughout the centuries (see Cottaar et al.: 1998). Fortune-telling as practised by Irish Travellers seems to have included similar techniques to those which have been ascribed to Gypsies and Travellers in other parts of Europe. In common with their counterparts in neighbouring countries Irish Travellers engaged in fortune telling as part of a family-based work strategy whereby it was ancillary to peddling and finding other work opportunities. An IFC respondent from County Down implied the interchangeability of nomenclature as applied to Travellers and said that those Travellers referred to as "Gypsies" were associated with fortune-telling:

> In this part of Down sometimes called "gipsies", sometimes tinkers — "a clique of tinkers". Often known as tramps. . . . Gipsies sell baskets, little tables (tripod) for flowers. They sell handkerchiefs, artificial flowers, lace. They "spey" fortunes.[11]

On arrival in a village the female Travellers who worked as fortune-tellers visited as many houses as possible to peddle items, to beg while simultaneously enquiring whether the inhabitants had any repair work that could be done. The women "tested the market" for the men and brought valuable information on potential work opportunities back to the camp. Fortune-tellers utilised a range of techniques including palm-reading (where the lines of the palm were said to indicate future happenings) or "tossing cups" (divining the future based on the shapes made by the tea leaves adhering to the bottom and sides of an emptied teacup). Playing cards were also used and were combined with astrology to predict the future. G. Gmelch (1974) says that many women would simply leave a deck of playing cards lying in their peddling basket within the vision of

---

[11] Iml. 1256: 221

the settled people who "came to the door". Cottaar et al. (1998) describes a similar technique as utilised in European countries where fortune-telling was repressed more seriously by the authorities than in Ireland:

> As fortune-telling was for the most part forbidden in Western Europe the women had to be careful. Some simply kept a deck of cards in their peddling basket so that it was in clear view of the housewife. If she rose to the bait the Gypsy would act. (1998: 169)

Fortune-telling as described in Irish descriptions tended towards the provision of "emotional services" (i.e. information about significant life events such as marriage, emigration, job possibilities, sickness and travel). The era prior to the twentieth century includes descriptions of a deeper, more magico-religious aspect to Traveller fortune-telling including advice in cases of theft, the bewitching of animals or people, the evil eye and problems with marital fecundity, etc. There are only a few twentieth-century descriptions of fortune-telling as provided by Irish Travellers, all of which imply its employment as a subsistence mechanism:

> If I was short of money and maybe I'd have nothin' to sell I'd go along and ask did they want their fortunes told. Well I'd read the cups and tell them all I could. I'd nearly know what to tell them. If it was a young person I'd tell them they were going to be married or were goin' to get money from friends across the water or they were falling into a bit of luck. Anything just to get a livin'. Other Travellers would get a bit of glass and pretend it was a crystal ball. We'd be lookin' through that and we'd tell them to look through it too. Sure, they'd see nothin' and we wouldn't either. We'd only tell them a pack of lies out of it. We didn't care once we got the price of food for our kids. In some houses, with what we'd call a foolish class of people in them, a Traveller could make good money at it. (Donahue in G. Gmelch, 1977: 20)

While employed as a subsistence mechanism the Travellers' "other" status meant that fortune-telling was a source of fear for some in the settled community. Many amongst the settled community who did not believe in it simply thought of the practice as a form of entertainment or deceit. Fortune-telling instilled fear in others, however, in part because of its association with magic and partly because of the Church's hostility to the practice. Traveller Nan Donahue (1986) describes hostility to her fortune-telling which she was forced to resort to in the poverty-stricken west of Ireland:

> I was nearly crying to the people. The Galway and Connemara people was very poor that time. . . . This [fortune-telling] was the only way I could get money in Connemara. . . . And when the mother went out of the room for something I said to the two girls, "Why don't you get your lucky fortunes told." "We don't believe in that," one girl said. "No one can do that, only God." "Oh, they can," I said, "take a wish and I'll tell your wish." But wasn't the old woman listening to me from the next room. She run in and took up the brush. "Get out! Get out!" she roared. "There's nobody can tell fortunes, only God. How dare you bring your unlucky words into my house." And she run me out with the brush and set the dogs on me. I had to fly for me life. (1986: 129)

Fortune-telling and the use of "emotional" magic was allegedly combined in with fraud on occasion according to Cottaar et al. (1998):

> As with all professions, itinerant or not, abuse was possible and occurred now and then. Some fortune-tellers used their skill to "lift" their clients, for example in cases of illness or bad luck (sick cattle), by suggesting that a spell had been put on the unlucky farmer. In offering to lift the spell they would advise their clients to gather all their valuables and bury them. After a set period of time the client was to dig these up again, after which the situation would be normal again. It needs little imagination to realise that in such cases the fortune-teller was ahead of the superstitious client. However, treasure-digging was not a common phenomenon. (1998: 168)

Similar stereotypical accusations of the deception of the "innocent" rural population by Travellers circulate in rural Ireland even today:

> P... who lives back the road there. You know he is a bit odd. A bit simple. He doesn't talk to anybody because his mother kept him at home from school when his father died. He can hardly read or

write either, the poor man. The tinkers called to him one day about
fifteen years back and he told them that he was lonely and he was
looking for a wife. They said that they would find him a wife if he
put £100 into a drawer that was in his kitchen. P., innocent as he
was did this. Sure enough, the money disappeared when he left the
house to go to the village for food. He never saw his wife or those
tinkers again. (Interview with Mary H., Limerick, 2001)

Stereotypes of Irish Travellers in relation to stealing, deception and using
begging as a part of a fraudulent strategy are likely to have been greatly
exaggerated. They could not afford to steal from or cheat the settled
community to any great degree since they were reliant on them for business and would return again and again to the same routes and villages.
That petty pilfering on the part of Travellers was engaged in only when
necessary for survival was implied by one IFC respondent who noticed
an element of "class solidarity" in its nature:

> Turf is often missed from reeks when tinkers are around, but it is
> also noticeable that it is always the well-to-do farmers' land
> which is grazed upon and the man with the large reek of turf —
> the small farmer or poor man is never interfered with.[12]

Another IFC respondent from County Kildare hinted at a more egalitar-
ian and symbiotic relationship between Travellers and the settled community, but it is probably a testament to the level of mutual suspicion
and prejudice that existed between both communities that sentiments
such as these are quite rare in the responses to the Questionnaire:

> Some tinkers are generous and grateful. If a farmer who has
> treated them well has a horse to sell at a fair, they'll do their best
> to try and get him a good buyer, and help to make a bargain. The
> women often put sugar stick and oranges into his car for the chil-
> dren in gratitude for giving them straw or potatoes in the camp.[13]

Some respondents to the Irish Folklore Commission alleged that the
goods which Travellers supplied were inferior in quality and implied that

---

[12] Iml. 1255: 27
[13] Iml. 1255: 393

Travellers were engaging in fraudulent behaviour on two fronts. On the one hand they were accused of duping "innocent" country people into purchasing poor quality products while simultaneously using this hawking as an excuse for begging, petty pilfering or other fraudulent activity. A housewife from Crossmolina, County Mayo who responded to the IFC Questionnaire implied as much:

> I can't say that they are honest, truthful or kind. They are unreliable. When they get repairs, they are sometimes known to change and take the article with them.[14]

The association of the Traveller with fraud and trickery was so widespread that it even entered the storytelling discourse of Travellers themselves and was used as part of the self-identity and boundary mechanisms that separated the Traveller community from the settled community as pointed out by Helleiner (2000):

> Men in the camp spoke proudly of their trading activities — vehemently denying that they ever lost out in deals. Male Travellers particularly enjoyed telling stories about exchanges with non-Travellers which demonstrated their skills of persuasiveness, cleverness, and/or trickery in making a profit. One housed male Traveller, for example, described to me how he outwitted a non-Traveller who had bargained him down to a low price by measuring linoleum in such a way that the person paid for a larger piece than he actually received. Another man told of how, after puncturing a car's tires, he would approach the non-Traveller owner to buy the car for a low price, then fix the tyres and resell it at its real value. Such stories of outwitting settled people or "conning the buffer" were often repeated and offered as evidence that house-dwellers were "soft" or "fools". (2000: 159)

Helleiner (2000) emphasised the role which stories such as this played in the maintenance of Traveller identity in the face of a primarily hostile environment. Traveller ingenuity and the ability to adapt to changing or adverse circumstances was not just a defence mechanism but was instead "evidence of a collective superiority" of Travellers over non-Travellers.

---

[14] Iml. 1256: 124

Helleiner (2000) cites an anecdote in Nan Joyce's autobiography *Travel-ler* as evidence of this "collective superiority", a superioritiy which en-sured survival in conditions of extreme adversity:

> People were burned out during the Cromwell evictions or they
> were made homeless during the Famine. The travellers were used
> to coping with cold and hardship and hunger, they could survive
> anywhere because they had their own way of working and their
> own culture. But the settled people weren't used to managing on
> their own, they slept in old sheds and barns and did a sort of slave
> work on the farms. (Joyce, 1985: 2)

It is interesting that similar allegations of fraudulence and deception were made against another "Other", i.e. the small minority of Jewish pedlars who hawked their wares in both urban and rural Ireland in the pre-industrial era, as indicated by the following allegation made to the Dublin Metropolitan Police by a government official who was worried about the increasing Jewish population in Ireland at the turn of the cen-tury. The same government official was concerned that these Jewish ped-lars were attempting to "hoodwink" Irish farmers with a view to acquir-ing their land:

> It has been stated that the Jews are in the habit of collecting from
> hotels, and other large establishments of the sort, used tea leaves,
> drying them, mixing them with deleterious drugs, and selling the
> compound to the poorer classes as tea; and it had been suggested
> that this product must be injurious to health, even producing
> nervous disease and insanity. (McDonnell in Keogh, 1998: 23)

Chapter 12

Mobility and Labour: The Nomad
as a Source of Suspicion

Lucassen (1987) has exposed the shallow nature of the "fraud" stereotype as pertaining to Travellers and Gypsies. He links its prevalence with European structural change that affected the nature of capitalism and economic competition between migratory and sedentary groups from the seventeenth century onwards. Contrary to those analyses which see mobility in terms of marginality, criminality and poverty, Lucassen emphasised the essential role of labour mobility within emerging economies and its absolute necessity for economic development. Cottaar et al. (1998) support Lucassen's findings and his negation of the stereotype tradition that saw Travellers work as marginal and a cloak for fraudulent activity:

> In spite of the often bad reputation of tinkers, knifegrinders, hawkers and pedlars, their work was important for the distribution of goods and services and many could make a reasonable living out of it. Hawkers and pedlars in the seventeenth and eighteenth centuries, for example, specialised in areas with a weak infrastructure and economically backward conditions. They were well organised . . . the accusations that these hawkers were workshy, only sold products of inferior quality and thereby deceived the simple country folk were mainly uttered by sedentary shopkeepers who were afraid of competition. Demetz (1987) argues that these allegations were generally false. Many of these hawkers also operated in larger places, where people could compare the quality with that offered by the shops. Moreover in the smaller villages they returned regularly enough so that they could not afford to cheat the villagers. (1998: 144)

Cottaar et al.'s comments are borne out by the comments of a number of IFC respondents:

> The Hourigans and Quilligans are, or rather were tinkers, that is tinsmiths. One no longer sees them pursuing their *tóin-céard* (Irish: "tin craft"). All I can say about them wares — tinware — is what I remember to have heard, that their "work" was better and cheaper than similar shop goods. I myself once bought a clothes break from a Callan tinker (from Kilkenny) for tenpence. That was all I had, and it was the best tenpence worth ever purchased.[1]

It is likely that the importance of Travellers as hawkers and pedlars in the era prior to mass urbanisation has been severely underestimated in social and economic history studies. Despite the widespread prevalence of reductionist stereotypes, many customers were dependent on the travelling seller. Many respondents to the Tinker Questionnaire pointed to the fact that the Travellers sold goods at more competitive prices than their sedentary counterparts in the village shops. There was also always the possibility of bargaining or bartering with the Travellers, options which were not available when dealing with shopkeepers in local towns. Cottaar et al. (1998: 157) expand on the possibilities inherent in these transactions:

> Even where several shops did exist people often preferred to buy from hawkers, many of whom were women. Most hawkers had a regular circle of customers and were therefore trusted. Moreover they offered cheaper goods and did not show the contempt that many workers were confronted with in middle-class shops. Consequently some shopkeepers were not all that popular with the working man. (1998: 157)

Despite the comments of Cottaar et al., the stereotype whereby the Traveller trader was associated with deception and mendacity had stubborn roots. Fraudulence and cheating was implied in relation to Travellers and horse-trading in particular, and the range of stereotypical stories and tricks allegedly employed by Traveller horse-dealers almost constitute a "genre". Some Travellers also acted as intermediaries for farmers in the horsedealing that went on at fairs such as Ballinasloe in County Galway.

---

[1] Iml. 1255: 170

These Travellers, sometimes known as "guinea hunters" acted as a buffer between the wary seller and the impatient buyer. An IFC respondent from Kerry gave a brief description of the work of the O'Briens, whom he referred to as "followers-up" in the selling process:

> The O'Briens' job in ponys and donkeys in a small way — at fairs they assist in clinching sales, sell halters, etc. They are mostly followers-up at fairs.[2]

Arensberg and Kimball (1937), two of the first scholars to undertake anthropological work in Ireland described the important role of these guinea-hunters in the clinching of horse deals:

> Time and time again he will drag back a buyer who rushes off in well-feigned disgust at an outrageous demand or push forward the hand of a reluctant farmer to be seized by the buyer in the hand-clasp that marks completion of the sale. Amid the encouragements of the bystanders, he repeats the old bargaining cries. He shouts, "Split the difference!" when taking-price and asking-price approach one another, and he wrings concessions from each party until agreement is reached. (Arensberg and Kimball, 1940: 292)

From early spring to late autumn those Travellers who specialised in horse-dealing travelled from fair to fair doing a brisk business. Some Travellers travelled to fairs with teams of horses which they sold on behalf of a particular farmer. Travellers known as "blockers" or "jobbers" specialised in the sale of the heavy work-horses and donkeys that were once a familiar sight on Irish farms and roads and which pulled milk carts to and from the creameries. Travellers' skills in horse-rearing, horse-medicine and horse-dealing were widely acknowledged to the extent that their horsetrading skills were sometimes seen as the catalyst for fairs and increased commerce incorporating the older Gaelic tradition of barter, as pointed out by this IFC correspondent from County Down:

> They sell horses. *Carraig-na-gCat* (Irish: "the Cats' Rock") fair is said to have been started by horse-dealers (tinkers) who helped to kill wild-cats in the district and became friendly with the people.

---

[2] Iml. 1255: 29

They barter horses. They are pitied in winter but seem to knock out
a good living in other seasons.[3]

An IFC respondent from County Limerick said that some Travellers used
to work both for the local gentry and big businesses such was the high
esteem in which their skills were held, skills which the Travellers themselves brought with them on emigration:

> The King's brother died some years previously. He was a good
> judge of horseflesh and was employed by the Dunraven family
> (local landlords) and other gentry to buy bloodstock for them. He
> even travelled to France for this purpose. He was employed by
> Messrs. Guinness to buy horses at the time when the city and
> town delivery was carried out by horsedrawn vehicles. . . . He
> (the King's brother) was nicknamed the "Blinking Boy" but his
> Christian name was Jack. He went to America and his descen-
> dants are now spread over America (USA) particularly in the
> West where some of them own big ranches. They specialise in
> horses following the old tradition. Some years before his death he
> came home, as he said to die at home. After his funeral several
> came by plane and called on the old Queen in Limerick . . . [4]

A respondent from County Clare highlighted the transnational nature of
the Travellers' dealing at a time when Ireland was still relatively insular in
terms of international economy and commerce:

> It was usual in my young days on fair days to see one portion of
> the fair devoted to the sale of donkeys. Tinkers bought, sold and
> bartered donkeys at the fairs. At the present time, I occasionally
> meet a tinker group driving some fifteen or twenty donkeys. On
> enquiring what they meant to do with them I learnt they intended
> to send them to Wales where they would be used in the coal
> mines. The donkey is almost an unknown quantity in this quarter
> now, his place has been taken now by handy ponies.[5]

---

[3] Iml. 1256: 221

[4] Iml. 1255: 357

[5] Iml. 1256: 55

Some, primarily older and worn-out animals were also exported to the Continent after being butchered. Horses like these, which were considered to be too old to be of any use as working animals, were referred to as "knackers" and some Travellers made money by driving them to the "knacker's yard" or slaughterhouse where the animal carcasses were later sold by weight. This was the original derivation of the word "knacker" which is used to refer to Travellers today in a pejorative sense.

Irish Travellers, like indigenous Travellers and Gypsies in other European countries were particularly associated with trickery in the doctoring or "sprucing up" of old animals for resale, as indicated by an IFC correspondent from County Westmeath:

> . The women often drive the horses and ponies. The harness used
> is very often mounted in silver and brass and bells are often hung
> on it. They are accounted excellent judges of horses and past
> masters in "doctoring" faulty animals for sale at fairs.[6]

Travellers' doctoring skills allegedly included the ability to "transform" an old or sick animal into a younger or healthier one to fool the gullible buyer. This involved trading a "young" animal for an old one, in addition to a few shillings, to some gullible countryman. If a particularly gullible customer existed it was alleged that the Travellers might bring him a number of exchanges over the course of a few weeks, always bringing the customer a "better" horse in exchange for the one they had already traded him. Additional money, sometimes known as "boot" or "luck money", passed hands in these exchanges and so the Traveller was making a profit on every transaction. The "doctoring" of older or "tired" animals involved a range of stereotypical tricks to make the animal appear more "lively" than it actually was. Some Travellers were said to place an irritant like mustard or pepper on a sensitive part of the animal (e.g. its anus or ears) to make the animal "jumpy", as recalled by a west of Ireland respondent:

> *Nuair a bhíonn said ag díol tada deirtear to gcuireann siad pio-*
> *bar dearg isteach i gcluasa an ainmhí agus cuireann siad gaoth*
> *ann ionnas go mbeidh sé ag breathnadh go maith.*[7]

---

[6] Iml. 1255: 409

[7] Iml. 1256: 24

(When they are selling anything it is said that they put red pepper
into the animal's ears and then they blow into them so that the
animal is looking well.)

Other alleged tricks to facilitate the appearance of a sprightly nature in the
animal included the driving of a tack into the animal's hoof or flank, the
placing of a small dose of arsenic in its food or the filing of grooves into a
horse's teeth to make it appear younger. (Cottaar et al., 1998), setting the
stereotype of the cheating Traveller horse-dealer within a European context, links its prevalence to the fears of border authorities regarding the
international aspects of this trade and the fears of sedentary dealers regarding competition from their nomadic counterparts. The transport of animals
across borders meant that the authorities in countries such as Holland,
Belguim, France, Germany and Britain feared that their countries would be
invaded by hordes of foreign Travellers/Gypsies when in actual fact only
relatively small numbers of Travellers, who were constantly travelling,
were really involved in the trade. The stereotype of the cheating Traveller
who fooled gullible farmers and sedentary dealers by "transforming" older
animals through such processes as singeing, clipping and other "beautifi-
cation" tricks holds little validity in the view of Cottaar et al. (1998):

> There are powerful arguments against the impression that Gypsy
> activity at horse markets was characterized by deceit. To begin
> with, it does not explain why customers kept dealing with people
> with such a bad reputation. Trading between Gypsies and others
> suggests a relationship of trust and respect rather than intolerance
> and abuse. There can be no doubt that "trickery" formed a part of
> horse trading (and trading in general), but it was not peculiar to
> Gypsies, not can it have been a general phenomenon. (1998: 160)

Lucassen's view is bolstered by comments on the mule-trade by a community of Irish-American Travellers from Georgia whose language,
which they referred to Cant, was studied by Jared Harper in the 1970s.
Harper (1977) found that Travellers were extra careful to cultivate a relationship of trust with their clientele:

> Mule trading required a variety of skills. The Traveller mule
> trader first of all had to be a public relations man. He had to relate

to all types of people and to judge his customers and their moods. Some almost seemed to have the ability to read a customer's mind and to know what his intentions were so that they might make some counter move to retain the advantage in trade . . . one ex-mule trader said:

"You figured your man and tried to gain his confidence. You made an effort to keep him satisfied. You left the man laughin' when you said goodbye. The goal was always to make a customer like you. Back then Country People trusted you, but if you did them wrong they would kill you with gun or knife. It was essential to keep them satisfied." (1977: 72)

As with many of the numerous stereotypes and allegations that were directed towards Travelling people it is clear that the stereotype of cheating or fraudulent behaviour in the horsedealing sphere was used to obstruct this activity on the part of Travellers and Gypsies. In the US Irish-American Travellers whose descendants had emigrated from Ireland during the Famine years were prevented from travelling about as mule-traders from the early 1900s onwards in the state of Georgia by legislation that was implemented on behalf of sedentary mule traders who were competing with the Travellers. Cottaar et al. (1998) point to a similar process in parts of Germany prior to the advent of the Second World War where stereotypes were used to incriminate and obstruct Gypsy horse-dealers:

In Germany we know of attempts by sedentary traders to protest against what they regarded as unfair competition, proof in itself that Gypsies already played an important role. In 1911, for example, Hannoverian horse-dealers asked the authorities to exclude Gypsies from their trade because they only aimed at deceiving their customers. The dealers' plea was not met, but authorities shared their opinion and promised to hamper Gypsy horse-dealers. A circular published in the German state of Wurtemberg in 1903 ordered local officials to prevent Gypsies from attending horse fairs as much as possible. In Bavaria, finally, Gypsies were in 1921 indeed excluded from horse-dealing because of their "dishonest" competition. (1998: 160)

In Ireland the stereotypical association of Travellers with fraudulent or illegal activities was given further sustenance by the role which Travellers allegedly played in smuggling and metalwork activities associated with the smuggling trade, including illegal whiskey stills. An IFC respondent from a remote corner of North Mayo described the part played by Travellers in the illegal whiskey or *poitín*-distilling business:

> In the past and even to the present, but in a limited sense, tinkers traded surreptitiously and illegally in the manufacture and sale of stills and distilling apparatus for the mountain distillers of Erris. Nowadays most of these mountaineers have developed their own technique and mechanical talent and can make their own machinery for distillation.[8]

Traveller nomadism was linked with the smuggling of items across the border between Northern Ireland and the Republic. The smuggling of items such as tin during the war years was regarded with jealousy by many IFC respondents who felt that many Travellers had enriched themselves greatly through smuggling activities, in particular through the smuggling of tin. A respondent from County Meath attributed the business success of a locally known family to cross-border smuggling during the war years:

> The best known tinkers visiting this district now are the Murray family. They originally came from Ballyjamesduff, Co. Cavan. The father — still alive — was not a tinker, but a dealer in live stock, e.g. horses, goats, etc., which went for a good price during the last war and left the Murray family quite respectable. His two sons learnt the tin-smith trade from a tinker in Ballyjamesduff and now practise the trade while the father deals in goats, etc. . . . During the war, they bought horses and goats specially and sold them over the Border, usually at about four times the cost price. They imported tin from across the border on their return journey, without going through the customs of course.[9]

The Traveller preference for nomadism was itself linked to the avoidance of the strict rigours of the law:

---

[8] Iml. 1256: 117-18
[9] Iml. 1256, 45

They prefer localities distant from Garda Stations and especially where warrants for fines etc. await them, usually avoiding that particular Garda Sub-District until the time limit has expired, a regulation evidently known to them. They often subscribe towards payment of a fine to save some member from gaol.[10]

TRAVELLERS AS SPIES

Jan Yoors (1967), who travelled with Gypsies on the continent during the war years and wrote an account of his experiences entitled *The Gypsies* described the way in which Dutch nomads also seized the opportunities provided by the social incohesion and the fluidity of territorial borders that characterised the Second World War to profit from black marketeering. Dutch Gypsies became involved in the Resistance movement, their knowledge of underworld life and survival tactics proving particularly useful. American folklorist Artelia Court (1985), who recorded life histories from Irish Travellers during the 1970s, described some Travellers who spoke of having sheltered Irish freedom fighters from British authorities during the upheavals of 1900–1921. The same Travellers also mentioned wartime profiteering, although Court claimed that "none ascribed these activities to conscious political motive" (1985: 223). The story of Travellers' involvement in the political struggles that have accompanied Irish partition is an aspect of Irish history where much greater study is necessary. That there were certain Travelling families from the Border area in particular who had a long history of "political" (Republican) involvement and had been imprisoned for subversive activities is well-known amongst the Travelling community. Smuggling, incorporating wartime profiteering, was linked with a very old stereotype relating to Travellers in the European imaginary, i.e that Travellers were spies who were somehow subverting the moral order. Some of the earliest European descriptions of the Traveller/ Gypsy depict them in roles incorporating sedition and treachery. Beier (1985) and Mayall (2004) link the association of Travellers with spying and sedition in Europe to the rapid social and religious changes and huge uncertainty that had accompanied the early modern era. The appearance of the first "Egyptians" travelling in

---

[10] Iml. 1256: 38

family groups fit this pattern. These groups were initially tolerated and even supported when they claimed to be pilgrims from "Little Egypt":

> Relying on the literature about the European history of persons designated in the sources as Gypsies, we find that at the time of their appearance in the fifteenth century they presented themselves as pilgrims from a country called Little Egypt. They did this in order to acquire safe conducts from higher authorities, even kings and the Pope, who assured them of safe passage through the countries of Europe. . . . In Europe during these years, however, there was a lively trade in travel passes and many (false) pilgrims roamed about. (Willems, 1997: 8)

When doubts about the pilgrim status of these "Egyptians" arose, these Travellers were suspected of being spies for the Turks and were soon stigmatised. Grellmann (1783), whose Gypsy "archetype" has held sway for centuries, claimed that Gypsies lent themselves readily to become the agents of treason in wartime. Although he found the accusations that their entry into Western Europe had been as spies for the Turks were likely to be far-fetched, he did not discount them entirely. Gypsies' indigent circumstances prompted the taking of bribes in his opinion and their happy-go-lucky character and wish to be liked could have tempted them to flirt with sedition. Mayall (2004) links the concept of sedition in a British Isles context with increased migrancy on the part of large numbers of nomadic and dispossessed Catholic Irish who were attempting to escape the war and eviction back in their native country during the Tudor era. The concept of sedition on the part of those who were "outsiders" or dispossessed became intextricably linked in the public imaginary with pestilence and crime, two problems which increased at this period and were associated with increased poverty, itinerancy and the disruption of existing social systems:

> The early modern period was a time of rapid change and extreme religious and political uncertainty, resulting in an often ill-defined fear or anarchy, popular risings and anything which might threaten or disrupt the existing social organisation. Concern about the consequences of disease, pestilence, crime and poverty was matched by the threat of sedition and the belief that Rome was sending

> Papal emissaries to England to provoke a Catholic revival. The
> link between these fears and itinerancy and nomadism was all too
> evident to contemporaries. Disease and pestilence were spread by
> nomadic carriers, various crimes were closely linked to an itiner-
> ant way of life, poverty and vagrancy were virtually synonymus,
> sedition was spread by itinerant colporteurs, and agents of the
> Pope were suspected of finding a cloak for their subversion in the
> camps of travellers and Gypsies. (Mayall, 2004: 60)

English colonists in Ireland made a strong link between sedition and nomadism because of the important role which the travelling bards played
in the fostering of Gaelic culture and in inciting the general population to
resist colonisation. Because of their nomadic lifestyle, Travelling people
in Ireland, but bards in particular, were often accused of being spies and
during the late 1500s many of them were executed. The British also issued many proclamations throughout the 1500s punishing both the poets
and anybody who might give them a welcome in an effort to stamp out
the traditional nomadism of large sections of the Irish population and the
traditional system of hospitality which supported them. The proclama-
tion of the "President" of the province of Munster, Sir John Perrot, issued in 1571, is a case in point:

> All carrows [gamblers], bards, rhymers, and common idle men
> and women within this province making rhymes, bringing of
> messages, and common players at cards, to be spoiled of all their
> goods and chattels, and to be put in the next stocks, there to re-
> main until they find sufficient surety to leave that wicked trade of
> life and fall to other occupation. (Perrot in Maxwell, 1923: 166)

The association of Travellers with subversive activity and spying remained strong in the Irish imaginary. One respondent to the IFC stated
his belief that some Travellers were the descedants of people who were
fugitives during periods of oppression in Ireland:

> *Teicheoirí ón dlí cuid aca in aimsir géarleanúna*[11]

---

[11] Iml. 1256: 15

(Some of them were fugitives from justice during times of persecution).

It was also a source of prejudice in the north of Ireland where the B-Specials, a Protestant (and predominantly Unionist) force were particularly discriminatory against Travellers because of their Irish Catholic (Fenian) background. The "double-prejudice" that Travellers encountered in the north of Ireland as a consequence of sectarianism is another aspect of Traveller history which has been hitherto severely under-researched. Traveller biographies such as Nan Joyce's (1985) and Pecker Dunne's (2004) all mention sectarian hatred and the suspicion of Travellers because of their "Fenian" background.

Pecker Dunne, a well-known Traveller musician, describes the frequent prejudice and harassment that Travellers suffered in the north of Ireland:

> Having a slag with the Garda Síochána was one thing. The north of Ireland was a different kettle of fish altogether. They had these *hornees* (police) up there called the B-Specials. I can think of a few words for them, none of which I will quote here. Many of them were a *cottiva* (bad) crowd. The bad ones were bigots and they hated Travellers or any Irish people from the southern part of Ireland. They referred to as Fenians and that was the most complimentary name they shouted at us, believe me! They would not let you alone all day. They harassed us non-stop. Things weren't too bad during the day. I remember coming to a town called Dungannon one time and I was busking on the street there. And people were passing up the street in cars and shouting out to me how much they were enjoying my music. That night was a different scenario though. That *darkee* (night) I remember being pulled out of *letty* (bed) at three o'clock in the morning. They dragged me along the ground and out of my tent. And they were shouting, "Come on, get out of here, you are not camping here. You Fenians and Taigs aren't welcome." They knew that most of the Travellers originated in the south, you see. It was as simple as that. Pure hatred. And I was only one of many Travellers who had that experience with them, let me tell you. (Dunne, 2004: 53)

Another Traveller, Chrissie Ward, who was born in Belfast in 1947, described the suspicious death of her father while in custody in the north of Ireland. Her experience was typical of many Catholics, both Traveller and "settled" during the "Troubles" in the North of Ireland:

> I think me father was about thirty-six when he died. They say me father was murdered but there was nothin' done about it because we were Travellers in the North an' Irish people, they didn't like people from the South. So Travellers was, they was kinda discriminated upon an' nobody ever med enquiries about it. So he was kilt in a police station. He was goin' up to see me mother one night in hospital. She was in hospital 'fore me sister was born. She was sick. . . . So he was comin' back and this night an' the police jus' dragged him in. . . . . So he was found dead. They left him all night swimmin' in blood in the police station an' they say it was a haemorrhage in the brain. But he was healthy, like, he was really, really healthy, healthy man . . . (Ward, 1992: 42)

Traveller activist Nan Joyce has given a good description of how both smuggling and subversion became intertwined in a divided Ireland whose border was particularly porous for a traditionally nomadic people:

> The travellers used to smuggle guns for the old IRA, because they were travellers and they wouldn't be searched. One summer's day, when he and his wife were very young, soon after they were married, they were going along the road with their ass and cart looking for a camp. His wife was sitting up in the cart and they had guns hidden under the straw. Years ago the men never used to sit up, they always walked. Two Black and Tans came along and they were getting ready to search their cart. Someone had told them about the guns. It was a real hot summer's day; the flies were gathered around the donkey and its tail kept swishing them away. The man said to his wife, "We have to make up a plan — if we don't we're finished, we'll end up our lives in jail." He told his wife to start stratching. She didn't know what he meant and she didn't want to do it. He said, "Scratch, or we're done out of all our happiness — here come the Black and Tans to search us", so she started scratching. He walked over to the two soldiers, scratching away, and he said to them, "Have you got any cure for

lice, sir? I'm walking alive." He pointed over to the ass, its tail swishing away the flies and he said, "Look at my old ass trying to beat them off and they're eating him alive." When the Black and Tans heard this they backed away, they wouldn't come near him and they wouldn't go near the cart. When the soldiers went off he lay down in the middle of the road, he was only young, and he cocked up his two legs jeering and he said to his wife, "Up Ireland, Mary, we won the battle that time!" It was just like the smuggling years ago because in the Free State they hadn't really got a lot. (Joyce, 1985: 26–7)

The musicologist Thomas Munnelly gave further substance to the smuggling motif by referring to a humorous song called *Smuggling the Tin* which was written by a Traveller and which referred to the important role of cross-border smuggling in the lives of Irish Travellers "during and after the Second World War when many commodities were rationed or scarce". According to Munnelly these smugglers dealt chiefly in "luxury items bought from bomb-damaged stores in that troubled area [Northern Ireland] and peddled in the Republic" (Munnelly cited in Court, 1985: 223). Another practice known as "coining", which was said to be indulged in by West of Ireland Traveller families, in particular, linked Travellers with notions of the illegal, deception and the acquisition of the "fast buck" through preying on the credulity of the peasant population. The folklorist Pádraig Mac Gréine (1934), one of the few Irish folklorists to have recorded material from Travellers, described how coining worked through the utilisation of a dummy mold for the minting of false coins:

The gladar box is a small box containing on either side a sheet of lead bearing the impress of a coin, generally a florin. On one of the outside edges is a small orifice leading to all intents and purposes to the mold inside. The operator usually approaches a countryman whom he knows to be fond of money, and not adverse to getting it easily. After a lot of beating around the bush he insinuates that it is quite an easy thing to turn a little money into a lot . . . if one knows how. Provided he is convinced that he has succeeded in creating the proper atmosphere, he produces the "gladar box". He then proceeds to give a demonstration. He produces a ladle and a quantity of solder. The solder is melted, the "gladar box" placed on a table, and everything is ready. Lifting the ladle, he prepares to pour the solder into the mold, but – "Get me water to cool the money," he says. While the victim turns to obey, a genuine florin is slipped into the mold and the boiling metal poured into the box. The box is opened and the hot coin falls into the water. Marvelling, the countryman examines the coin. He has already made up his mind to invest some of his earnings. It is not often he gets a chance like this: twenty pounds for five. The tinker takes the money and promises to return on a certain day. He never does. (1934: 261–2)

An IFC respondent from Kilfinane in County Limerick stated that coining had a history that went as far back at least as the turn of the century when the British were the administrating authority in Ireland, in the form of the RIC (Royal Irish Constabulary):

I was often astonished to find people and wise people at that having a belief that occult powers are possessed by these people. . . . In other ways we find the tinkers playing on their credulity. Some time ago there was a tinker named McDonagh up for swindling an old farmer and his wife out of ten or fifteen pounds. The farmer had some bad scrap. The tinker asked for a piece and said that he would make money out of it. He returned the next day and showed some new silver pieces. Then opposite the farmer's eyes he cast a few pieces. The farmer then gave him all the lead and ten pounds to produce some stated amount of coin. I believe the *bean a' tighe* (Irish: "woman of the house") gave five pounds. As the tinker didn't turn up the farmer complained to the guards and the case came before the court. A somewhat similar case of swindling occurred some years ago. I forget names and details. In the old RIC days members of the tinker class were occasionally in trouble with the "law" over the coining and passing of false or debased coin. Tinkers were, I needn't say, not the only offenders in this regard.[12]

---

[12] Iml. 1255: 202

Chapter 13

Idleness: An Irish Predilection?

One of the most common stereotypes as reiterated by many of the respondents to the IFC Tinker Questionnaire was the notion that Travellers were a lazy people by nature. In this Irish people accorded with the archetype of the Traveller or Gypsy as defined in the European imagination and as outlined by the "father" of the Gypsy archetype, Anton Grellmann. All the sources which Grellmann consulted for his "masterwork" *Die Zigeuner* (1787) agreed that the root cause of Gypsy poverty lay in their lazy natures and their love of ease:

> That they had no bread on the shelf and resorted to thievery and conning operations he attributed to their laziness, forever after an iradicable element of the Gypsy image. (Willems, 1997: 55)

The attribution of a lazy nature was directed so frequently at Travellers and Gypsies that they even told it as part of a "story against themselves" as outlined by this explanation for Gypsy origins recorded from a Gypsy storyteller in Spain in the early 1970s:

> The Lord, when he was about to go to heaven, first called an assembly of all the peoples of the world in the Great Plaza. He said, "Tomorrow I am going to heaven, and those who want to come here before I go, to them I will assign their position in life. Whoever gets there too late won't get any." And that way before he left, he assigned everyone a position — a schoolteacher, a doctor, all. And there were two Gypsies who were very lazy, and one said to the other, "Look, cousin, the Lord is leaving today. He is going to heaven, and everyone has already gone to get their destinies. We are going to be late." And so they started running to the

Great Plaza, and when they get there, the Lord was already leaving because they were so lazy. They called to him, "But father, you have assigned a destiny to everyone in the world. Are you just going to go off and leave the Gypsies here without an assigned place?" The Lord said, "You get on any way you can." And so he left us, and so we get on any way we can. This legend is mine, but it is a reality. The Gypsies live or eat by their wits. They have no real assigned place in the world.

A similar association of laziness with Traveller origins was implied by a number of IFC respondents who linked Irish Traveller laziness with their alleged noble origins:

Deir siad féin gur ós na taoisigh Gael a ghluaiseadar agus go bhfuilid ró-uasal, ró-galánta chun obáir a dhéanamh.[1]

(They say themselves that they are the decendants of the Gaelic chiefs and that they are too noble and too grand to work.)

They are not Gipsies at all but just Irish. . . . Nobody here is so interested as to think of them at all. I believe that they are the descendants of deposed Irish chiefs, who having lived among their clansmen for a generation or two, and being unable or too proud to resort to ordinary labour, took to the soldering iron.[2]

The discursive categorisation of Travellers as lazy was said to be such a defining characteristic of their natures that it was almost part of their physiological make-up and their nomadic nature:

Dath ruadh dhearg a bhíonn ar a gcuid gruaige agus cuma na leisce orthu. Labhrann siad garbh gránna.[3]

(They have a rusty red coloured hair and the look of laziness about them. Their speech is ugly and rough.)

Níor shocruigh aon duine aca síos san gceanntar riamh mar bhí siad ró leisceamhall le aon obair a dhéanamh.[4]

---

[1] Iml. 1255: 43

[2] Iml. 1256: 236

[3] Iml. 1256: 28

(None of them have ever settled down in the locality because they were too lazy to do any work.)

This form of categorisation can be linked with the strong anti-Irish discursive tradition whereby colonial writers attributed laziness to the Irish population as a whole, as outlined by Leersen (1996):

> God with the beames of hys grace, clarifie the eyes of that rude people that at length they may see theyr miserable estate: and also that such, as are deputed to the government thereof, bend their industry with conscionable pollicye to reduce them from rudenesse to knowledge, from rebellion to obedience, from trechery to honesty, from savagenesse to civilitie, from idlenes to labour. (Cited in Leersen, 1996: 43)

> [The Irish] . . . are uncivilised in some areas; who, by a remarkable freak of nature, both love idleness and hate quietude; and who are only too indulgent in headlong amorousness. (Cited in Leersen, 1996: 45)

> . . . the mountaines would yeeld abundance of Mettals, if this publike good were not hindred by the inhabitants barbarousness, making them apt to seditions, and so unwilling to inrich their Prince and Country, and by slothfulnesse, which is so singular, as they hold to basenesse to labour . . . (Cited in Leersen, 1996: 51)

The attribution of the sobriquet "tinker" to the Travelling commuity in Ireland has meant that a focus on tinsmithing was central to the claims of many in the settled community that Travellers were becoming lazy because they did not practise their "assigned" trade. In reality tinkering as a trade was dying in Ireland even as early as the 1930s, as G. Gmelch (1974) outlines:

> The demand for tinsmiths declined first in the more prosperous East where new consumer products were first acquired. As early as 1937, Travellers in County Wexford complained that new enamel buckets were hurting their trade. . . . By the mid-1950s, tinsmithing had become obsolete throughout the eastern half of

---

[4] Iml. 1256: 28

Ireland and survived only in the under-developed areas of the
West. (1974: 42)

Even as revered a source of reference as the *Oxford English Dictionary*
defined tinsmithing as the sole occupation of Travellers. A dictionary
reference to tinkers from the 1896 edition referred derisively to tinkering
as the only "ostensible trade" of the tinkers — the subtle implication being that they actually survived by means of theft. An IFC respondent
from County Cork said that settled people sometimes distinguished between Travellers by following their surname with the word "tinker",
thereby highlighting the importance of the tinsmithing trade with the settled people's construction of what a Traveller actually was:

> They are generally distinguished by the addition of "tinker" to their
> surname, e.g. "Driscoll the Tinker", "Foley the Tinker", etc.[5]

The focus on the Traveller as "tinker" has been central to the claims of
prejudiced settled people that Travellers were lazy or that they were previously industrious but the disappearing economy for tinsmithing had
transformed Travellers into a lazy or "parasitic" group who "lived off the
backs" of the "settled" community. This sentiment is found again and
again in the responses to the IFC Tinker Questionnaire:

> Tinkers, according to him, were originally a respected sect of local
> society until the British Government levied five pounds on their
> smelting pot and reduced them to beggary.[6]

> In their time they worked at their trade. They had only a few don-
> keys and cars to carry the women and children. They made money
> and spent it faster than they made it. They are tinkers no more.
> The present crowd are only tricksters and pedlars. It is at the fairs
> they do anything now, making bargains and swapping animals.[7]

> Many of the women have the reputation of being notorious beg-
> gars while the men folk are considered more decent and industri-

---

[5] Iml. 1255: 66

[6] Iml. 1256: 257

[7] Iml. 1255: 64

ous. But all are neer-do-wells. And when they have a few shillings in their pockets they go to town and drink it all. These
spending bouts end in great quarrels where the children suffer
more than the adults.[8]

*Bíonn céard ag fo-dhuine acu. Deinid áraistí stáin agus deisig-
heann siad iad. Bíonn ciseán ag cuid de na mná ag gabháil tim-
cheall agus díolann siad lasáin, cnaipí, snáth, cupáin agus fo-
chupáin, iallacha bróg agus rl. Tá alán acu ró-leisgeamhail chun
aon obair a dhéanamh, bailighid roinnt airgid agus siúd leo ag ól
annsan. Is maith leo "Gaoth adtuaidh agus grian andeas, claidhe
cluthais agus bolg lán".[9]*

(The odd person amongst them has a trade. They make tin items
and fix them. Some of the women have baskets and go around selling matches, buttons, needles, cups and saucers, shoe laces, etc. A
lot of them are too lazy to do any work; they collect some money
and then they go off drinking. They like "The wind on the north
and the wind on the south, the shelter of a ditch and full stomach".)

The supposedly frivolous and parasitic Travellers of modern times were
contrasted with the "true" tradesmen of the past who took pride in their
tinsmithing skills, sentiments which were an uncanny Irish echo of the
gypsiology tradition incorporating the concept of the "true" Gypsy:

*Fadó nuair a bhíodh na tincéirí ag deisiú corcán is aruistí mar
sin bhídís an-sholmanta; ní bhíodh focal ná gáire ná eascaine le
clos uatha ar eagla go raghadh aon mhíseol ar an ngoradh. Á
mbaineadh aon cheataighe don ghoradh níor mhaith do dhuine
bheith n-a gcómhghar.[10]*

(Long ago when the tinkers were fixing pots and other items like
that they were very solemn; they didn't laugh or curse in case
anything funny would go amiss with the heating iron. You
wouldn't want to be near them if something went askew with the
heating iron.)

---

[8] Iml. 1255: 230
[9] Iml. 1255: 272
[10] Iml. 1246: 222

I do not see any budgets now carried on the shoulders of men and very few call at my house to find out if there are any pots and kettles to mend or umbrellas to settle . . . I do not profess to know much about the present race of Tinkers. I will say however that they are an entirely different lot to those whom I knew in my young days when they were in the habit of going about from place to its neighbour mending and patching various articles of household value, like kettles and saucepans and so on. Those tinkers were always welcome and they were easily paid, as they took eggs, potatoes, meal, vegetables etc. in lieu of money.[11]

The customs of tinkers have waned much for the past half-century. Fifty years ago these roving tinkers camped in some disused or idle house which they happened to find in some out-of-the-way place. They had no vans or lorries or portable houses of any kind at this time. In this house they worked at their trade as tin-smiths making gallons, buckets and household articles in use at the time, such as quarts, pints, peggins, etc. [12]

This focus on the Traveller as "tinker" has situated Travellers within the framework of the coeval, as a group who have been left behind because of the obselence of the tinsmithing trade. It has also ignored the Travellers' own folk history of "who the tinkers were". Helleiner (2000) says that the traditional folk cateogorisation of the Traveller as tinker has perpetuated a particular view of Travellers' occupational history, a view which Travellers' own accounts frequently contradict. Travellers' accounts of their history tend to emphasise occupational flexibility and the ability to access diverse niche markets as occasion demands, as opposed to a singular reliance on tinsmithing:

A Traveller was quoted by Court, an American folklorist, as saying: "Well, a Tinker is a man who does every class of a job, and he's tinking on every job, tinking on every job. It comes along that that's how we got the title (Court, 1985: 88). In this etymology (dependent upon the fact that "think" and "tink" are often homophones in Irish English), Travellers' cleverness as "think-

---

[11] Iml. 1246, 160
[12] Iml. 1255: 140

ers" is emphasised rather than the occupational specialisation of the tinsmith. A similar account was recorded by S. Gmelch in the 1970s: "A tinker was a man years ago who thought of a hundred ways of surviving . . . This was the real tinker, not just the tinsmith. He was a better survivor than the rest" (S. Gmelch, 1975: 28). In these accounts from male Travellers, the economic ingenuity and self-reliance of Travellers was emphasised rather than a particular occupational identity. (Helleiner, 2000: 132)

In spite of this, a declining demand for tinsmithing was often central to outsiders' claims of Travellers' occupational obsolescence and inactivity. A 1959 editorial in the Galway newspaper *The Connacht Tribune* is a good example of the new orthodoxy whereby the formerly legitimate tinker "craftsman" had metamorphosed into an illegitimate and parasitical "nuisance".

The Irish Census returns show an increase in the number of tinsmiths and sheet metal workers in this country but it is obvious to everyone that the itinerant tinsmith is almost no more. The craftsman who mended pots, kettles, and pans has virtually disappeared from the roads. On the other hand there has been no fall in the number of tinkers of the type usually in mind when that word is used. They are on every road and a nuisance in every town.

These tinker groups rarely ply any trade. . . . The men, for the most part, are lazy louts and depend on their women folk to cadge and crave money, food and clothes.[13]

Local Opinion [regarding Tinkers]: "Harmless but entirely useless parasites".[14]

Similar sentiments were echoed by some respondents almost a decade earlier as indicated by the comments of this IFC respondent who recommended that the Tinker "nuisance" be eradicated so that Ireland could progress as a newly industrialised nation:

---

[13] Iml. 1255: 253

[14] Iml. 1255: 358

I think that while not endeavouring to wipe out completely the Tinker Tribe an effort should be made to control the whole class and make them do more work for the nation at large. Ancestrally the Tinkers may claim a sort of protection but when one sees that as a class they will become a damned nuisance unless some steps be taken to put a limit to their number we shall soon have such an increase in their ranks as will cripple the present efforts of our rulers to make our people into workers for the country's good. Tinkers are, as you know idlers and we want no idlers at this junction in our efforts to advance the nation. I do not know if you have noticed that our workers now do as little as possible to speed up any kind of work they engage in. I observe this habit among workers here in Killarney at present and somehow I fancy that they say to themselves "Why should we work hard when we see so many of the Tinker Class idling about and having a good time?"[15]

Similar sentiments incorporating the attribution of laziness to Travellers continue today, as indicated by newspaper headlines such as the following.

"Judge says Travellers have too much spare time" (*The Irish Times*, 1998)

In 1998 a County Councillor from the west of Ireland allegedly suggested that Travellers should be "tagged" so as to monitor their movements and also described Traveller men as similar to "pedigree dogs" who spent the day sunning themselves rather than undertaking work re-training pro-grammes (see *The Irish* Times, 2 March 1999; and *The Irish Times*, 13 May 1998). This Councillor was subsequently brought to court under the Incitement to Hatred Act but escaped prosecution. One IFC respondent put forward the belief that Travellers' perceived "laziness" had its roots in the fact that time did not appear to be as important to them as to workers who worked in "settled" or "nine-to-five" jobs:

I never passed their camp without their asking me what time of day it was. This curiosity on the part of people to whom time seems of

---

[15] Iml. 1255: 62

> little concern and who have plenty of it at their disposal always ap-
> peared strange to me whose life is directed by timetables.[16]

Cottaar et al. (1998) have linked the attribution of laziness to Travelling
and other "marginal" groups to the changing nature of discourses concerning poverty and poor relief in Western Europe from the Middle Ages
onwards. Class analyses of socio-economic developments in Europe by
scholars like the Belgian historians Lis and Hugo (1979) explained the
increased criminalisation of nomadism and Travelling groups that accompanied the end of feudalism and the advent of modern notions of
capitalism. Increased attention to the control of the labour force on the
part of the governing classes in European states were part of an effort to
control the labour force in order to keep wages down and labour available. The growth of capitalism had increased poverty by the proletariani-
sation of the mass of the European population. Summarising the work of
Lis and Hugo (1979), Cottaar et al. (1998) describe a situation where
there was a great increase in the criminalisation of begging and wandering from the fifteenth century onwards.

> They [Lis and Hugo] show that poverty is no longer deemed
> normal and is now equated with vagrancy and criminality. At the
> same time an elaborate stereotyping of the alleged criminal anti-
> society came about. The "social problem" was associated with
> idleness, criminality, etc., to be solved by the creation of work-
> houses. In order to regulate the labour-market the cities created a
> system of poor relief. In this climate the idea of vagrants could
> easily become the symbolic apogee of antisocial behaviour and it
> was extended to everybody who refused to work for a (low)
> wage. The aim was not so much to catch the real criminals, but to
> stigmatise the wandering poor. (1998: 142)

While Ireland's colonial and island status may have meant that certain
structural differences existed between attitudes towards the Travellers
and other "wandering poor" in Ireland as compared with our European
neighbours, it is safe to say that the general thrust of Cottaar et al's
analysis regarding the increased criminalisation or disapproval of the

---

[16] Iml. 1256: 45

"wandering life" also applied to Ireland, and involved a slow evolution from the medieval era onwards. Perhaps most pertinent to the context of Irish Travellers and their stereotypical "laziness" is Cottaar et al's observation regarding the association of "laziness" with what was perceived to be a countercultural "threat":

> The aim was not so much to catch the real criminals, but to stigmatise the wandering poor as disorderly and antisocial. The church did the same and the middle groups soon took over the hostile attitude. Especially from the seventeenth century on, the alleged resistance of the poor against wage-labour was regarded as structural. Marginal groups were thought to be extra dangerous because they could persuade others to go astray. (1998: 142)

Chapter 14

"A Society within a Society"

*And for much more might the whole island be beholden unto it
[i.e. the English conquest], in case upon a certain peevish and
obstinate love they beare unto their owne country fashions, they
had not stopped their eares and shut up their hearts against
better governance. For, the Irishry are so stiffly settled in
observing the old rites of their country, that not only they be
with-drawn from them, but also are able easily to draw the
English unto same. (Cited in Leersen, 1996: 46)*

The second major discourse evident in the discursive construction of
Travellers as "Other", as outlined by the responses to the IFC's Tinker
Questionnaire, depicts Travellers in terms of a countercultural threat.
They are seen to disturb the moral order because they are perceived to
inhabit an exclusive and secretive society which operates in symbiosis
with and yet on the margins of the settled community. This discourse
implies the existence of a mutually exclusive "society" which has a certain internal structure incorporating leaders/kings and a range of customs, superstitions and ceremonies that exhibit an absence of coevalness.
This belief system incorporates constructions of Travellers that place
them "outside of history" and frozen in certain folkways that have been
abandoned by the "civilised" or "progressive" settled community. According to these constructions Travellers are "Other" because they are
nomadic and allegedly engage in cultural practices that are considered
anachronistic by the settled community, including a range of beliefs and
taboos associated with social organisation, death, marriage, the use of a
"secret" language, and a refusal to integrate into the wider community,
etc. To break into this "separate" world was the project with which the

British Gypsiologists of the first half of the twentieth century had tasked themselves, in an effort which bore remarkable similarities with the cultural "reclamation" task to which the IFC Commission dedicated themselves. The task which the Gypsilorists had set themselves in relation to the Travellers/Gypsies had been considered all the more vital given the "non-literate" culture of the Travellers/Gypsies and the notion that this culture was doomed to extinction with the advent of industrialisation:

> The apparent absence of the self-produced sources and the related silence of the Gypsies created an impression of a separate people whose way of life and culture were largely impervious to intrusion by non-Gypsies. Indeed it heightened their mystery and relative invisibility, which for many are among their most intriguing and beguiling qualities. In some accounts their separateness was said to be conscious and deliberate, with the Romany language used as a means of excluding the non-Gypsy speaker and of asserting the distinctiveness of Gypsy identity. The reluctance of Gypsies to reveal the secrets and intimacies of their lives to potentially hostile outsiders stemmed largely from the justifiable belief that information is a source of power which could be termed against them. The task of the Gypsiologist was to break down these barriers and overcome the silence . . . (Mayall, 2004: 38)

A similar reticence, as a function of exclusivity, was indicated in relation to Irish Travellers by some "settled" community members who tried to find out more about their community:

> I repeat that they seem most averse to intermarriage or intercourse with outsiders. It is most difficult to prise information from them, normally, but they seem anxious to repay a good turn. They do not absorb individuals outside their own class.[1]

THE PISREÓGS

The archives of the Irish Folklore Commission show that prior to the advent of more wide-scale industrialisation Ireland had an intricate system of psycho-magical and animistic belief that was interwoven with its two

---

[1] Iml. 1255: 317

"official" religions, i.e. Catholicism and Protestantism. Many of these psycho-magical beliefs manifested themselves in *pisreógs* (superstitions or "traditional" beliefs) which governed social and individual behaviour in relation to a wide range of aspects concerning everyday life. When folklorists and other intellectuals initiated attempts to record the folklore of Ireland towards the middle of the twentieth century much attention was given to the recording of this aspect of Irish native belief. Examples of the alleged superstitious nature of the Irish Travellers and the coeval superstitions or *pisreógs* practised by them were many, as recorded by the respondents to the Irish Folklore Commission. Virtually all of these superstitions had in common that they situated the Travellers in a position of timelessness. Travellers, like most groups who are perceived as "Other", were seen to exist outside of history and practised superstitions that had allegedly disappeared amongst the Irish rural population.

An IFC respondent from County Galway described the Traveller fear of ghosts in the following manner:

> *Cáil ar chuid aca freisin faitíos mhór a bheith ortha roimh thaibhsí nó neacha ón saol eile a chastáil ortha.*

> (They have a reputation as being very afraid of meeting ghosts or beings from the other world.)

> I heard that tinkers are very superstitious. They believe in ghosts. Cases have been known where they changed their camping ground, on account of having seen some strange objects at night in that place.[2] *(An IFC respondent from Monasterevan, Co. Kildare)*

A Galway man described another practice that related to death or the otherworld:

> *Agus nuair a bhíonn said ag teacht amach as teach an phobuil cuireann an fear an bhean amach i dtosuigh mar bheadh sé ag ceapadh gur bé féin a gheibheadh bás.*[3]

---

[2] Iml. 1255: 391

[3] Iml. 1256: 23

(And when they are coming out of the Church the man puts the woman out first. If he didn't do so he would be afraid that he might be the first to die.)

Some of the Traveller customs which situated them in a "coeval" time-frame in the eyes of the settled community related to "rite of passage" or major life events such as birth or death. A commonly cited cultural attribute of Travellers that was seen to "other" them was the custom of burning the caravan and/or possessions of the deceased. Few IFC respondents ventured an opinion as to why this practice was carried out although Mayall (1982), who notes the existence of many references to this belief as applied to English Gypsies, states that its origin may have been due to a variety of causes:

> There are numerous reported instances of the custom of the burning of the property of the dead, which variously included every item associated with the dead person, from his horse and van to his fiddle, to just a few selected items. The custom was still carried out even if it meant that the living members of the deceased's family were reduced to poverty. The motive for this practice was said to be due to a variety of causes, some superstitious and others practical. Those who wished to emphasise the mystical side of the gypsies' beliefs put the causes as a desire to avoid the taboo of the corpse, and, associated with this, the ghost of the dead man was to be placated by providing, in an ethereal form, the goods needed by him in the spirit world. (1982: 156)

Traveller "separateness" was reinforced for the IFC's settled community respondents by the fact that death as a "rite of passage" was marked much more "overtly" amongst the Traveller community, an overtness that was extemporised in the use of more "traditional" coping mechanisms that were dying or had died out amongst the settled community.

One coping mechanism observed by many in the settled community was the practice of moving away from the area where somebody had died in an apparent effort to avoid being reminded of the tragedy. Non-Travellers observed that Travellers tended to move away from a camping place where someone had died, and generally did not return there again.

This cultural tradition was observed by Helleiner (2000) only recently in her anthropological fieldwork amongst Travellers in Galway:

> Despite improved child survival rates, the still common experience of infant and child mortality ensured a pervasive sense of the precariousness of children's lives. . . . At least some children also appeared to view their own early mortality as a possibility. . . . Aware of the preference for a change in residence after a death in the home, one boy volunteered to me that he would be sure not to die in his family's trailer because then his parents would have to move. One doctor also indicated to me that Travellers had a high rate of hospital admission because when their children were ill in the night they would bring them in immediately for fear of them dying at home. (2000: 213)

Overt forms of lamentation such as keening over the body, which was still common amongst the settled community in the early 1900s, seems to have survived as a cultural practice for a longer time amongst Travellers:

> The "King of the Tinkers", Mike Ward, was buried in Aughrim, Mount Bellew. The funeral was attended by the townspeople. Later the tinkers erected a tombstone to his memory. They mourn their dead in the old "caoining way".[4] *(IFC respondent from Menlough, Ballinasloe, County Galway)*

> A death of a tinker, Mrs Cauley, occurred in this district about two years ago. She was attended by the local priest in a little tent on the roadside. The funeral was delayed so that relations could be got in touch with. A very large number of tinkers attended the funeral. They arrived in all sorts of vehicles. A scene took place in the church during Mass when a daughter of the deceased became hysterical. She had only arrived in time for Mass and wanted the lid of the coffin removed to see her mother. A month's mind Mass was offered up for the deceased and all the relations attended.[5]

Traveller activist Michael McDonagh (2000b) has written that the (sometimes) lack of an overt expression of grief on the part of settled

---

[4] Iml. 1256: 31

[5] Iml. 1256: 232

community at funerals was something which was actually the basis of a reverse-prejudice on the part of Travellers *vis-à-vis* the settled community. When writing of the importance of the extended family and kinship to Travellers in times of sickness and death he says:

> Working at your family ties is the key to Traveller identity so we will turn up at all meetings of the extended family, for weddings, for funerals or when visiting the sick in hospital. If you even look at what happens in hospital when someone's sick or dying, everyone gathers together and visits the hospital, and the nurses are going haywire over the huge number of Travellers there. I think that it's very important to understand that for Travellers this is a sign of respect that shows the person who is going to die that their life was worthwhile and that their life just didn't go by unnoticed. In addition to this there is also the whole grieving process whereby we openly mourn for the person who has died. This explains the reason why for generations there has been a prejudice on our behalf where we see settled people go to a funeral and we say to ourselves, "God they mustn't have loved the people they're burying because they're not crying or expressing strong emotions very visibly and openly." It's important for Travellers to actually be allowed to express their grief because it's part of the grieving process. (2000: 31)

Death amongst Travellers was a rite of passage which was marked by the type of mourning with which many Europeans are now only familiar from their television screens when viewing the very "public" grieving that is common to many Middle Eastern and Islamic countries.

> . . . and that morning where they found the place where, in the long plaited grasses by the river where she was drowned, may God rest her soul . . . and I had a pot of stew hanging on the fire waiting ready hot for to give her. I threw it out on the grass rather than give it my dead, my dear, dead, daughter . . . Oh my poor dear dead daughter, may God rest her. I hurled myself at her grave. I wrecked myself. I drank myself. I threw white paint and ashes at me mouth. I didn't want to live after and I swore I'd have no more children after. But I got ten children now, God bless them all, but it's not the same as my Bridget, may God rest her!

(Anonymous Traveller woman in Ó Fearadhaigh and Wiedel, 1976: 58)

Anthropologist Jane Helleiner (2000) highlighted this aspect of Traveller life when commenting on some of the coping mechanisms relating to child mortality amongst Travellers in Galway city in the 1980s:

> The deaths of children after infancy were the most traumatic events experienced by women and men alike. Some parents were described by others as being consumed by grief and despair by the death of a child and efforts were made not to remind them of the tragedy. In some cases bereaved parents destroyed all photos of the dead child, while in others such photos were featured in a central location. Anniversaries of children's deaths were, like the death anniversaries for adults, marked by rituals of remembrance by the immediate family and wider kinship group. Wealthier families erected large and ornate headstones to dead children in the cemetery. . . . The widely shared experience of child mortality ensured that the illness of a child was intensely experienced by many beyond the immediate family. (2000: 214)

In addition to engaging in cultural practices that might be considered anachronistic by some members of the non-Traveller community the Travellers' role as "outsiders" meant that it was commonly believed that they had a "*fios*" (insight) which the "settled" community didn't have. The Travellers' alleged emphasis on "superstition" meant that they were in possession of curing/socio- magical knowledge of which the "settled" community was bereft:

> One woman, a McDonagh, told of a cure for whooping cough in a child. She said they used it themselves. A person was to run to a river, catch a trout with the hands, race back to the child or have the child convenient, allow some of the water from the fish to drip into the child's mouth, and then race back to the river and return the fish alive; and this was a cure: if the fish died during the ritual, the cure was ineffective.[6] *(IFC respondent from County Tyrone)*

---

[6] Iml. 1256: 255

TINKER KINGS

Many respondents to the IFC constructed Travellers' "aloofness" and lack of integration as indicative of the existence of a separate and mutually exclusive "society" which had a certain internal structure and leadership including kings. The notion that Travellers, Gypsies and other nomads had their own "kings" went back to the very first archetypal images of Travellers and Gypsies in the European imaginary, the German "gypsiologist" Grellmann considering this belief to be a projection of the social structures of the "civilised" world:

> Since their initial appearance in Europe Gypsies were said to have travelled about in bands under the leadership of chiefs. Down through the years these headmen were referred to in annuals by such titles as *woiwoden* (a Polish term for governor or leader), knights, counts, dukes and kings. Grellmann derided these designations as the ridiculous aping of titles that Gypsies encountered in "the civilised world". An advantage of the title *woiwoden* that he acknowledged, however, was that in time of war the state could call upon these "leaders" to supply fighting men. The leader's actual power was, according to Grellmann, slight and he was said merely to serve as an intermediary between his old followers and the government. Still, Grellmann added, perhaps one thing he may well have done in their own interest was to administer justice. That was also, to his mind, the reason why Gypsies preferred to settle their own affairs, because then everybody, at least in their own circle, fared better. (Willems, 1997: 51)

While more historical research is necessary it is sometimes claimed that the fact that they had high-sounding dukes, counts and lords among their group, and the fact that they claimed that to be on a religious pilgrimage, eased the passage of the first Roma Gypsies when they arrived in Europe, an initial welcome that quickly turned sour:

> In 1519 the Earl of Surrey is reported to have entertained gypsies at Tendring Hall in Suffolk and to have given them safe conduct. Also it is said that they held letters of recommendation from both James IV and James V of Scotland. (Mayall, 2004: 57)

In Ireland similar notions of a historical travelling "nobility" were linked more with the concept that the Travellers were the remnants of "fallen nobility" who had lost status during the various periods of dispossession associated with the colonisation of Ireland.

Travellers whose surname was McCarthy were described in the following "romantic" manner by a schoolteacher from County Cork:

They claimed to be descended from the royal McCarthys of Munster, and to see their splendid figures and handsome features one could believe this. Could we not believe it also from our sad history, when these nobles were outlawed and crushed.[7]

That they exoticised themselves on occasion so as to gain greater acceptance from the settled community is likely, a process that was explained as follows by anthropologist G. Gmelch (1977):

Although Tinkers sometimes claimed to settled Irish that they were divided into "tribes" and elected their own "kings", these were only public fictions probably intended to enhance the Traveller mystique. (1977: 35)

A Traveller woman from County Limerick linked "noble lineage" with fortune-telling and linked the "Other" status of the Travellers with both the mysterious and the exotic:

She said the Queen (Sheridan) had the "knowledge of the truth in life and could fortell things. She (the Queen) is the person that won her case against the Limerick Corporation lately. The King died in 1952.[8]

A Traveller whom a "settled" person spoke to in Enniskillen, County Fermanagh implied the existence of a ruling structure and a king and seemed to also use the occasion for some "point-scoring" against other Travellers:

---

[7] Iml. 1255: 271

[8] Iml. 1255: 332

Here is an account of what a gipsy told me in reply to my questions. In reply to tinker society. Yes, we have a chief or king to whom we give allegiance. I can't mind his name but I think he is Ward. No, there are no classes within our ranks. Yes, some of us are richer than others. We are mostly Roman Catholics. We practise our religion. Keshes, Lockes, Stewards, Prices and Whites are mostly Protestant. No, they do not practise their religion.[9]

These sentiments were repeated by a Traveller from Munster who implied the existence of democratic structures in the election of a king:

The old lady said that there would not be an election for a King, and that nothin' would happen for a long time. I think that a selection would be made from some of the King's family if some of them showed outstanding merit and gained the good will of the rest — otherwise things would be put on the long finger.[10]

The comments of another "settled" person who responded to the IFC Questionnaire make reference to the alleged existence of rulers amongst the Traveller community and can be seen as a "projection" of the class structure that existed among the settled community:

Up to the present, I only know that the present king of the tinkers is named Patsy Joyce and the queen is his wife Biddy. There certainly seem to be classes within the tinker world.[11]

The idea of a separate society with its own class structure was mooted by a range of Questionnaire respondents. As with the settled community, class divisions were often perceived to fall according to gradations of wealth:

They seem to have greater and lesser social status within the gang for a member of the Wards was asked about a brother of his and the answer he gave was, "I know nothing about him, he married into the Gavins and we don't recognise him".[12]

---

[9] Iml. 1256: 257

[10] Iml. 1255: 334

[11] Iml. 1255: 315

[12] Iml. 1255: 214

> These clans or factions have absolutely no dealings with other tramps (poor creatures travelling about singly or in little family groups). If one were camped as near as five yards from the other, which is unlikely, one party would not speak to that other. As far as I can make out, these single or family groups live in dread of falling foul of a faction.[13] *(IFC respondent from County Carlow)*

> There are evidently various classes in the tinker world considering all the bartering and bargaining that usually precedes a tinker's wedding. Negotiations go on for a considerable time before the match is finally fixed.[14] *(IFC respondent from County Clare)*

The notion of a separate "Travelling society" that was presided over by its own rulers and was the subject of separate and secretive practices and taboos had very old roots in the European imaginary. Fears over the countercultural threat posed by the nomadic "dispossessed" go as far back as the early modern era. Changes in population structures and the transition from feudalism to capitalism resulted in greater migrancy and more repressive attitudes towards nomadism on the part of governments tending towards the centralisation of the state. The literature of Gypsiology stressed the marginality of Travellers and Gypsies to the dominant social order, as indicated by Mayall (1982), in relation to British Gypsy-Travellers:

> Few commentators were able to write about the gypsies without stressing the marginality of this separate and secretive race to the dominant political and social institutions. Essentially, the gypsies were said to be uninvolved in the politics of the wider society of which they were a part, and had instead their own organisations that depended on dark and mysterious meetings, which called to mind freemasonry practices. (1982: 208–9)

Related to the belief that Travellers were an aloof and "exclusive" group, then, was the notion that they had their own political structure that operated externally of the politics of the host society. Travellers in Ireland were considered to be similarly "apolitical" regarding developments in

---

[13] Iml. 1255: 214

[14] Iml. 1255: 241

"settled" society as described by this respondent from County Mayo who mooted possible foreign origins as an explanation for this situation:

> In their society, among the people, the tinkers are a very exclusive set. They have never merged into the fabric of the general population, through marriage or affinity. . . . Neither have they been known to absorb any outside individuals into their own pattern of society. Political or social questions never seem to trouble them. Problems such as emigration or falling population never worry them. They never participate in public amusements such as athletic sports, football, dances, etc. They are not, of course, popular with the people and the aversion is equally reciprocated by them. . . . . They are a distinct people following their own exclusive way of life. In this respect they are somewhat on a par with the Red Indians of America with the difference that while the latter are aboriginal, our Irish tinkers are supposed to be the descendants of an alien tribe. Certainly, whatever their origin or history, our tinkers are seen to be a very ancient class in the Irish community.[15]

It is no coincidence that the notion of separate and "exclusive" class with its own social structures and organisation seems to have come to the fore generally in contexts whereby large groups of Travellers were gathering together in one place. Funerals, weddings or fairs seem to have been occasions for the proliferation of the "king" stereotype and are possibly indicative of the countercultural threat in the subconscious of the settled community occasioned by large gatherings of this "Other" group:

> The groups had a king or leader whose word was law, but since his death a few years ago I do not know if a successor was appointed.[16]

> Paddy Maughan was King of his tribe. Had a wealth of horses and left legacies when he died . . . Since Maughan died the local groups didn't bother going to Ballinasloe and they had no King since.[17] *(IFC respondent from Templeboy, County Sligo)*

---

[15] Iml. 1256: 119

[16] Iml. 1255: 239

[17] Iml. 1256: 130

> Davy Joyce seems to be the head of the Joyce Clan. When Hubert
> Nevin died there were £69 "offerings" at his funeral.[18] *(IFC re-*
> *spondent from County Westmeath)*

> They have no local "King" here but a few years ago hundreds
> came to a tinker's funeral in Tullamore and the "King" travelled
> from Galway and was royally received.[19]

Notions of kingships, and a "separate" society with the mainstream Irish
society fed into countercultural motifs that had a long tradition. They can
be linked to the sixteenth-century phenomenon that was the "literature of
roguery", a literature that influenced English playwrights such as Christopher Marlowe. This was an elaborate literary genre which developed in
Britain under Queen Elizabeth, which portrayed wanderers as members of
a dangerous criminal subculture or underworld. According to the popular
literature this subculture was made up of highly organised wandering
gangs, groups who had their own canting language and who spread sedi-
tious ideas while travelling. Beier says that the literary portrayal of vagrancy and the stereotyping which it engendered should be taken very
seriously because it was a popular form of literature and was believed:

> The literature of roguery went beyond the learned tradition,.
> however, to describe a highly organised vagrant underworld. In
> 1552 Gilbert Walker said vagabonds were a "corporation"; to
> Awdeley they were a "fraternity", a "company" with orders; to
> Harman a "fleeting fellowship" in which "rufflers" and "upright
> men" were top dogs. At an annual beggars' convention in
> Gloucestershire a Lord of the Fair was supposed to be elected; a
> Chief Commander and officers for regiments were also reported.
> A new recruit, Thomas Dekker wrote, had to "learn the orders of
> our house", to "recognise that "there are degrees of superiority
> and inferiority in our society". Even women and children had
> their assigned places in the vagrant pecking order. This anti-
> society was specialised, too. Some vagrants went in for horse
> theft, others pretended to be shipwrecked, and still others feigned

---

[18] Iml. 1255: 222

[19] Iml. 1255: 232

epilepsy. They had a special underworld vocabulary — canting, or Pedlar's French. (Beier, 1985: 8)

Although this literature of roguery was primarily a British phenomenon it is interesting that many of the same countercultural motifs were to be found in the Irish oral tradition even at a much later date. These included a range of beliefs concerning the existence of a beggars' or wanderers' counterculture. According to this discourse beggars and nomadic people generally were allegedly divided into well-organised communities akin to trade unions, some of which organised themselves so as to keep "foreign" beggars from their own area of operation. Countercultural motifs such as "fraud", the use of an anti-language or "canting" jargon and organised groupings under a specific leader or "king" remained remarkably consistent, as evidenced from the following description given by witnesses from the west of Ireland to the pre-Famine Poor Inquiry known as the *First Report of His Majesty's Commissioners for Inquiring into the Condition of the Poorer Classes in Ireland* (1835). These witnesses from Galway reported seeing the following amongst the "begging" community at country fairs:

> That man gave his daughter £30 fortune. He is like a king over the others, and people say that he has a tribute from each of them. I saw him, at the fair of Kilcreest take off the bandage in a drunken fit, and defy any man in the fair to try him at the stick. (478–9).

An IFC respondent from County Monaghan linked the "nobility" concept with ritualised fighting which continues as the most prominent vehicle for the proliferation of the "king" stereotype in the public imaginary of modern Ireland:

> Once when I was at the Connemara Show in Ballinasloe in October I saw hundreds of gipsies or tinkers there. It seemed to be a real reunion of the tribes from the various parts of Ireland. On that occasion the new king of the gipsies had to be chosen for the previous one had died. The choice was made when the eligibles from each family fought for the kingship. The champion who was

successful in overcoming all his rivals was declared "King of the Gypsies" as long as he lived.[20]

The notion of kingship was linked to a stereotype which implied an alternative, "pagan" form of marriage which operated outside the sanction of the Church. A retired schoolteacher from County Kerry who responded to the IFC Tinker Questionnaire described Traveller marriage like this:

> Marriages do not take place before a Priest and the common belief is that when a pair wish to become man and wife they meet someone in authority; an authority that they believe in — such as a King or Queen appointed by themselves, and that a part of the ceremony is the "jumping over the Budget.[21]

The teacher's comments were given some support by the following description from County Westmeath:

> I was told of a tinker wedding which took place on the roadside, an old member of the clan performing the ceremony. He stood between the shafts of an unyoked cart, the young man on his right hand and the young girl on his left. I could not get further information about it, as regards words said, etc.[22]

A similar practice incorporating countercultural motifs and marriage of a casual nature was ascribed to those people referred to as "beggars" who met at fairs as described by a "settled community" observer who answered the British-instigated *First Report of His Majesty's Commissioners for Inquiring into the Condition of the Poorer Classes in Ireland* which had oral hearings throughout Ireland in 1835:

> There is a place near Strokestown, where they assemble every year in immense numbers; at this fair, called the fair of Ballinafad, the beggars are married for a year. The ceremony is performed by joining the hands of the parties over a pair of crutches,

---

[20] Iml. 1256: 227

[21] Iml. 1255: 60

[22] Iml. 1255: 216

and hundreds return to have the rite renewed year after year.
(Great Britain, 1835, xxxii: 513)

Interestingly, the countercultural motif in the latter example has a resonance which can only be understood with reference to the Irish language.
In the rites of passage as described there is a suggestion that these beggars have their own religion since there is a convenient pun between a
crutch and a cross, a pun which also worked through the medium of the
Irish language, as crutches are known in Irish as "maidí croise" or "cross
sticks".

Chapter 15

Countercultural Motifs and the Essentialisation of Traveller Identity

The lewder sorte, both clearkes and lay men are sensuall and over loose in livying. The same being virtuously bred up or re-formed, are such mirrors of holynes and austeritie, that other nations retain but a shadow of devotion in comparison of them.
(Description of the Irish people by sixteenth-century English writer, Edmund Campion in Leersen, 1996: 41)

The people are . . . for the most parte Papists, great gluttons, and of a sensuall and vitious lyfe, deepe dissemblers, secret in displeasure, of a crewel revenging minde, and irreconsiliable.
(John Dymmok, 1842, in Leersen, 1996: 50)

SEXUAL AND MARRIAGE PRACTICES

The association of Travellers with sexual immorality in the European imaginary has deep roots. One need only consider the image of the "fiery" Gypsy as depicted in Spanish culture and as associated with flamenco. That the image of the Gypsy woman as an object of sexual allure has been central to artistic impressions of Gypsy life is unquestionable. Mayall (2004) describes how this image fed into "real" constructions of Travelling people in nineteenth-century England:

> There is no doubt that many people deliberately impersonated the gypsy of the Romantics in the manner and style of dress in order to secure specific ends. At times it would have been beneficial to adopt the gaujified[1] image of the gypsy to facilitate economic

---

[1] "Gaujified" is Anglo-Romany for "settled person's image".

transactions. For example, London prostitutes were said to have dressed up as gypsy women in order to attract clients at Epsom during Derby week. This served to confirm the popular impression of the gypsy as immoral and lacking any sexual scruples. (1982: 189)

The association of Travelling people with an imagined sexual licentiousness and a romantic concept of "freedom" is also evident in constructions of Irish Travellers as outlined in the folklore tradition. The allegedly "casual" attitude of Travellers regarding marriage, courtship and sexual congress gained popular currency partly through the medium of the theatre. The Anglo-Irish playwright J.M. Synge based his play *The Tinker's Wedding* on popular perceptions of tinker marriage incorporating "pagan" wedding rites and as recounted to him by country people in the west of Ireland. Synge described how a man had told him of a "tinker" couple who had never been married (Synge, 1980: 53). Similar accounts were collected by folklorist and writer Lady Gregory in the west of Ireland during the same period. One country person allegedly told her that "the tinkers sell their wives to one another; I've seen that myself . . . [and that] as to marriage, some used to say that they lepped [leaped] the budget [bag of tinsmith's tools], but it's more likely they have no marriage at all" (Gregory, 1974: 94). The notion of a "pagan" marriage that involved the jumping over or passing some sort of boundary was mentioned by many respondents:

> The phrase I always heard in my girlhood as to tinkers getting married was "jump the bucket", i.e. when the couple jumped over the bucket they were then married in their own ceremonial.

> Another vague custom re: a marriage of tinkers in "the quarry hole" in Crockanboy, one side of Donnelly's. Only information so far available is that the couple being married "had to jump in and out of a ring. *(IFC respondent from County Tyrone)*

The possibility that these accounts are an echo of some form of pre-Christian marriage ceremony requires further investigation. The boundary mechanisms implied in these accounts are reminiscent of marriage rituals in other non-Christian societies. It is noteworthy that it is actually a Traveller who describes another pre-Christian ritual as employed in

marriages in England many centuries ago. Nan Joyce (1985), commenting on her travels in England with her family described a visit to Gretna
Green in Scotland in the following manner:

> We travelled all over England and Scotland. . . . We came to
> Gretna Green where boys and girls would go if they ran away to-
> gether and got married quickly. Father showed us the big anvil
> they would hit with a hammer when they were getting married.
> (1985: 27)

> There used to be a story told when I was young that a tinker's
> marriage had taken place by extending hands over the Cross on a
> donkey's back — the ceremony being presided over by the
> Tinker King or family head.[2]

While quite a few of the people who responded to the Tinker Questionnaire mentioned the notion of a "pagan" wedding ceremony it is debat-
able to what extent this idea was believed in the Ireland of the early 1950s
when some of these observations were recorded. It seems more likely that
it was a stereotype that had belonged to the recent past as most respondents who described Traveller marriages described Travellers as marrying
in the Church in the same way as the "settled" community:

> *Caitlicidhthe iad go léir agus póstar san Eaglais iad. Chuaidh beirt
> acu lá go dtí an sagart paróiste i gCúil Mín chun iad a phósadh. Ní
> raibh ór ná airgead ná fáinne acu. Chuir an sagart an cléireach
> amach go dtí an geata chun an eochair a thabhairt isteach chuige.
> Bhí fáinne iarainn san eochair agus dhéanfeadh sé an gnó.*[3]

> (They are all Catholics and they get married in the Church. Two
> of them went to the parish priest in Coolmine to get married.
> They didn't have gold or silver or any ring. The priest sent the
> sacristan out to the gate to bring the key into him. There was a
> iron ring in the key and that did the job.)

One IFC respondent implied possible "exoticisation" of the "old" stereotype on the part of a Traveller he had spoken with:

---

[2] Iml. 1255: 244

[3] Iml. 1255: 270

> We believe all Tinkers do marry though they say they don't. They
> have their family pride and are glad of being noted for not break-
> ing their word and for their being never indicted for stealing.
> Long ago I heard old Tom Coffey saying: "Yerra the devil a mar-
> riage for us. If we find a wan willin' to jump the Budget what
> more about it". Some of the women really jumped the man's
> Budget showing that they were willing and ready for marriage
> which always took place. There may be exceptions of course.[4]

The intertwining of both Traveller and settled community mores is made
clear by the fact that the phrase "jumping the budget" became synono-
mous with elopement amongst many in the "settled" community:

> There was a strong conviction among the people of not so many
> years ago that their nuptials took place without any religious
> ceremony whatever. There was a contract entered into verbally
> and it was considered — by the ordinary people — to be of a very
> permanent and binding type and though it almost smells of heresy
> to say so it was further believed that this contract was held as
> binding by the Church. There was some kind of ritual observed at
> the marriage, which was known as "jumping over the budget" —
> the budget being the tinsmith's kit of tools. Whenever an elope-
> ment took place in our part of the world — that is among the ordi-
> nary people — the neighbours said that they (the eloping couple)
> had only jumped over the budget.[5]

Sentiments such as those expressed in the above statement gave the impression of Traveller immorality and fed into the image of the "sensual"
or sexually licentious Traveller/Gypsy of the European imaginary. The
Traveller preference for endogamy and the existence of matchmaking
traditions amongst certain families when these cultural practices were on
the wane amongst the rural Irish population also bolstered the impression
that Travellers were casual about marriage. The Traveller practice of
swapping or bartering which encompassed everything from horses to
jewellery was seen as an anachronism in an increasingly capitalist-
oriented economy and this too was incorporated into the myth which at-

---

[4] Iml. 1255: 78

[5] Iml. 1255: 141

tributed sexual immorality to them. J.M. Synge described how a country person had given him an eye-witness account of how the "tinkers" swapped wives "with as much talk as if you'd be selling a cow" (Synge, 1980: 31). Similar sentiments were echoed by some of the IFC Questionnaire respondents a half a century after Synge had written his play. A respondent from County Kerry who described Traveller "customs" alleged that the men abducted the women, once again echoing a practice that had been common in some parts of rural Ireland until the late 1800s:

> *Sé an nós a bhíonn aca nuair a bhíonn said ag dul ag pósadh ná an fear an bhean a ghoid leis.*[6]

> (The custom that they have regarding marriage is that the man abducts the woman.)

Myths regarding Travellers' preference for endogamy and more "traditional" practices such as "matchmaking" still hold sway today as evidenced by recent efforts to "set the record straight" on the part of Traveller activists. In 2003 a report concerning Traveller consanguinity and cousin-marriage outlined the fictitious nature of many stereotypes concerning Traveller marriage patterns. Responding to a recent survey urging genetic counselling for Traveller cousins who were about to marry, Nora Lawrence, a Traveller working with Travellers' Resource Centre, Pavee Point, made the salient point that settled people were often more preoccupied with concerns and some stereotypical myths concerning Traveller intermarriage than Travellers were and commented:

> We've never seen anything wrong with it. The settled people have a lot of myths about it, but it wasn't an issue for us. We've always had cousins marrying. It's a myth that people are thrown together and forced to get married. People make up their own minds. (*Irish Times*, 1 May 2003)

The greatest irony regarding stereotypes of alleged Traveller immorality in the sexual sphere was the fact that rules concerning gender relations and the interaction of the sexes were extremely strict with monogamy the norm before marriage. Virtually every Traveller biography/autobiography writ-

---

[6] Iml. 1256: 23

ten to date (e.g. Joyce, 1985; Dunne, 2004; Maher, 1972) makes mention of the strict moral code prevailing in Traveller families and the way in which this strict moral "sphere" impacted on Traveller self-identity, social relations amongst Travellers and even patterns of nomadism. Helleiner (2000) has described how purity in the sexual sphere, encompassing severe strictures on women's social behaviour continues to be at the core not only of Traveller identity, but of the ethnicised boundaries between Travellers and the settled community:

> . . . women's practices of purity were linked to their embodiment of an ethnicised boundary between Travellers and non-Travellers. This was also evident in discussion of arranged marriages and restrictions on female sexuality, both of which were signified not only as markers of individual and familial reputation, but as sites of Traveller moral superiority and ethnic purity. (2000: 193)

In the IFC Questionnaire responses Travellers were frequently "othered" as dirty, a dirt that was said to encompass both the visual and moral spheres, as indicated by the following comments in the responses to the IFC Questionnaire:

> *Ní chaitheann siad ach éadaí salach a bhíonn ag tuitim dóibh.*[7]
>
> (They only wear dirty clothes that are falling off them.)
>
> *Anam chomh dubh le hanam tincéarai.*[8]
>
> (A soul as black as the soul of a tinker.)

A number of IFC respondents hinted at Traveller immorality linking it with the concepts of dirt and shame and the belief that some tinkers allegedly cohabitated rather than getting married in the Church:

> I have never heard of tinkers being married in Church, I would put it down to shame of their rags and lowly condition.[9]

---

[7] Iml. 1256:28

[8] Iml. 1256: 120

[9] Iml. 1255: 277

"Othering" incorporating the notion of "dirt" even came to be used as an argument for Traveller "settlement" when assimilationist policies were advocated in Irish political rhetoric in the decades between the post-war years and the 1980s (see Helleiner, 2000) whereby Travellers were identified more broadly as dangerous to the nation's public health, economy, and "social order". Alleged "dangers" posed by the Travellers's "dirty" status included trespass, allegedly dirty campsites, theft and even the spread of disease. The purity of Traveller women was the cornerstone on which allegations of immorality or dirt were countered. Helleiner (2000) mentioned hearing Travellers on more than one occasion, reciting a story of their origins which linked their origins with a "pure" Irish identity, a story which well-known Traveller spokesperson Margaret Sweeney referred to in a television interview:

> [my father said] that the Travellers went back to the time of Cromwell when he first came into this country . . . That Travelling People didn't have any money to pay for the rent and that a lot of the landlords of those days used to take over the young daughters of the settled community. And I feel that the Travelling People had it in them that they wouldn't let this happen and rather than that happen they took to the sides of the road and they went to other counties where they wouldn't be known. (Sweeney in Helleiner, 2000: 194)

The invoking of Traveller women as markers of "pure" Irish and Traveller identity clearly illustrates how, in the course of publicly contesting racism and exclusion, Travellers asserted an account of Traveller origins that claimed both a pure Irishness and a pure form of sexuality. Helleiner's (2000) study in Galway confirmed the strong cultural tenets regarding inter-sex segregation, courtship and concepts such as clean/dirty, etc. She contextualised such claims within the context of resistance, a resistance which in her view also worked to bolster forms of patriarchy:

> [They] represented important forms of resistance to imposed stigma while simultaneously legitimising gendered practices in the areas of work, marriage and sexuality that can be seen as supporting male privilege. (2000: 194)

It is also possible to link the invocation of concepts such as sexual purity to the ritual practices of some Traveller and Gypsy families in Ireland and Britain in relation to cleanliness and washing, practices which also serve to distinguish between Travellers and non-Travellers. These practices include the use of "clean" bowls for the washing of dishes and utensils and "dirty" bowls for the washing of clothes, the floor and the body. (See Helleiner, 2000; Joyce, 1985; and Okely, 1983 for further discussion of the significance of these concepts.) Inter-sex segregation and the concepts of pure women / pure Irishness as a form of resistance also involved a process of reverse "Othering" on the part of the Travellers according to Helleiner:

> Travellers frequently contrasted "clean" Traveller women with "dirty" settled women through stories about how settled women would go out with several men before getting married and in doing so prostitute themselves. Settled women, it was said, performed strip teases and were swopped around by their husbands. (2000: 193)

A few IFC Questionnaire respondents who knew Travellers well were aware of the moral and religious strictures regarding segregation, courtship and marriage that were characteristic of Traveller culture:

> Tinkers don't get into trouble with the law more frequently than other folk and usually when they do the case is often very trifling. They salute clergy respectfully and beg from them at the same time. I don't know anything against their moral character but local people believe that they live good moral lives. I heard a local man once saying: "When a boy and girl begin to keep company amongst the tinkers they are brought to the priest at once" (to marry them).[10]

> Most of these tinkers are Catholics, nominally at any rate. They are married in Catholic Churches and can always produce certificates of Baptism. They do not, as a rule, attend Divine Service on Sundays. I heard of one very fine old lady — grandmother of these Cawleys and now dead — who was very strict with her

---

[10] Iml. 1255: 371

family. . . . She was also very strict about the courtships and would not allow any unseemly conduct around her tent.[11]

Similar strictures in relation to Catholic religious practice were commented on by at a number of settled people:

> . . . a priest told me of an experience he had when a tinker woman came to him to arrange for the baptism of a child. He asked when she wanted it baptised and she said she would like to get it done that day. He asked her when the child was born and she replied that it was born about two hours at that time. The priest told her that it would be time enough to bring it along the following day. The woman got annoyed and said they would like to have it baptised that evening as they would not like to leave the poor thing too long "in the dark". Another story told me by the same priest shows the anxiety of tinker parents to have their babies baptised as soon as possible after birth. This happened in Co. Fermanagh to another priest. About 12 o'clock one day a woman with a baby arrived at the priest's house and asked to have the child baptised. The priest asked the woman if she was acting as sponsor. The woman replied "No, you see I'm the mother". When the child was produced it was completely naked.[12]

Nan Joyce's (1985) biography *Traveller* provides what is probably one of the best insider accounts of a courtship ritual incorporating the segregation of the sexes and the "asking for the hand in marriage" that was characteristic of many in the wider Irish population generations earlier:

> When the dealing was over there'd be a big camp fire in the middle of the field and the men would gather round and start drinking. There'd be music and singing and storytelling till morning. A boy might meet a girl at a fair and fall in love with her and he'd be trying to ask her father could he marry her. If he didn't ask for her now maybe he wouldn't see her again for a year and she might be married to somebody else. He would sit beside her father and maybe he'd be a large rough man and the boy would be

---

[11] Iml. 1256: 240

[12] Iml. 1255: 223

half-afeared of him. He'd be handing him the drink and cigarettes to coax him up. "The girl would be ogling the boy from behind her shawl and she'd by saying. "Ask him now, ask him now," because her father might be in good humour when he was drunk. The boy would edge up and ask him and maybe the father would give her but if he was a real contrary fella it'd be "Get off outa that!" — he wouldn't give her. In those days boys and girls didn't go out together. Even if they were allowed in to places as travellers, their parents wouldn't have let them go to a dance or to the pictures on their own, they always had chaperones, especially the girls. . . . You were never allowed go anywhere but when I was growing up we never just thought about it. (1985: 15–16)

STEREOTYPES OF VIOLENCE AND DISORDER

Notions of dirt and separateness were linked to the concept of disorder as applied to Irish Travellers, a concept that had strong affiliations with Travellers' ascribed "status" in the world, as outlined in the Irish folktale tradition generally (See Ó Héalaí, 1985). This concept of disorder that was most obviously made manifest in the stereotype of Travellers as a people who were inordinately given to fighting, a fighting that was held to be an external manifestation of their apparently "primitive" or uncivilised lifestyle. The association of Travellers with fighting and feuding continues to be one of the strongest images of Traveller life in the Irish imaginary today. Many IFC respondents gave "in-depth" descriptions of Traveller fights, some describing Traveller groups as "factions" and often utilised the same imagery that had been ascribed to the faction fights that were common in Ireland throughout the nineteenth century. Indeed many descriptions of Traveller fights as outlined by the settled community represented them in terms that echoed the ritualised nature of faction fighting and in terms whereby this fighting was seen to enhance the "separate" or distinct nature of Traveller society:

> It is never safe for an outsider to interfere in brawls between tinkers, even as peacemaker, for all turn against him.[13] *(IFC respondent from County Mayo)*

---

[13] Iml. 1256: 120

I remember the wholesale use of sticks, stones, soldering irons and even iron bars, and the wholesale wounding of men and women whose shouts and curses made a bedlam that roused the whole neighbourhood. Some of the wounds made me shudder in disgust. The injured men boasted of their prowess during the battle and the words of encouragement from their women seemed to placate them the pain of their injuries. Those who were the best fighters, always the least wounded, hobnobbed over pints of stout in one of the local pubs and spoke of the wounds they inflicted on their opponents. . . . In such rows there was much blood to be seen and afterwards many bandaged heads and limbs, but somehow it struck me that they started such rows to keep up their credit in the country and to instill the fear of the Tinker in the neighbourhood with the usual result of getting a better reception, through fear in their usual daily, weekly or yearly rounds to the farmhouses.[14]

There was a fierce battle between the Nevins and the Joyces at Umma about two years ago. The local residents were terrorised. Apparently the Joyces defied the Nevins to cross the Shannon at Athlone to go to Ballinasloe Fair.[15] *(IFC respondent from County Westmeath)*

The local people have a wholesome dread of the tinkers and justly so. They would terrorise us only they are afraid of the law.[16]

Special names or knicknames — Some of them are known by special names. A well-known Tinker woman of the Maughans is known about here as "Mary the stick". She is middle-aged; of amazonian type, and strongly built. Her sobriquet, has, I believe, been derived from her dexterity and prowess in the use of the stick in many a brawl.[17] *(IFC respondent from County Mayo)*

---

[14] Iml. 1952: 60

[15] Iml. 1255: 244. The town of Ballinasloe is now principally recognised for the Great October Fair. This horse fair has been conducted under Letters of Patent since the early eighteenth century. However, the Gaelic name for the town, Béal Átha na Slua, would suggest far greater antiquity for this location, as a recognised gathering place. The name means Mouth of the Ford of the Hostings. A village therefore developed near the fords and close to two castles which were built to control the fords.

[16] Iml. 1255: 215

[17] Iml. 1256: 116

> They quarrel with themselves but never among the people.[18] *(IFC respondent from County Wicklow)*

> After a horse fair the tinker clans sometimes fight but only among themselves.[19] *(IFC respondent from County Wexford)*

Travellers' alleged skill and propensity for fighting was also linked to the strong role they, like many Irish people, have played in military campaigns. This is an aspect of Traveller history that deserves more in-depth research. This IFC respondent from County Cork described the Travellers' influence in the military when Ireland was still under British rule:

> Mallow was the centre for the North Cork Militia. I knew them well in my young days. They were all tinkers and officered by the local half-gentlemen, Purcell, Ware, Good, Atkinson, Love, etc. 'Twas the same in 1798 . . . The North Cork Militia slaughtered on Oulart Hill, were all tinkers and their officers were all half sirs of Duhallow, whose descendants are there still, or were till recently.[20]

The ritualised nature of Traveller fights and the fact that women also joined in the fights was highlighted by some IFC respondents. While the settled community appeared to be shocked that Traveller women sometimes took part in the fight there are many sources which indicate that settled women also sometimes took part in ritualised "faction fighting" particularly in the mid- to late nineteenth century:

> *Bhíodh mná ag troid freisin, bheadh stocaí acu agus cloch thíos sa stoca agus dá bhfeicfidís a gcuid fir féin, nó fear ar bith eile a mbeadh aon mheas acu air dhá sháinniú, rachaidís ag cuidiú leo leis na stocaí.*[21]

> (The women would be fighting also, they would have socks and a rock down in the sock and if they saw their own men or any other man that they had respect for being cornered, they would go to his help with the socks.)

---

[18] Iml. 1255: 358
[19] Iml: 1255: 362
[20] Iml. 1255: 356
[21] Iml. 1205: 145-7

References to the way in which Travellers were often friendly to one another after a fight reinforced this idea of ritualised fighting as an indicator of cultural separateness:

> Tinkers are very violent when they fight among themselves. No-one would interfere in a tinker's fight. People say "tinkers tear other to pieces tonight and are great as pickpockets tomorrow".[22]

So too did many descriptions of both group and single combats:

> *Uaireanta sa tsean aimsir bhíodh aighneas is clampar idir cómhlucht tinncéirí. Go mórmhór nuair thágadh dhá threibh díobh le chéile. Bhíodh árd am aca. Bhailídís le céile i sráidbhaile éigin agus dólaidís go dtí go raibh a gcuid arigead caite nú nach mór caite. Bhíodh idir fir is mná ar meisce agus sa deire na dála d'éiríodh easaontas agus rí-rá agus bhiodh cómhrach aon fhir ar siúl agus uaireanta deintí úsáid den "soldering iron".[23]*

> (In the old days, sometimes there would be arguments and trouble between different companies of tinkers. Especially when two tribes would meet up. They would have a high time of it. They would meet together in a certain district and they would drink together until they had spent all or nearly all of their money. Both men and women would be drunk by the end of it and there would be disagreement and fighting and there would be single combats between men and sometimes they would use the soldering iron as a weapon.)

The descriptions of "single" combats between Traveller men indicate a certain similarity with the cultural traditions of the settled community, however. It is interesting, for instance, that there are many recorded instances of Traveller fights which refer to challenges and single combats. This is consistent with the challenges and "one-on-one" barefist fighting which some Traveller families "specialise" in today. Travellers' former prowess at the art of stick fighting was also noted by many in the majority community. It appears that some Travellers made a living from attending fairs and challenging men to "take them on" in the art of stick

---

[22] Iml. 1255: 45
[23] Iml. 1255: 72

fighting. Stick fighting was a specialised sport, similar to "martial arts" today and there were special schools, such as the one described below, with *maistrí pionsa* (fencing masters) who taught this sport:

> The practice of stick-fencing was common in South Tipperary down to about the forties of the last century. The contestants observed a code of noble bearing analogous to the customs of duelling. A champion of the pastime in South-East Tipperary was nicknamed "The Rudaire" apparently from his honourable bearing in action. Professional teachers of the art seem to have been numerous . . . (Cited in *Béaloideas*, XII, I-III, 1943: 269)

AN ANTI-LANGUAGE

One of the final cultural attributes that served to "Other" Travellers and situate them within a countercultural discourse was their use of "secret" forms of communication. According to the IFC respondents Travellers utilised two forms of secret communication. One involved a spoken language known as Cant or Gammon. The second form of secret communication was a sign language that took the form of physical "markers" left out to communicate with other Travellers. The markers included rags, sticks and embers which were left in a highly particularised manner so that "readers" would immediately know news concerning the direction a family may have taken on the road, the favourability shown to beggars by locals, the arrival of a new horse, the death of family members, etc. The significance of what was known by Romany Gypsies as the "*patrin*" is explained by Irish Traveller, Nan Joyce:

> Travellers had their own codes too. If a group of them were coming along the road some of them would have better horses than the others and the one with the lazy horse would be left behind. Since a lot of the travellers didn't know how to read, a signpost was no use to them for telling them where to go. The group who came to the main road first would pull three sods of grass — and the sods had to have plenty of mud on them — and they would throw them on the road in the direction they were going. The sods wouldn't blow away and if a car drove over them they wouldn't go off the road for days. This was the travellers' signpost and the three sods of grass

were the Father, the Son and the Holy Ghost, because prayers came into everything. (Joyce, 1985: 18)

A rather "romantic" description of the *patrin*, implying Traveller trickery as befitted the literature of Gypsiology, was provided by John Sampson, a member of the British branch of the Gypsy Lore Society in 1891:

Sometimes a tinker woman, travelling a little in advance of the band, begs a night's lodgings at a farm-house under the pretence of being alone. Then, if successful, she hangs out her *patrin* [a sign left on the road to give information to those who are following] and the rest of the band, on their arrival, descend upon the house, which they occupy during their stay in the neighbourhood, defying removal. This practice is, however, so well understood in the west and south of Ireland, that tinker women are seldom received as guests. (Sampson, 1891: 205)

A number of IFC correspondents commented on the use of this private sign language:

Rags are hung on the hedges by a group when leaving and these serve as a sign to the next comers. It is also said that gipsies can leave a secret sign on each inhabitant's gate to indicate to the next group of gipsies the kind of reception to expect from the inhabitants of those houses.[24]

It is said that they have a means of following each other from signs left by the first party. Broken twigs or marks on trees or crossroads.[25] *(IFC respondent from Enniskillen, County Fermanagh)*

I am told that they tie a red cloth or string to the willow or alder bushes that they used and other gypsies or tinkers who came that way were supposed to not cut any of those bushes.[26] *(IFC respondent from County Cavan)*

---

[24] Iml. 1256: 228

[25] Iml. 1256: 262

[26] Iml. 1256: 277

Relatively little modern research has been undertaken into the functions of Travellers' spoken language, known in academic parlance as Shelta but referred to by Travellers as Cant or Gammon. Opinions vary as to the exact functions of Shelta, whether it was always a "secret" language or whether it should be defined as a language or a linguistic register (see Binchy, 1994, 2002; Ó Baoill, 1994; etc.) Binchy (2002) describes three contexts in particular where Shelta is used, but there are probably others, indicating that further research is needed into Traveller language use. The first of these is when Travellers wish to communicate privately in the company of settled people, a function of the language which has been provided by Traveller writer Nan Joyce (1985):

> Father . . . could read anything and he knew Irish and our own language that we've had for hundreds of years. Some of us call it gammon, and more of us call it cant — it depends on which tribe you're from. . . . When I would go out hawking with my mother she'd be selling things from the basket and she might say to me, "*Gage the byor for a few collyins*," that meant, "Ask the woman for a few potatoes." Then she'd say, "*Gage the yorum*" and I'd ask the sup of milk. This was the way the language was used. When the police would come down to shift us or to hunt us on we'd say, "*Oh, the wobs, the gammy wobs*." ["Oh, the police, the bad police."][27] (1985: 5)

The second context where Shelta is used, according to Binchy (2002), is when Travellers are buying and selling with the settled community and endeavouring to gain an upper hand in terms of price. The third context is when Travellers are discussing subjects which "according to Traveller norms cannot be spoken about openly, such as women's health and matters relating to childbirth" (2002: 13). That Shelta is acquired by children in infancy and is switched to unselfconsciously within the community indicates a broader range of usage, and the importance of Shelta as a marker for Traveller identity.

   None of these aspects of Traveller language use were noticed by the IFC respondents to the Tinker Questionnaire, who generally saw Shelta as an example of the conscious and deliberate separateness of Travellers,

---

[27] This sentence is my own translation. *Wob* can mean "policeman" or "soldier" in Shelta.

who wished to exclude those who were not able to understand their language. Shelta, as described by the few IFC respondents who mentioned it, was generally defined in terms of an "anti-language" as described by Halliday (1976) and Yinger (1982). Halliday (1976) described an anti-language as a form of language generated by an anti-society — that is, "a society that is set up within another society as a conscious alternative to it" (1976: 570). As examples of anti-languages he cited the "pelting speech" of the vagabond counterculture that characterised Elizabethan England; the argot used by the Calcutta underworld; and an anti-language used in Polish prisons. The few IFC respondents who noted the existence of Shelta placed emphasis on this "anti-language" function of Shelta, highlighting its secretive and "exclusive" aspects, a fact which served to emphasise the cultural "Othering" of Travellers as a separate or "countercultural" group.

The same members of the "settled community" also recognised the substantial Irish-language underlay in Shelta and, like Nan Joyce (1985), indicated that many Travellers were trilingual:

> People say they have a language of their own. Have been heard speaking to each other in houses they had called in: people thought it sounded like Irish, but couldn't understand or interpret it when they listened. Tinkers known to speak Gaelic. Patrick McCullagh spoke to two youths who said they were of the McDonagh clan. They had Gaelic. Then they spoke in their own language to each other. McCullagh did not know any words or expressions of the speech.[28]

> Tinkers have a certain language which they use when they do not want others to understand the meaning of especially when they are making bargains. I spent some time about a year ago with a Tinker who was making saucepans at the entrance to one of those picturesque Killarney lanes, and I wrote down a good deal of it. I put it aside and must have hidden it too well as I cannot put my hands on it right away.[29]

---

[28] Iml. 1256: 258

[29] Iml. 1255: 61

This use of a "secret" language as a form of exclusivity had a romantic and conspiratorial air to it and descriptions such as the above were common in much of the Gypsilorist literature (discussed in Chapter One), as applied to Gypsies and Travellers in Britain. For instance, James Simson (1884), one of the early members of the Gypsy Lore Society, described the "secret" use of Romany amongst British Gypsies and Travellers as follows:

> The Romany is emphatically a language of secrecy, and the more mixed its phrases the more bewildering it becomes to the uninitiated and valuable to a race of people which socially has the hand of respectability against it and its hand against respectability. (Simson in Mayall, 1982: 195)

CONCLUSION

In the previous chapters I have mapped the contours of a reductionist "discourse of difference" in Irish tradition where the Traveller is depicted as a negative "Other". This discourse takes the form of a construct or myth of Traveller identity that defines Travellers in terms of a reductive essentialism. This essentialism represents Travellers as culturally "Other", an "Other" who are defined in terms of secrecy, dishonesty, licentiousness, violence and "a society within a society". The great bulk of the material reviewed here has seen Irish Travellers as subsumed within a reverse ethnocentrism, an ethnocentrism based on essentialist binarisms as rigid as those which had been promulgated under the essentialist discourses of colonialism. The discussion of the material available in the IFC Tinker Questionnaire has served as a bulwark to this volume as a whole with the Traveller "Other" being identified as a "constructed" identity redolent of frequent and reiterated stereotype. Travellers as defined by the settled community are an element of Irish identity itself, but an element whose perceived degraded attributes condition certain responses to Travellers as a group. Even today these responses continue to have important ramifications for the interaction between the settled community and the Traveller community and the modern-day categorisation of the latter.

Chapter 16

Traveller Advocacy and the Emergence of the "Traveller Voice"

As previously outlined in this book the issues of ethnicity and racism in Ireland have assumed importance for those scholars and activists whose concerns encompass the national and international dimensions of the Traveller "question" and similar issues as applied to an increasingly multicultural Ireland. Much of this work is similar in intent to what has been attempted in this book. It is an attempt to identify the specificity of Irish racism and prejudice as it has been constructed against the "Other" in Irish society in both the historical and contemporaneous contexts; irrespective of whether this "Other" is Traveller, Jew, Muslim, or one of the myriad of new and immigrant ethnicities that now make their home in Ireland. It can be argued that the most fundamental value inherent in this new questioning of Irish identity and the identity of the Irish "Other" is that it challenges long-standing perceptions, within both the official and public spheres, that Ireland was always an ethnically homogenous monocultural state that was devoid of any seriously overt and long-standing prejudices. (See the work of Helleiner, 1998; Ó Síocháin et al., 1994; Lentin and McVeigh, 2002; McGréil, 1977, 1996; McVeigh, 1992, 1994, 1997; Power, 2004; etc.)

It was from some of the activists most concerned with the position of Travellers in Irish society that much of the impetus, both theoretical and practical, to challenge the fallacy that Ireland was a homogenous and monocultural entity devoid of any obvious and sustained forms of intercultural prejudice. While members of the settled community were often the most active in initiating this new "dialogue" with the margins in Irish life, Travellers themselves have mobilised within the past few decades to fight for political and cultural recognition and change. To examine the manner in which the Traveller community has done this it is necessary to assess the context to this politicisation, one which has encompassed sweeping societal change within both the Traveller and settled communities, within Ireland and indeed within Europe itself.

In 1960, only ten years after the issuance of the IFC's Tinker Questionnaire, whose discourse we have just examined, it is estimated that over 90 per cent of Travellers were living a "traditional" lifestyle, the living conditions of which encompassed tents and horsedrawn wagons (Report of the Commission on Itinerancy, 1963). The vast majority of these people were nomadic for some or all of the year. While more research is necessary into Traveller employment and travelling patterns in this era, it seems very likely that the majority of Travellers moved in a fairly restricted circuit of villages and towns within their own county and occasionally within neighbouring counties. Travellers were perceived as a people who were united into a single community, a community predicated on their mode of economic and social life and their "marginality" from the settled community. Within each Irish county and province there were Traveller families linked through social and kinship networks, with Traveller society organised on a very similar basis as it is today — i.e. the basic structural unit (which is also the primary unit of production and consumption) of the nuclear family, which is in turn part of a larger group of married siblings and parents who live together, this larger group often numbering no more than five or six families. As with today, marriages between cousins were frequent, a pattern which sees endogamy, stability of marriage, a sense of mutual dependency and support and greater economic power as strong cultural criteria. Groups of Travellers that were larger than this extended nuclear family group were consequently organisationally fluid, their size and composition indicative of a variety of individual and situational responses to changing social and economic opportunities, travelling patterns and pressure exerted from outside — e.g. threat of eviction. Ironically, today it is the settlement patterns instigated by local authorities which sometimes involve the grouping of non-related families together which, in addition to promoting a more sedentary life, are also the instigation for increased tension between families within the Travelling community.

The late 1950s and 1960s saw the large-scale migration of Traveller families to the larger urban centres like Dublin, Cork, Limerick and Galway. This migration was to a large degree a response to the changing demographics in Ireland as a whole and the disappearance of much of the Travellers' "traditional" economic base. Mass-produced goods such as plastic and enamel containers saw the disappearance of the tinsmith trade and increased mechanisation impinged on Travellers' piecework for farmers. Infrastructural change in Ireland saw the expansion of better road networks and rural transportation in the form of expanded bus services and increased ownership of private vehicles, factors which all contributed to the death-knell of the subsistence peddling and itinerant tradeswork that had been mainstays for Travellers prior to this. The speed of change that accompanied Irish urbanisation saw the appearance in the late 1950s of large numbers of Travellers camped in wagons and tents on wasteland and commonage that skirted Ireland's major towns and cities. This era can now be seen as the beginning of an era of sustained tension between both the Traveller and settled communities, a tension that continues unabated until today. Complaints began to emanate from urban residents alarmed at what they perceived to be large and unsightly camps and the potential health hazards they might harbour. By the year 1960 the complaints of the settled community had become such that a group of government health inspectors submitted a formal request to the government requesting it to investigate the Traveller "problem".

The publication of the government-commissioned and heavily influential *Report of the Commission on Itinerancy* (1963) marked the beginning of a sustained and focused examination of the Traveller question in Ireland and the attempted assimilation of Travellers in Ireland. This assimilationist ethos was rooted in the perceived status of Travellers in Irish society, in particular the question of whether theirs was a distinct cultural group with a distinct identity. The Commission on Itinerancy stated unequivocally that Travellers did not, in their view, constitute a single or homogenous community within Ireland. Nor were they considered to constitute an ethnic group. This left the Commission free to pursue an unashamedly assimilationist policy towards the Travelling community, this assimilationism being couched in terms of nationalist and rehabilitative rhetoric that constructed Travellers within the modernisation and culture of poverty theories fashionable at this time — i.e. that Travellers belonged to a disaffiliated and under-socialised community encompassing attitudes and a lifestyle that was primitive, anti-social, uneconomic and irrational.

As was the case with other indigenous Travelling groups in Europe at this juncture, humanitarian considerations combined with the emergence of the welfare state and increasingly technocratic methods of social organisation, all of which produced a drive towards assimilation. From the 1940s onwards and in virtually every European country, the disappearance of the nomad or Traveller problem was to be achieved through a hegemony that was portrayed as consensual. Liberal and universalistic categories that frequently ignored the ascriptions that indigenous travelling groups applied to themselves and downplayed their cultural tenets were invented so as to legitimate assimilationist policies throughout Europe. In Ireland, for instance, officialdom replaced the, by then, pejorative term "tinker" with "itinerant", ignoring the term "Traveller", which Travellers preferred to use to describe themselves. Travellers were constructed within imagery that implied destitution and social deviance, a tactic whereby "through judicious use of imagery cultural specificity is reinterpreted as a 'social problem'" (Liégeois, 1994: 150). This version of Travellers paved the way for policies which Kenny (1996) described as "welfare policies which undoubtedly relieved misery, but at the price of dependency and cultural degradation" (1996: 11).

In an Irish context the ethos encoding this assimilationist trend found expression in publications such as the newsletter *Settlement News*, and to a lesser extent the newsletter of the Association of Teachers of Travelling People. The 1963 Report of the Commission on Itinerancy had included a recommendation that itinerant "settlement committees" be formed and 1965 saw the formation of the first "itinerant settlement committee" in Dublin. This spawned a nationwide network of volunteer-organised settlement committees whose aim was the settlement of Travellers and their absorption into the settled community.

The year 1969 saw the formation of an umbrella organisation named the Irish Council for Itinerant Settlement comprised of settled community representatives from each Irish county. These settlement committees continued to be active well into the 1980s when ideological changes, including increased Traveller self-determination and the failure of the settlement policies themselves, came to be increasingly acknowledged. Initially, though, the immediate aim of the settlement committees was the provision of serviced campsites including *tigíns* or small houses which would have running water and electricity. The long-term aim was more ambitious and was aimed at the permanent "settlement" of Travellers on halting sites and in conventional housing and the enrollment of Traveller children in local schools. This, it was felt, would be an inducement for Travellers to abandon nomadism and "integrate" with the settled community.

By 1981 it was estimated that nearly half the Traveller population in Ireland was "settled" in some form of accommodation including the *tigíns* that are a common sight on Traveller halting sites and conventional housing that most frequently took the form of local authority housing. Ironically, and in spite of these changes, the number of Travellers living on the roadside today is probably larger than before the settlement movement began. This is in strong part due to the fact that the settlement ethos was usurped by a new literature of Traveller advocacy and self-determination from the 1970s and 1980s onwards. While the public articulation of this phase lagged well behind developments in academia, the early 1980s in particular saw a movement away from the perception of Travellers as a "problem" in need of a solution to a more "rights-based" approach predicated on the tenets of interculturalism and the toleration of difference.

This change in perception and approach to the Traveller question was already evident by the mid-1970s when the nomenclature of the National Council on Itinerant Settlement was changed to the National Council for Travelling People. Travellers and their fellow activists from amongst the settled community now began to identify and articulate the assimilationist approach for what it was — yet another form of hegemony and cultural disappearance — and increasingly identified the treatment of Travellers as unacceptable and racist. The rhetoric that exemplified this new approach now saw groups like the National Council for Travelling People begin to lobby for policies the rhetoric of which would enable Travellers secured basic human and civil rights and a sense of "self-determination". Terms such as "itinerant" disappeared from usage in official Irish public discourse and in the media and were replaced with Traveller, as is the case today. Officially, at least, Irish government rhetoric in relation to Travellers has changed. Travellers are now seen as "an identifiable group of people . . . with their own distinctive lifestyle" who have an acknowledged right to "retain their own identity and tradition" and for whom "full integration with the settled community" may not necessarily be regarded as a "desirable goal" (Report of the Travelling People Review Body, 1983: 62).

Developments in the official sphere have also acted as a catalyst for a certain amount of academic research on Travellers (see Chapter 3) including the studies undertaken by American anthropologists such as the Gmelches (see Boyce, 1996; S. Gmelch, 1975, 1990; Gmelch and Gmelch, 1976; McCarthy, 1971; Helleiner, 2000) and overviews of the Traveller issue by social workers (Ó Nualláin and Forde, 1992; Ó Riain, 2000; Phipps, 1986; etc.). The 1970s and 1980s also saw the production of a few ethnographic-type books (Barnes, 1975; Court, 1985; Griffin, 1999; Ó Fearadhaigh and Wiedel, 1976; O'Toole, 1973), a number of which echoed the "older" folkloric, "New World" or Gypsilorist literature, including the brief accounts of Irish Travellers written at the turn of the century (Arnold, 1898; Sinclair, 1908).

The early 1980s was a fruitful period for Traveller–state interaction with several Travellers being appointed to service on the government's advisory body on Traveller affairs. It also saw the foundation of a group entitled the Committee for the Rights of Travellers, which took place in Dublin in 1982. In its initial stages, this group combined offices jointly held by both Traveller and non-Traveller counterparts, but two years later it evolved into Mincéir Misli (Travellers' Movement) a Traveller-run body that organised demonstrations, protest marches and lobbied the news media in particular regarding events like evictions, which were an impediment to Traveller self-determination and which were contributing to the erosion of Traveller life. Mincéir Mislí regularly sent spokespeople to meetings of local government and community groups and in 1982 the organisation backed the first Traveller ever to run for a seat as an elected representative. This was Nan Joyce, a Traveller woman who was unsuccessful in her attempt to secure a seat on Dublin City Council but who secured 581 first-preference votes, outperforming a local opponent who had campaigned on an anti-Traveller platform.

Contemporaneous with this mobilisation effort was the initiation of a range of projects by a few key social workers who aimed to give Travellers the opportunity to achieve the confidence and skills to articulate their own interests, and the foundation of Pavee Point, a partnership of Irish Travellers and settled people working together to improve the lives of Irish Travellers through working towards social justice, solidarity, socio-economic development and human rights. This Dublin-based organisation was founded in the early 1980s by social activist John O'Connell.

A range of activities such as adult literacy classes, personal development classes and communications workshops saw a new generation of Travellers training as community development workers. While these initiatives were initially based primarily in the Dublin area, the momentum from them helped forge a stronger sense of group identity amongst the Traveller community, a process which eventually spread throughout the country. The settlement-inspired literature of old was replaced by a new literature of advocacy from Traveller community and support groups, with Traveller-produced publications acting as a particularly important organisational tool (see Belfast Travellers' Support Group, 2000; Kerry Traveller Development Project, 1996; Sheehan, 2000).

The mid-1980s saw the emergence of Traveller-produced publications such as the monthly newsletter *The Pavee*, concerned primarily with the documentation of harassment against Travellers, and a more comprehensive newspaper entitled *Mincéir Staméir* ("Travellers' Paper"), first published in Dublin in 1985. An important addition to this literature of advocacy were autobiographic and ethnographic accounts of Traveller life and culture as produced by Travellers themselves (Joyce, 1985; Maher, 1972) an important development which has continued into the modern era (Cauley and Ó hAodha, 2004; Dunne and Ó hAodha, 2004; Gorman, 2002), a more detailed discussion of which follow in Chapter 17.

DEFINING TRAVELLERS:
PERCEPTIONS OF TRAVELLERS AND THE MEDIA

While the emergence of Traveller-produced publications, often as an indirect outcome of other advocacy initiatives, has been an extremely valuable aspect of Travellers' efforts to achieve parity of esteem in modern Ireland, it remains the case that the Traveller "question" is debated solely by the "settled" community and the Traveller–settled interface takes place more often than not through the prism that is the Irish media. Indeed it can be argued that the modern-day representation of the Travelling community as incorporated in media sources is often the only arena where the non-Traveller community has any sort of sustained contact with the Traveller community, the Traveller "question" and the debates which underlie the relations between the non-Traveller and Traveller communities.

Ironic as it may seem, were it not for the all-pervasive media influence in Irish life, the Irish Traveller community might continue to be viewed as a "hidden" or undocumented community. Traveller isolation and their historical absence from those modern political and media outlets which would enhance their opportunities for cultural expression are all issues that have already been touched upon in this book. In tandem with an increased academic growth in issues associated with migrancy and minorities in Ireland today, there is also a parallel expansion of public interest in these issues and consequently in the position of Travellers both in past and present societies. The "wall-to-wall" media saturation by television and newspaper sources that Irish people nowadays so often find intrusive has brought with it certain benefits, amongst which is a certain "opening up" of Irish society to debates on issues which encompass both the local and the international. Global television networks and the newspaper press have brought issues which previously might have remained hidden to the attention of much wider audiences in Ireland — for instance, the sometimes hostile treatment of Travellers by local authorities in Ireland, the complex issues that surround the issue of Traveller accommodation and the contemporary persecution and migration of Roma (Gypsies) from Eastern Europe to the West. The airing of these and a range of other related issues in the arena external to the rarefied atmosphere that is academia is important since it is the representation and definition of Travellers and their place in wider Irish society which is particularly significant. Responses to minorities including Travellers in the public sphere in Ireland are frequently dependent on their image or the perceptions of them as communities, factors which are increasingly debated almost solely through the lens that is the modern media.

Media coverage of Travellers and Traveller-related issues spans the whole gamut of attitudes, ranging from the overtly hostile to a minority of articles which portray a positive view of the Traveller community — albeit that these views frequently construct Travellers within a class-related framework that emphasises those values considered important to the mainstream community (e.g. Traveller achievements in education or news relating to the "successful" settlement of Travellers and their integration with the settled community). The manner in which Travellers are most frequently constructed in the media today, however — most notably in the tabloid reportage of the newspapers — is in many ways an example of élite discourse as theorised by scholars such as Van Dijk (1993, 1997).

It is most often the case that Travellers are discussed in terms which encompass the latest "moral panic" regarding Travellers, New Age Travellers or other new and "outsider"/immigrant groups who have attempted to make a home for themselves in Ireland. The impetus for these moral panics as relating to Irish Travellers show a remarkable consistency with representations from the past, including many which have already been alluded to in this book as part of the overview of the Irish Folklore Commission material. This fact only highlights what has been the central concern of much of this book; i.e. the fact that anti-Traveller prejudice and the representation of the Traveller "Other" can only be viewed with reference to the past. While frequently depicted as a relatively new phenomenon, anti-Traveller sentiment is not something new but draws on a tradition of anti-nomadic sentiment and action that has deep roots in the Western European imaginary. While the intensity of anti-Traveller sentiment will differ relative to a range of interacting factors at a given historical juncture (e.g. the dominant political ethos of a given period, levels of unemployment, tension over land use and changes in the health of the economy), it is nevertheless the case that moral panics which encompass a strong anti-Traveller sentiment draw on a long and rich history of moral and political anxiety concerning "Other" groups perceived to be rootless or external to the social order, as emphasised by Sibley (1981):

Contemporary representations of the Other are always the product
of historical legacy and active transformation in the light of
prevailing circumstances. (1981: 40)

An overview of national and local newspapers within the past decade
shows the re-occurrence of a range of themes and perceptions that have
been applied to Travelling people since time immemorial. Irish media
interest in the Traveller "issue" today generally involves any situation
where "large" numbers of Travellers are seen to encroach on the lifestyle
of the settled community in some way or exhibit a refusal to "integrate"
with the norms of the majority population. These controversies can range
from allegations regarding revenue or social welfare fraud, attempts to
house Travellers either within or anywhere near housing estates that are
traditionally home to members of the settled community, or other situations which involve the visibility of groups of Travellers, e.g. marriages,
funerals, internecine feuding and the summer "invasions" when a minority of Travellers attempt to travel, go on pilgrimage (e.g. to Knock in
County Mayo) and travel between countries, most frequently between
Ireland and Britain.

It remains the case that representations and imagery concerning Travellers as exemplified in the modern-day media frequently differ little from
the "inferiorised" or degraded discourse that was prevalent in aspects of
the folklore tradition of the past and which this book has attempted to
highlight. As in previous decades, the way in which Travellers are represented in cultural discourse, and as exemplified through the medium of
the print and electronic media, continues to be largely determined by outside forces. As the print media is the source with the most regular commentary on Traveller-related issues, the cultural discourse that circumvents the Traveller community can be seen to function on two levels, both
active and reactive. Print media have a role that is much wider than the
simple presentation of factual material. In modern Ireland it is widely acknowledged that today's print media have an increased role in the formation of public opinions and attitudes as compared with the situation in the
recent past.

It is an undeniable reality that the print media, as with other forms of
communications technology, is indelibly rooted in the cultural discourse
of the moment. As such it does more than simply mirror those views

prevalent amongst the chattering classes. It also has the power to distort these views, tabloid journalism being a prime culprit in this regard. It can be argued that in much the same way as the folk tradition consolidated the way manner in which Travellers were represented in the pre-literate era; it is the print media that consolidates and perpetuates the popular perceptions and representations of Irish Travellers today. Much of the good work that has been done to date in the area of inter-community relations is frequently tarnished by simplistic or ill-informed reportage which deliberately ignores any sense of objectivity with an eye on newspaper sales and the values of the marketplace. While the Irish media can be commended on a clear shift in the interpretation of societal difference as embodied in the nomenclature used to refer to Travellers — e.g. 1960s references to the "itinerant problem" have generally been replaced with the term "Traveller community" — the rhetoric that is the substance of many newspapers articles and television reports frequently continues to focus on the stereotypical and the sensational. Resident groups and Traveller activists represent the growth of pressure politics in Irish society and the splintering of what was the previously assumed monolith of Irish identity into differences that are discussed in terms of ethnicity and cultural dialogue.

Bhreatnach (1998), who studied a representative example of Irish media reports as they referred to the Irish Traveller community between the 1960s and 1990s found a substantial increase in the number of reports that discussed the Traveller community in terms of race, discrimination and dialogue. While the new acknowledgement of a "sense of difference" as applied to the Traveller community was to be lauded, she found a strong emphasis on sensationalist reporting which gave undue prominence to Travellers in terms of crime and violence.

Increased representation of Travellers and acknowledgement of cultural difference was undermined by the continuance of Traveller stereotyping and a decontextualisation of the "real" issues common to tabloid journalism, which only served to reinforce prejudice and increase hostility towards them as a community. She found that the issues of crime and violence as applied to the Traveller community continued to draw on a well of reductionist imagery that has been drawn upon for centuries. This reductionism was linked to a new fracturing of Irish identity along ethnic lines where "difference" as expressed between communities was increasingly viewed as undesirable and irreconcilable.

This perceived sense of "difference" between the Traveller and "settled" communities was exacerbated by a lack of personal contact between both communities, as compared with the situation in a previously "rural" Ireland. The government task force entitled the Travelling People's Review Body (1983) and the *Citizen Traveller* campaign (2001) both pointed to increased isolation of the Traveller community as a consequence of rapid social change and the "unfounded fears" generated within the settled community by this same lack of interaction between both communities. It is no small irony that a similar sense of "difference" based on a perceived lack of cultural compatibility is currently being used in relation to many immigrant groups by those elements in Irish society who would deny full citizenship rights and privileges to Ireland's increasing immigrant population.

While guidelines have been implemented in media sources which acknowledge cultural difference as pertaining to Travellers and outlaw the use of inappropriate language — for instance, terms such as "itinerant", "tinker" and "knacker" have been deemed offensive by the National Union of Journalists (NUJ) since 1996 — the challenge of recognising ethnic difference without resorting to the use of stereotypes remains a big one for many media outlets. The worst tabloid elements aside, it is the case that media discourse has undeniably shifted to a considerable extent away from past perceptions of Travellers as a socioeconomic problem to a perception where their ethnic difference is acknowledged in more positive terms. However, all too often it continues to be the case that while ethnic difference is ascribed legitimacy, the recognition of Traveller ethnicity is demeaned by the implication that Traveller cultural expression is irreconcilably different with that of other non-Traveller communities and that the Traveller community is consequently deserving of further polarisation.

Chapter 17

The Occluded Voice

While media and "settled" community perceptions of Travellers have a somewhat longer history, the public articulation of Traveller identity on the part of the Irish Traveller community itself is a relatively recent phenomenon. It is a phenomenon that has focused in particular on a number of core aspects of the Traveller experience. These aspects are ones which Travellers themselves have identified as contributing to the deliberate erosion of their culture when operating in tandem with an overtly assimilationist ethos as directed towards their community. One extremely important element in this new articulation of identity on the part of Travellers themselves is the increase in Traveller self-representation through the mode of autobiography.

Travellers' liminal position in Irish society has commonly meant that representations of them had largely been effected from without. However, recent decades have seen the emergence of an increasing number of powerful evocations of Traveller identity from within the community itself. In this canon of work, the voices of Travellers themselves are heard for the first time in the public sphere and their culture is celebrated in a unique and intimate fashion. These evocations are all the more remarkable when one considers the high levels of non-literacy, social exclusion and the denial of access to the dominant means of self-representation that have been characteristic of Traveller life until very recently.

While Irish writing has had a fascination with the Travelling community since at least the late nineteenth century, Travellers have, in the works of such well-known writers as Synge, Yeats, Pádraic Ó Conaire, James Stephens, Liam O'Flaherty, John B. Keane, Bryan MacMahon, Jennifer Johnston and Richard Murphy, normally been made to fit a generic image. This image, frequently the mirror-type of the colonial "stage Irishman", has included that of the happy-go-lucky vagrant, the criminal, the drunk, the storyteller and the outcast. Recent Traveller literature has emerged, however, to challenge this static and stereotypical way in which Travellers have been reproduced culturally, politically and ideologically and to forge a "place" for Travellers in modern Ireland, one that is no longer on the margins.

It can be argued that Irish Travellers have in the past had little consciousness of their culture and language as distinctive attributes. These publications are an example of a fundamental change in this regard, however. A number of common themes have emerged in these texts that form the core of this challenge and which seek to undercut the common view of Travellers' perceived liminal position in Irish culture. They form an important challenge to those "official" or written histories of Ireland which have ignored groups whose culture has been primarily oral. They also function to forcefully reject the "drop-out" theory of origin that continues to haunt much modern-day representations and treatment of Travellers.

Other themes that emerge strongly in this autobiographical work by Travellers include a focus on education and inclusion in Irish society on Travellers' own terms, a strong prescience and fear of cultural annihilation and an ever-present anxiety that the negative stereotypes about Travellers have been internalised by Travellers themselves, in particular younger Travellers, thereby damaging irreparably their cultural self-identity. A strong emphasis is also placed on documenting instances of abuse and discrimination that have led to Travellers' exclusion from Irish society. These writers frequently express bewilderment at the levels of prejudice and hostility exhibited by the Irish "settled" community towards Travellers and exhibit a longing for the acceptance of nomadism, now frequently referred to as the "nomadic mindset", which is the kernel of Traveller identity.

Books such as Maher's *The Road to God Knows Where* (1972), Nan Joyce's *Traveller* (1985) and Pecker Dunne's *Parley-Poet and Chanter* (2004) are all very aware of their quasi-oral status, one which generates a unique and creative tension between print and speech. Both Maher's and Dunne's books are littered with folk-anecdotes, songs and superstitions, all of which highlight the educational function that the oral tradition occupies within the Traveller community as regards the cultural transmission of knowledge. They indicate the high value placed by the Traveller community on the skills of the storyteller who effectively disseminates Traveller values and historical tradition. The oral tradition as elucidated in these narratives functions as a coping mechanism whereby the past can be communicated with and the present can be dealt with, as Maher (1972) makes clear:

> . . . you must remember that storytelling is our only means of communication with the past. We on the road can't write our deeds, but we do remember them and pass them down faithfully by word of mouth. (1972: 68)

The self-educated Maher wrote his manuscript with his own hand, unlike Joyce, Cauley and Dunne, whose stories were recorded on tape and subsequently transcribed.

Irrespective of the methods of cultural reproduction employed by the Travellers, each of the narrators has succeeded in preserving a sense of orality in print. All four Travellers belong, in a sense, to the Gaelic tradition of the *seanchaí* (storyteller) as their books all record and describe stories and traditions which are not to be found elsewhere. Their books also expose a range of common stereotypes about Travellers that continue to have a strong resonance in Irish public opinion. One example of this type of rebuttal, for instance, is the under-cutting of the long-standing stereotype that Travellers were always nomadic and never lived a sedentary existence for any significant length of time.

This usurpation of such a Traveller stereotype cannot be underestimated when one considers that much assimilationist policy as directed towards Travellers has assumed a permanent form of nomadism to be the Traveller norm. Maher, Dunne and Cauley all provide rebuttals to this common misconception about Traveller nomadism, with Maher (1972) describing his family's nomadism as seasonal in nature:

> Most of the bad winters, my parents would abandon the tent or the wagon and move into a spike[1] for a few months. In those days there was one in every large town in Ireland . . . I liked the spikes very much during the cold winter nights, for I could sit at the turf

---

[1] "Spike" was another word for the poorhouse or "County Home".

fire with my father and all the old men . . . Night after night in the
spike he would hold me on his lap near the blazing fire and sing
and tell stories to the other men there. (1972: 9–10)

An emphasis on the importance of Traveller literacy so that their community can function with dignity within modern Irish society is also a theme
which emerges in this autobiographical canon, with both Maher and Joyce
expounding on their struggles in this regard and the importance of this aspect of human dignity to the articulation of a community's "true voice":

It's an awful sad thing to have no education . . . If I knew how to
write properly and had good spelling I wouldn't have done this
book on tape. Anna Farmar [the book's editor] recorded it and
wrote it out for me — if I wrote a book myself whoever published it would need a medal for bravery! (Joyce, 1985: 95)

The mediation between print and speech which serves to emphasise the
orality central to Traveller culture is given a new awareness by the inclusion of various Shelta words in these autobiographical works, a pattern
that has been given added impetus in some of the most recently-
published Traveller literature, including Peter Brady's novel *Paveewhack*
(2001) and, latterly, in the works of Cauley (2004) and Dunne (2004). It
can be argued that the written use of Shelta, a language into which very
little research has been undertaken and which appears in the past at least
to have had a strong secrecy function, is "political" in the sense that it
serves to highlight the "sense of difference" that is felt by a community
who, when it has been convenient, have often been dismissed as having
no fundamental cultural attributes to distinguish them from the "settled
community" in Ireland.

A significant increase in the use of Shelta in the most recent Traveller publications may also be indicative of the huge assimilative pressure
that the small minority that is the Traveller community is currently ex-
periencing alongside the frantic pace of societal change that is affecting
all members of the Irish population, be they Traveller or non-Traveller. It
may also be indicative of the feeling of foreboding that pervades the
texts of these Traveller writers, who, it should be noted, are elderly in
terms of their own community, a foreboding highlighted in the fear of
their possible cultural disappearance as a separate group in Ireland.

Maher, Cauley and Dunne all make reference to the weakening role of the Traveller language(s) as a cultural marker within the Traveller community, a fact which cannot be separated from the decline of many "minority" languages in an increasingly globalised world, but one which in the context of the Travelling community's history cannot be divorced from the sustained undermining of Traveller identity that has accompanied the modernisation of Ireland. Maher, whose autobiography was published over thirty years ago, includes a brief glossary of Shelta words at the end of his book, a glossary which is prefaced with the warning that this language is "now almost extinct", while Dunne and Cauley preface the different sections of their books with phrases in their respective Cants, complete with English explanations, including for example:

> The drom in the clammy pani – *On the road in bad weather* (Dunne with Ó hAodha, 2004: 19)
>
> Our dhíls scurlimed — *Burning us out* (Cauley with Ó hAodha, 2004: 26)

Dunne (2004) warns of an absence of interest in this aspect of Traveller culture amongst the younger generation and links this with the damage that has been inflicted on Traveller self-identity and the transference of Irish identity as a whole:

> The way I see it the Travellers here don't speak the Cant very much anymore. More's the pity. That's what I say. They are letting it die you see. A lot of Travellers in Ireland are not speaking our own Cant because they are ashamed of it. They don't want to be called the "knacker". I don't understand this. They should be proud of who they are and who their ancestors were. It's a bit like those people in the West of Ireland who have lovely Irish but who won't use it or pass it onto their children for fear that people might think they are ignorant. It's a lovely thing to know the Cant and it is a very old language. (2004: 51)

While these autobiographies are extremely positive in many respects and include many vignettes that emphasise the joy, resourcefulness and adaptability of Travellers in often-adverse circumstances, the books also intimate that the threat of language death may be indicative of a greater cultural disappearance. The ambivalence in the title of Maher's book *The Road to God Knows Where* (1972) is followed by apocalyptic "warnings" that the road may not lead anywhere or that the destination is ultimately one of assimilation or cultural disappearance.

> You see, son, life is becoming more difficult and the road as a way of life is finished . . . (1972: 100)

> The time shall come too, brothers and sisters, when the travelling people of Ireland shall be no more. (1972: 78)

It is the death-knell of the most defining Traveller cultural attribute, nomadism — that which is inherent in the very nomenclature by which Travellers refer to themselves — that many of the writers identify as the most serious threat facing their community. Both Maher (1972) and Joyce (1985) identify the disjuncture between the Traveller and "settled" views of nomadism as the roots of much of the prejudice that has been indicative of settled–Traveller attitudes and relations:

> We lived in a house for a very short period when I was young, but my parents could not adapt to settled life. In the town where we lived we were not wanted; there was always a great amount of prejudice among the townspeople, especially those who lived near us. For my father it was not too bad because he went out the country each day with the pony and cart. For my mother, however, things were different. She was always alone in the house; none of the neighbours would even talk to her — let alone come into our house for a visit or a cup of tea. To the townspeople we were dirty begging tinkers and no respectable person would visit us . . . (Maher, 1972: 15)

> My third little boy, Patrick, was born in St. James's and he was christened when we moved over to Finglas. We stayed there for about two years until Elizabeth was born but the Corporation kept shifting us, from one field to another. People say to us, "Will you not settle down?" but we don't get the chance because we're hunted from place to place . . . (Joyce, 1985: 80)

Joyce also describes the activities of the police and vigilante groups in Northern Ireland where Travellers were doubly prejudiced against for sectarian reasons:

> Some of the police were very hard on us. They would come up at ten o'clock of a winter's night and it didn't matter if it was snowing or freezing, the travellers would have to pack up. The women might have walked miles for two buckets of water to cook the food and wash the children. They might have spent an hour trying to light the fire . . . If you had any brain at all you knew that the travellers weren't wanted. Once in the North we stayed with two families for about a week, near Warrenpoint. One man's horse jumped through a gap into a farmer's field. A group of men came up about twelve o'clock of a winter's night with shotguns that they use for hunting foxes and rabbits. They shot this man in the legs and he was in terrible pain. We shifted but it was so dark we didn't know where we were going. (1985: 40)

While Joyce highlighted the phenomenon of eviction, an aspect of Traveller life which has recurred with increased regularity since the introduction of the Housing Miscellaneous Provisions Act (1992), Cauley (2004), a landscape painter by profession, spoke of the psychological difficulties induced by Travellers' forced settlement in the absence of transient sites or any provision for those who wish to remain nomadic and the destruction of Travellers' "collective memory" through the deliberate blocking off of traditional campsites that had been used regularly by generations of the same family:

> I wonder how many older Travellers became depressed because they weren't allowed to travel anymore? How many of them became depressed when they saw their traditional camping places being blocked up and they ended up drifting from the countryside into houses and the cities? . . . A number of my siblings who are now dead suffered from depression while they were alive. I think the city life may have had a lot to do with it. Freedom and travelling was in their blood and being cooped up in the city affected them and made them sick. I have heard that the same thing has happened to many other traditionally nomadic people who have been forced by circumstance to live in the cities — people like the

Native American Indians and the Aborigines in Australia . . .
Someday I will try and capture this misery in a painting. I will get
a huge canvas, the biggest one I can find, and when the painting is
done I will show it to the press and the government so as to make
a statement to them. "Look it, this is how the government ignored
us back through time. This is how you hurt these peoples' minds
then, a hurt that later changed into a depression. At a later stage
you forced them into houses. You blocked up their roads." I will
put all my energies into that painting. Everything. (2004: 23–4)

In the same book Cauley compares his identity as grounded in a nomadic
tradition with a nature that has been befouled by rapid and often-forced
social change:

I was often asked if I was born again what would I like to be.
Well, the first thing that comes to my mind is a swan. Yes, I
know it's a strange thing to say but I have my own reasons for
that answer. When you look at how peaceful a creature the swan
is, it seems to have no worries, it comes and goes as it pleases.
And most of all it has rights. No one tells it to move on; no one
tries to control it. (2004: 109)

The importance of nomadism, even to younger Travellers who have
never had the same opportunities to travel as their parents and grandpar-
ents, is powerfully highlighted by a young Traveller named Martina
Joyce, interviewed for a series of essays on Traveller life and culture and
produced as *Traveller Ways, Traveller Words* (1992) by Pavee Point.
She expresses a longing for nomadism and highlights the alienation and
lack of social contact that accompanies enforced settlement:

You get ta see more an' ya meet up with different Travellers that
you never seen before. You mix better. You wouldn't be always
around your own that ya do be around in the sites and that.
You're always nearly with your own people. Mixin' with the extended families and that. And ya could pick up things and do
things like. Pick up like doin' things in markets an' that. Travel to
the markets an' the fairs an' things like that. Out sellin' in houses
an' things. Well, nowadays you don't have the freedom to travel.
Like, if you go to the camps most o' them are all bowldered up

with stones in front o' them an' that. The sides o' the roads is all
done. And then if you go tiv a site nearly all the sites is full up
because there again the wans that's in it can't go movin'. And
then if y'are aan the side iv a road or in a field you're put out o'
them mostly with the guards an' the people who owns the land. I
don't know, if you've no skips or an'hin' to put the rubbish in
they'll say that you're pilin' the rubbish an' you're gatherin' dirt
an' this, that an' the other an' you're ruinin' the countryside an'
they have ta put ya goin. An' then when you go, then, you've
nowhere else ta go because all the sites are full up with the Travellers that's 'ithin in them. So wha' else will ya do? You'll only
have ta go because they'll drag you out of it if ya don't go.
(Pavee Point, 1992a: 72–3)

Much Traveller autobiography expresses incomprehension at the level of
prejudice that is often evinced by the "settled" community towards Travellers, the roots of which frequently lie in ignorance and fear. Both
Dunne and Cauley describe an anti-Traveller prejudice that blighted their
memories of childhood:

It is funny but no matter how hard you try you will remember to
your dying day those moments when people were prejudiced towards you. Every human being wants to be respected . . . The
worst part of prejudice like this is when your childhood inno-
cence is destroyed by it. I remember seeing people shouting at us
when I was a child. "The Tinker isn't wanted here, go away," and
all the rest of it. They made a distinction between us and the rest
of the Irish people. That's the best way to describe it. And you
were aware of that distinction from the moment you were born. I
knew what it was from the moment I was able to walk. The bad-
ness in some people . . . This prejudice is an old thing in Ireland
and there isn't any sign that it's going to go away. I was talking
to a few fellas there recently. They are Gypsies, travelling people
from Eastern Europe. Roma or Romanies is what they call themselves. I was asking them what they thought of Ireland and one of
the first things they said to me was, "My God, but this is an awful
racist country." "Tell me more about it," says I to them. "If anybody knows about the racism here, it is me. I have seen it since I
was born, since I came from my mother. Against me and people

like me. And I can't explain fully what the reason is behind it."
(Dunne with Ó hAodha, 2004: 37)

Maher (1972) admits that his interest in literacy and the thirst for a "formal" education which tormented him for much of his youth was as much
a means of attempting to understand the prejudice against Travellers as it
is a natural inclination for learning:

> You know . . . I keep thinking about people. I keep asking myself,
> why do people have to hate each other? I keep thinking how nice it
> would be and how happy everyone would be if they did not hate
> each other. I don't know why I keep thinking like this; perhaps my
> father is right when he says that I'm a funny one. There are times
> when I go and beg from house to house for old books. (1972: 101)

Cauley (2004) expresses his bitterness at the intolerable burden that is
the prejudice against his community by taking refuge in his imagination.
He describes one of his occasional "flights of fancy", which functions as
a form of escapism from a reality that is a good deal more grim:

> Sometimes I feel very bitter about the way Travellers were
> treated in Ireland. When I was younger I sometimes hoped that I
> could just disappear out of this country. In my mind I used to
> wish that I someone would kidnap me so that I could escape from
> some of this hardship! (2004: 74–93)

Joyce (1985) situates her autobiography within a context whereby the
roots of much Irish anti-Traveller prejudice can be firmly identified as
having its roots in ignorance. Her description of a public meeting with a
group of Irish university students is an unbelievable indictment of the
levels of ignorance that exist regarding Traveller culture in an Ireland,
where stereotypes have become so reified as to almost assume the status
of "truth":

> Some of the students — and they were Irish — knew nothing
> about the travellers, it was as if we'd if we'd come from the moon.
> The questions they asked! "Do you marry?" They didn't know if
> we got married or if we lived together, if we had the children on
> the roadside of if we went to hospital. It was like speaking to

something from out of the world. They could tell you the history
of the North American Indians but here were the Irish travellers in
their own country and they could tell you nothing about them,
their history or their traditions. And these are the people who'll be
running the country when we're all gone. (1985: 108)

She calls both for younger Travellers to jettison their feelings of inferiority and for the "settled" Irish community to make themselves more aware
of the minority in their midst:

I would like all the travelling children to have self-confidence and
to grow up proud of what they are because they are very special
people with their own traditions and their own way of life. But
the way they've been treated and discriminated against they grow
up ashamed of their own parents. It used to be that the one time
you heard about travellers was when they did wrong; nothing
about us was ever taught in schools and when children came by
our camp they would just run by — they were afeared of the travellers. Even today some people are afeared to come near us and
chat with us — it's a fear of the unknown. (1985: 118)

Virtually the entire Traveller autobiographical canon challenges the way
in which Travellers have traditionally been precluded from discussions
of modern Ireland. This is unsurprising given that many canonical historical texts, by both nationalist and revisionist historians alike, have
simply excluded all mention of Ireland's oldest minority. In the very few
cases that Travellers are alluded to at all they tend to be depicted primarily in the role of passive recipients of the historical process, a group
whose perceived position as drop-outs — i.e. victims of colonial eviction
and/or the Great Famine — rendered them uninterested in such issues as
Irish nationalism or the fight for Independence or uninvolved in Irish
history generally. As a consequence, perhaps, Traveller authors have
been at pains to emphasise their Irishness and their critical role in the
development of Irish cultural processes. Cauley (2004) cites the Irish
predilection for genealogy and "Where are you from?" to provide a
counter to the manner in which Travellers are ostracised in Irish society.
He combines the Irish obsession with genealogy with a healthy sense of
humour in an attempt to obviate the sense of bitterness that grips him

when he dwells on the manner in which Travellers have been denied a place in the Irish historical "record":

> ... Sometimes in this country they treat you like an alien because you are a Traveller . . . That's how bad-minded some people are towards Travellers. They hate us for some unexplained reason. In my time I have been mocked and jeered at, because I am a Traveller. But I got used to it and later on I passed no heed to them . . . We Travellers are a different people so we stand out from the crowd. People think because we have a different culture that there is something wrong with us. It is sad but that is the way that life is. And the strangest thing of all is that Travelling people and settled people are often buried beside one another when we pass on. Is that the only time that we communicate with each other? You have Cauleys in this country for centuries, for example. There are Cauleys who are settled people and Cauleys who are Travelling people. Do you mean to tell me that the settled Cauleys and the Travelling Cauleys aren't related somewhere back along the line? Of course they are. But so many settled people act as if we, the Travellers, never had any connection with them. It's like President like President Kennedy, President Clinton or President Reagan in America. It's pretty obvious from their names that they are related to people back here in Ireland somewhere back though the generations. Even Pierce Brosnan — I doubt if he was born James Bond! There are connections between all the Irish families if you look back through the history records — whether you are a McCarthy, an O'Driscoll, an O'Reilly, a Cauley — or any other name that is common amongst the Travellers here in Munster. If they are not Irish names then I will have to go back to whatever planet I'm supposed to have landed from! (Cauley, 2004: 74, 93)

Maher and Joyce both refer to the importance of oral tradition in Traveller culture and point to its tenets to assign themselves a *"dinnseanchas"* or "sense of place" in Irish society. This sense of orality that has been passed down faithfully by "word of mouth" is set against the official or "written" history of Ireland which would assign to Travellers a place in the footnotes of Irish history, a place where if they are considered at all, it is only as helpless victims of poverty and dispossession, the detritus of colonialism and a tragic Irish past who are only a strange nuisance or anachronism in the modern nation-state. Maher (1972) cites the Traveller known as the doll-man – the strange, shaman-like figure with whom Maher has a dialogue regarding the position of Travellers in the modern world – as an exemplar of the challenge to the official or "establishment" view from the oral culture of those who tell their stories "from below" or from the margins of society:

> . . . The written history is very warped in its composition and truth. The history that has come down through the travellers, however, is more than reliable. It is told night after night around camp fires . . . (1972: 97)

Maher links Traveller nomadism with the Irish hagiographic tradition and with the travelling of Christ and the saints, thereby providing an alternative and counter-hegemonic "take" on Irish popular tradition, one which usurps the image of the Traveller as degraded or peripheral. His narrative provides a wealth of stories and anecdotes, many of which the Travelling community may have used to "sustain" themselves and "validate" their existence in the face of the prejudice and marginalisation of their community. These stories, many of which were probably narrated to the "settled" community in the pre-industrial era, link the Travellers with a pantheon of other "more respectable" "Travellers" including St. Patrick and St. Kevin. The Travellers' links with Ireland's hagiographical tradition provide a "validation" for their existence and are a celebration of their nomadic culture. Instead of being a people "cursed by God" the hagiographical tradition intimates that the Travellers are in fact a "chosen people" whose wandering is reminiscent of other sometimes-ostracised groups such as the Jews. Rather than the "settled" community it is they, the Travellers, who are the "respectable" people as Irish saints like Patrick and Kevin have chosen them to employ their nomadism as a vehicle for spreading Christianity throughout Ireland. The exclusion and prejudice that Travellers suffer is unsurprising according to this discourse as it is natural and inevitable that a "chosen" people should suffer at the hands of the "majority" community.

The urbanisation of Ireland in recent decades has meant that the vibrancy of the oral tradition which was described by Maher has waned amongst Travellers and "settled" alike. As a consequence, it is unsurprising to find more recent Traveller writers have focused on those aspects of modern Irish culture which continue to be keenly contested in the post-independent and increasingly multicultural Ireland of today — i.e. questions of identity, nationhood and cultural legitimacy. Women Travellers like Joyce (1985) and Sweeney (cited in Helleiner, 2000: 245) reject Travellers' alleged non-involvement in the course of Irish history and point to Travellers' agency in the political and social struggles that formed the Irish nation while the recent literature of male Travellers such as Cauley and Dunne has provided new insights into Traveller language and history which serve to challenge the perception that Travellers were/are always a homogenous group. Their insights into the history of the various Traveller languages as spoken in Ireland serve as an important reminder of the way that the culture of an indigenous Irish group such as the Travellers has been intimately interwoven with the development of Irish culture generally. Dunne (2004) undertakes a brief survey of the range of different Traveller languages that were still spoken in Ireland when he was growing up in the 1940s including:

> . . . the Cant or Gammon of the Travellers that people called Tinkers, there was the Tailors' Cant of the Travelling Tailor which I never heard spoken myself and there was the Circus/Showmans' Cant of the Circus and Carnival people. Finally there was the Buskers' Cant of Travelling people like myself. Today two of those Cants have croaked [died]. There is no-one now who can speak the Stonemasons' Cant which was called the Béarlagair or Béarlagair na Saor and there is no-one either who can speak the Tailors' Cant, the language that the tailor would use when he was talking privately to his apprentice. (2004: 50)

He rejects many of the notions of secrecy and exclusivity that have surrounded discussions of the language and been promulgated by those who would exoticise, denigrate or discuss Travellers in terms of some kind of a counter-cultural or semi-criminal group and points instead to the use of Traveller language as a form of solidarity and group identity:

> A lot of people call Cant a "secret" language. There is a kind of a romantic notion that it was a language that was only used for se-

crecy and scheming and all the rest of it. Sure it was a "secret" language in the sense that a lot of people did not know it, but the main reason for speaking Cant had nothing to do with scheming or being very "secretive". It was a language like any other and the Travellers spoke it because it was their own language and it kept them close together. Some families would say their own prayers in Cant. Even the Travellers who emigrated to America around the time of the Famine kept up the Cant long after they had left Ireland. It was like their own sign of the fact that they were Travellers and that they were proud of that. (2004: 53)

Cauley's (2004) insights into the origins of Traveller language also question some common hypothetical constructions of the historical function of this language as previously considered within Irish culture. He links its origins with the bardic culture of the Irish Travelling Poets or *Filí Taistil* who were once central to Gaelic culture but whose history, like that of the Travellers, has been occluded through a combination of colonialism and neglect:

It is a part of our culture that most Irish people don't know much about. The word Cant comes from the Irish word "Caint" which means "talk" or "speech". The word Gammon is also from Irish. It means "twisted" or "disguised". That is because many of the first Travellers were poets who were highly educated scholars. They were skilled with words and one of their pastimes was to disguise words and twist them around. Sometimes they did this for fun. Other times they did this so that they speak to each other privately in their own language. This was at the time when Cromwell was massacring Irish people all over people. People forget that Cromwell slaughtered thousands of people, including a lot of Travellers. The English colonisers hated anyone who travelled for a living, whether they were poets, musicians, tinkers or herbalists. They were afraid that Travellers, especially travelling poets would be encouraging the people to rise up and rebel against them and so they killed them in their hundreds. When the Gaelic culture was strong in Ireland the poets were one of the most widely respected groups in Irish society. They used to travel the country playing music and performing poetry and it was unlucky for anyone to refuse them lodgings. After the Battle of

Kinsale in 1601 everything changed for them. The Gaelic princes
were gone and the poets could only beg from place to place. A lot
of the poets mixed in with all the other different Travellers on the
road. There were so many Travellers on the roads at that time, it
is hard to know where to start. There were travelling tinsmiths,
travelling shoemakers, travelling carpenters, travelling monks,
travelling stonemasons, travelling weavers, travelling nailers,
travelling musicians and travelling healers. You could go on forever! All of these people were the ancestors of today's Travelling
people if you go back far enough. (2004: 88)

His comments echo those of other Travellers such as Joyce (1985) and
Sweeney (cited in Helleiner, 2000: 127) in affirming Travellers' agency
in the political and social struggles of Ireland and locate Travellers
firmly within the foregrounding of Irish culture:

Some words that we have were disguised by the Travelling poets
in times gone by. The word *laicín* meaning "girl" is the Irish
word "*cailín*" twisted around. A light is a *glimmer* or a *lodus*, and
lodus is from the Irish word *solas*. Even the word that describes
myself "*Noiceall-feen*" (Candle-man) is a word that was disguised by the poets, because it comes from the Irish word "*coin-
neall*". When people look down at Travellers or treat them badly,
how many of them realise that they are putting down the culture
of the old poets of Ireland?!

Chapter 18

Modern Ireland, Social Inclusion and the Question of Identity

No longer is it acceptable to say that Travellers were settled people and therefore it's perfectly alright to resettle or re-assimilate them. Now you must look at Travellers as having an identity and culture to be celebrated and resourced.
(Traveller spokesperson Michael McDonagh, 2000: 21)

The emergence of Traveller autobiography has coincided with a newly emergent and multicultural Ireland that has in the past decade seen the immigration of migrants from at least one hundred different countries and ethnic groups. It has also coincided with a re-engagement on the part of the Irish people with the questions of identity and cultural difference in an era where increasingly globalised societies are seeing transformations and new complexities in the cultural interactions between different peoples and cultures. The literature of Traveller advocacy has developed in tandem with the emergence of an articulate and politically conscious Traveller leadership in the form of groups like Pavee Point and the Irish Traveller Movement, a development which academics such as Jim MacLaughlin (1995) have argued as "perhaps the most significant development in Traveller society" in the modern era. These groups have enabled a new movement towards self-determination evident amongst Travelling communities themselves. Traveller activist Martin Collins (1994) explains that they represent:

> a new and growing awareness among Travellers. This new awareness is about having a clear understanding of the reasons for the differences between Travellers and settled people. These

differences are cultural and do not mean being either inferior or superior — just different but equal. More Travellers are rejecting the culture of poverty theory and the policies and practices which follow it because we see ourselves as a distinct ethnic group. This enables us to put into words, and to have concepts which explain, our experiences and what has been happening to us. There are important implications from this. It means that we can be clearer about our rights and that we can be confident in making demands. (1994: 132)

In addition to helping to improve the position of Travellers in Ireland, advocacy groups like Pavee Point, the National Travellers Women's Forum and a wide number of regionally based Traveller support/development groups have been to the forefront in both leading and organising a broader anti-racist coalition in the 1990s, one which has expanded in cognisance of both ethnic and racial tensions as a consequence of Ireland's economic growth and the arrival of new immigrant groups to Ireland. This formation of coalitions with other like-minded groups is echoed "on the ground" amongst traditionally nomadic groups such as Travellers and Roma throughout Europe where new alliances of solidarity see Traveller and Roma (Gypsy) groups departing from what may have traditionally been more fragmented forms of social organisation to form alliances in pan-national political movements. The public articulation of Irish Traveller identity in this new environment demands a re-assessment of the Traveller community and the way in which this community has been represented and articulated in cultural and ideological terms since the foundation of the Irish State. It also demands a more sustained engagement with the controversial question of rights and responsibilities as they apply to both the Traveller and non-Traveller communities.

These questions are controversial ones in a modern Ireland where the swift migration of a formerly primarily rural Irish population to the large urban centres of Dublin, Cork, Limerick and Galway has placed huge pressure on the country's social and environmental amenities and led to emotive social conflicts in relation to such issues as housing and the usage of land. In very recent years the question of Traveller/settled relations and the rights and responsibilities of both communities towards one another has increasingly been played out in the media where different media elements have used conflictual situations to signify a variety of different purposes and agendas. It is generally acknowledged that the media is not the most appropriate forum to resolve issues which generate tension between both communities. This applies in particular to the Traveller cultural tradition of nomadism and the question of "unofficial" Traveller encampments on the part of the Travellers who wish to travel during the summer. That conflicting arguments in relation to issues such as this are played out in a "tit-for-tat" manner through media sources frequently serves only to exacerbate tension in situations where Traveller-Settled relations are already strained or highly emotive.

Recent advocacy literature which has emanated from Traveller activists, as opposed to Traveller writers of ethnography and oral history, has sought as a basic preface to many of the aforementioned controversies that Irish society come to an acceptance and acknowledgement of the social and cultural importance of Travellers to Irish society. Such an acknowledgement would help create a meaningful engagement between the Traveller and settled communities in the long term, one which would recognise that Travellers have both rights *and* responsibilities as citizens of Ireland. Works such as *Travellers: Citizens of Ireland* (Sheehan, 2000), an earlier edition of which was entitled *Do You Know Us At All?* (Hyland, 1993) elucidates the double-stressed nature of the demand that meaningful participation in a civic society entails. In many ways that book can be seen as a watershed in the struggle towards Traveller self-definition and self-determination including as it does essays by Travellers on all aspects of their culture including such issues as "nomadism", "ethnicity and culture", "the Traveller economy", "healthcare", "education", "family, marriage and faith", "Traveller spirituality", etc. The essays argue the evolving nature of Traveller culture and ethnicity in Ireland and rejects the "sub-culture of poverty" or "dispossessed peasant" prism through which the Travelling community has been viewed by the majority. The Traveller activists in this book argue that the members of the settled community in Ireland need to recognise that Traveller identity is not determined by a history incorporating a "drop-out" origin and a history of dispossession. This view of Traveller origins, which has dogged the attitudes of the "settled" community towards Travellers, has dictated the services that have been provided for Travellers and provided a justification for their attempted assimilation. This approach is no longer acceptable, as outlined by activist Michael McDonagh (2000):

> No longer is it acceptable to say that Travellers were settled people and therefore it's perfectly alright to resettle or reassimilate them. Now you must look at Travellers as having an identity and culture to be celebrated and resourced. (2000: 21)

What is needed instead is a comprehensive review of attitudes towards issues as complex as nomadism, accommodation and difference so that Travellers may be accepted as fellow-citizens with a distinct cultural identity and a legitimate ethnic inheritance. A new acceptance of such an approach on the part of the majority or "settled" community will, in turn, provide a further incentive for Traveller groups to engage with and address questions of civic responsibility.

EQUALITY AND ETHNICITY: THE SITUATION TODAY

While the question of Traveller identity and self-representation has been subject to a new re-engagement, the same cannot be said, as yet, concerning the everyday living conditions with which many Travellers "on the ground" still have to contend. To date, most advocacy work on the part of activist and rights-based groups has unsurprisingly been directed towards the situation of those Travellers living in particularly disadvantaged and marginalised circumstances. Official analyses continue to show the precarious nature of the average Traveller family's everyday existence with the fairly widespread acknowledgement that Travellers in Ireland fare poorly on every indicator used to measure disadvantage: unemployment, poverty, social exclusion, health status, infant mortality, life expectancy, illiteracy, education and training levels, access to decision-making and political representation, access to credit, insurance and accommodation, etc.

To outline the thrust of Traveller advocacy campaigns in the past two decades, it is necessary to review the progress of official and state responses to the Traveller "question". While official responses are slow in their effect, their import eventually percolates into the public sphere over time. In Ireland, the first purposeful examination of Irish Travellers — i.e.

the 1963 *Report of the Commission on Itinerancy* has been followed by a number of other official analyses and recommendations (1983, 1995 and 2000), all of which have seen a slow but gradual acceptance of Traveller cultural self-determination. The 1983 *Report of the Travelling People Review Body*, while rejecting terms such as "itinerant" did not accept the cultural validity of nomadism and saw, for example, the movement from a house to the travelling life as a form of regression. Neither did this report tackle the pressing issue of anti-Traveller prejudice or discrimination, a subject which was a central aspect of the *Report of the Task Force on the Travelling Community* (1995) twelve years later. This report described the manner in which anti-Traveller discrimination impinged on all aspects of Traveller life e.g. relations with the settled community, education, training, the provision of accommodation, Traveller culture, the Traveller economy, Traveller health and the position of particular groups within the Traveller community such as Traveller women and the disabled. This report was the first official document since the foundation of the state to accept the validity of Traveller culture, whose tenets included such markers as nomadism, Traveller language and the organisation of the Traveller economy and the importance of kinship and the extended family within Traveller culture.

The cusp of the millennium witnessed the launch of an Irish Traveller Movement initiative entitled *Citizen Traveller*, an integrated communications initiative whose catchphrase was "supporting Travellers as an ethnic group". This 1999 initiative aimed to promote the visibility and participation of Travellers within Irish society so as to lead to a greater understanding between the Traveller and settled communities. The programme also set out to nurture Traveller self-pride so that Travellers could have a sense of community identity that could be expressed both internally and externally. This three-year initiative came to an end in 2002.

Initiatives such as *Citizen Traveller* and the Traveller Rights Movement in general have drawn sustenance and added legitimacy to their cause with their definition of Travellers as "a separate group with its own culture, language, values, norms, models, structures" (Ennis, 1984: 5). However, the concept of ethnicity as applied to Irish Travellers has yet to receive acceptance either legislatively or in public discourse. This has led to the strange anomaly whereby Irish Travellers are considered an ethnic group in Britain and Northern Ireland (*Case of Mandla v. Lee*

(1983), House of Lords) and not in Ireland. While the ethnic concept is generally accepted as applied to Irish Travellers in the academic arena this is not the case in social policy and may not be for a while yet. In October 2003, for instance, the current Irish Minister for Justice, Mr Michael McDowell, stated that it was his view that Irish Travellers did not constitute a distinct ethnic group.

Traveller advocacy groups continue to have a high profile within the contemporary politics of anti-racist campaigning in Ireland. In spite of this the progress of Travellers towards the recognition of their economic, cultural and poltical rights has been very limited. Amongst the more positive developments have been the ratification by Ireland of the UN Convention on the Elimination of All Forms of Racial Discrimination. This treaty was ratified by Ireland in December 2000 and entered into force on the following month, January 2001. The Convention, which was originally opened for signature in 1965, is a multilateral treaty embodying obligations on UN Member States to ban racial discrimination and is part of the United Nations' ongoing efforts to tackle racism and racial discrimination. The terms of the Convention require that the Irish State has in place at a domestic level an effective means of redress for those who may experience racial discrimination, a process which occurred with the enactment of anti-discrimination legislation, namely, the Employment Equality Act, 1998, and the Equal Status Act, 2000.

Ireland now has in place an anti-discrimination legal code and an Equality Infrastructure to support it in the form of the Equality Authority and the Office of the Equality Tribunal, with the Equality Tribunal acting as the first forum for redress under the Acts for those individuals who have experienced racial discrimination. The Housing (Traveller Accommodation) Act (1998) has ensured the requirement of each local authority to set out how they will fulfil the accommodation needs of the Travellers in their area over five-year periods. Despite these legislative developments there has not been a significant improvement in the circumstances of Travellers in Ireland. Between 1995 and 2002 only 129 new halting site bays were provided out of the 2,200 units needed. In 2003, 1,000 families were still living on the roadside without access to basic services such as water and toilets. The level of discrimination experienced by Travellers does not appear to have decreased if the high level of cases and queries from Travellers handled by the Equality Authority are a reliable indicator. In the year 2000, approximately 500 families nationwide were served with eviction notices without being offered alternative accommodation.[1] In these circumstances families are given only 24 hours to move and must try to get legal representation and establish their case within this period. In practice it has proved impossible for Travellers in most such situations to obtain legal representation. Ironically, the persistence of evictions of Travellers who have nowhere else to go flies in the face of Irish governmental commitments as outlined in treaties such as the aforementioned UN Convention on the Elimination of All Forms of Racial Discrimination. The situation "on the ground" has been further compounded by the government's introduction of the Housing (Miscellaneous Provisions) Act, which criminalises trespass on public and private land. This has meant that over 1,000 families camped on public land are trespassing — in the majority of instances, due to no fault of their own — and can be prosecuted. This Act also criminalises those Travellers who wish to continue their traditional nomadism and would prefer to continue travelling.

The erosion of Traveller culture continues through a wilful ignorance of their history and culture and the introduction of other legislative devices which act to suppress the expression of their cultural identity; the Control of Horses Act, 1997, for example. The past few decades have also witnessed a substantial deterioration in the relationship between the Traveller community and the "settled" community as officially represented in the form of local authorities. The reasons for this deterioration in social relations are complex and have to do with struggles in relation to class, changes in economic relations between the Traveller and settled communities, the thorny issue of land use in an increasingly urbanised country and the increased attempts on the part of the state to intervene in what has often been defined as the Traveller "problem". A *Citizen Traveller* survey undertaken in 2000 located the disjunction between the Traveller and settled communities in a lack of communication and contact between both communities, with their disturbing finding that over 80

---

[1] Statistic taken from reports available on the ITM (Irish Traveller Movement) website, www.itmtrav.com, accessed 6 July 2006.

per cent of the Irish "settled" population had never spoken to a Traveller, making a mockery of much of the jingoistic jargon concerning multiculturalism that is currently common in Ireland's official circles today.

The reality is that concrete progress on Travellers' struggle to achieve parity of esteem in Irish life remains very slow. Significant improvement in the structural neglect of Travellers in terms of accommodation, education, health and social services has been minimal, a fact which is highlighted in the disproportionate levels of poverty, long-term unemployment and early mortality still evident in the Traveller community.

As outlined here, it can be evidenced that the Travelling community and the way in which the majority or settled community interacts with it has, in recent decades, been defined principally in terms of legislative responses, responses instigated on the part of the state and in the form of the local authority. This is not so different from what took place in the recent past where the history of Travellers and other traditionally migratory groups was more frequently constructed with a view to their categorisation and assimilation and as a legislative response to the phenomenon of nomadism. As this book has attempted to show, the manner in which Travellers are treated legislatively and in the official sphere provides the clearest instance of the way in which responses and category definitions or representations are inextricably connected.

Recent historical research on Traveller and Gypsy history on mainland Europe points to a similar conclusion. Dutch historians such as Willems (1997) and Cottaar et al. (1998) have highlighted the historical legacy of prejudice or what they term "stigmatisation" in the formation of official and popular antipathy to Travelling or marginal groups. Roma activist and linguist Ian Hancock (1987, 1992) and the French activist on behalf of the Roma (Gypsies), Jean-Pierre Liégeois (1987) both pinpointed the inextricable nexus that exists between persistent stereotyping and hostile imagery as applied to Travelling groups and the subsequent treatment of these groups in the legislative and official spheres, with Liégeois (1987) arguing that "the image of Gypsies as forged by non-Gypsies has done much to incite a fear that in turn serves to justify and inspire rejection . . . rejection is bound up with the public's image of nomads and Gypsies" (1986: 134). Liégeois's comments are also an appropriate summation of both historical and current-day perceptions as applied to the Traveller community in Ireland and the long and complex history of Othering as applied to this cultural minority.

There is today a greater acknowledgement in Irish socio-cultural discourse that the manner in which the Traveller "question" has been considered in the arena of social policy has been intimately connected with Travellers' perceived status as a distinct group within Irish society. As elucidated in this book Traveller identity is a "constructed" one, a false identity which has involved the repetition of stereotypes and as operated through myth. Like all stereotypical constructs its evolution and repetition has involved the combined repressions of politics and history, so that a series of social and historical events have culminated in a literary and cultural production of mythic proportions. The condensing of these various myths through the stereotypical Other that is the Traveller image has, however, involved the creation of an imaginary discourse with very real effects — the rationalisation of hostility and prejudice and the perpetuation of economic inequalities and social exclusion.

The damage inflicted by decades of mythmaking and stereotype has been twofold and acted to the detriment of both the Traveller and settled communities in Ireland. The advancement of those false constructs that have been considered the "truth" about Travellers has had serious repercussions for the objects of stereotypical regard — the Travellers — but also for non-Travellers, whose interaction with the Other has been curtailed by an ideological wall of stereotype. This wall has acted as an insurmountable barrier to productive social interaction, over both time and space. Irish representations of the Other are deeply rooted in the sedimented layers set down by past cultural practices. They are representations which have become entrenched as powerful social myths and it is only by a serious re-engagement with the questions of identity and Irishness that a more realistic and holistic view of the question — "What does it mean to be Irish?" — can be reached.

A new interrogation with the identity "constructs" that are "Irish" and "Traveller" is long overdue and it is to be hoped that this book may go some small way towards acting as a catalyst for such a process. Such a process can only be beneficial in unearthing those rich and varied layers that have contributed to the fashioning of Irish identity in the postcolonial era. A particular focus of any such interrogation should be directed towards those "liminal" zones of culture — a number of which have been considered in this book — those contested spaces at the interstices of Irish identity where Irish Otherness has been formulated. The Irish Other is a conception which should be celebrated and engaged with on a reciprocal level. A respectful dialogue with the Irish Other is all the more important given that the Irishnesss that is Irish Traveller identity — the Traveller Other — is, in reality, an "alterity within identity". It is an alterity that has intersignified with the construct of Irish identity itself. It is a unique identity and one which is analogous with Kristeva's (1991) description of the "stranger" in our midst:

> . . . the stranger is neither a race or a nation . . . we are our own strangers — we are divided selves. (1991: 268)

Bibliography

Acton, T. (1974) *Gypsy Politics and Social Change*, London: Routledge and Kegan Paul.

Acton, T. (1994) "Categorising Irish Travellers" in S. Ó Síocháin et al. (eds.) *Irish Travellers: Culture and Ethnicity*, Belfast: Institute of Irish Studies, Queen's University of Belfast.

Adorno, T. and Horkheimer, M. (eds.) (1973) *Dialectic of Enlightenment*, London: Allen Lane.

Alexander, J. (1988*) Durkheimian Sociology: Cultural Studies*, Cambridge: Cambridge University Press.

Althusser, L. (1971) *Lenin and Philosophy, and Other Essays*, London: Monthly Review Press.

Arensberg C. and Kimball, S. (eds.) (1937) *The Irish Countryman: An Anthropological Study*, London: Macmillan.

Arnold, F. (1898) "Our Old Poets and the Tinkers" in *Journal of American Folklore*, Vol. 11, pp. 210–20.

Arnold, H. (1958) *Vaganten, Komodianten, Fieranten und Briganten,* Stuttgart: Verlag Georg Thieme.

Arnold, H. (1965) *Die Zigeuner. Herkunft und Leben der Stämme im deutschen Sprachgebiet,* Freiburg: Walter-Verlag.

Ashcroft, B. and Ahluwalia, P. (eds.) (1999) *Edward Said*, London: Routledge.

Ashcroft, B. et al. (eds.) (1995) *The Post-Colonial Studies Reader*, London: Routledge.

Atkinson, P. and Hammersley, M. (eds.) (1992) *Ethnography: Principles in Practice*, London: Routledge.

Babcock, B. (1978) *The Reversible World: Symbolic Inversion in Art and Society*, London: Ithaca.

Bakhtin, M. (1968) *Rabelais and his World*, Massachusetts: MIT Press.

Bakhtin, M. (1981) *The Dialogic Imagination: Four Essays*, Texas: University of Texas Press.

Banton, M. (1998) *Racial Theories*, Cambridge: Cambridge.

Barnes, B. (1975) "Irish Travelling People" in E.F. Rehfisch (ed.) *Gypsies, Tinkers and Other Travellers*, London: Academic Press.

Barry, A. et al. (eds.) (1996) *Foucault and Political Reason: Liberalism, Neo-liberalism and Rationalities of Government*, London: UCL Press.

Barth, F. (1969) *Ethnic Groups and Boundaries*, London: Allen and Unwin.

Barth, F. (1975) *The Social Organisation of a Pariah Group in Norway* in E.F. Rehfisch (ed.) *Gypsies, Tinkers and Other Travellers*, London: Academic Press.

Barth, F. (1995) "Ethnicity and the Concept of Culture", Paper presented to the Conference *Rethinking Culture*, Harvard.

Barthes, R. (1993) *Mythologies*, London: Vintage.

Bartlett, R. (1982) *Gerald of Wales: 1145–1223*, Oxford: Clarendon.

Bateson, G. (1958) *Naven: a survey of the problems suggested by a composite picture of the culture of a New Guinea tribe drawn from three points of view*, Stanford: Stanford University Press.

Battaglia, D. (1995) *Rhetorics of Self-making*, Berkeley: University of California Press.

Bauman, Z. (1991) *Modernity and Ambivalence*, New York: Cornell University Press.

Beckett, S. (1979) *Molloy, Malone Dies, The Unnameable*, London: John Calder.

Beier, A. (1985) *Masterless men: the vagrancy problem in England 1560-1640*, London: Methuen.

Belfast Travellers' Support Group (2000) *In Our Own Way: Tales from Belfast Travellers* (ed. J. Keenan and D. Hines) Belfast: BTSG.

Bergson, H. (1911) *The Idea of Nothing. Creative Evolution*, New York: Rinehart and Winston.

Bergson, H. (1956) "Le Rire" in W. Sypher (ed.) *Comedy*, New York: Doubleday.

Bewley, V. (1974) *Travelling People*, Dublin: Veritas.

Bhabha, H. (1986) "The Other Question: Difference, Discrimination and the Discourse of Colonialism", in F. Barker (ed.) *Literature, Politics and Theory*, London: Methuen.

Bhabha, H. (1990) *Nation and Narration*, London: Routledge.

Bhabha, H. (1994) *The Location of Culture*, London: Routledge.

Bhabha, H. (1996) "The Other Question" in P. Mongia (ed.) *Contemporary Postcolonial Theory: A Reader*, London: Routledge.

Bhreatnach, A. (1998) "Travellers and the print media: words and Irish identity" in *Irish Studies Review*, 6:3.

Binchy, A. (1993) "The Status and Functions of Shelta", Unpublished Ph.D thesis, Oxford: Oxford University.

Binchy, A. (1994) "Travellers' Language: A Sociolinguistic Perspective" in S. Ó Síocháin et al. (eds.) *Irish Travellers: Culture and Ethnicity*, Belfast: Institute of Irish Studies, Queen's University.

Binchy, A. (2002) "Travellers' Use of Shelta" in Kirk and Ó Baoill (eds.) *Travellers and their Language,* Belfast: Cló Ollscoil na Banríona.

Bobcock, R. and Thompson, K. (eds.) (1985) *Religion and Ideology*, Manchester: Manchester University Press.

Boyce, D.G. (1996) *The Irish Question in British Politics, 1868–1996*, second edition, Basingstoke: Macmillan.

Brady, P. (2001) *Paveewhack*, Dublin: New Island.

Breathnach, R.B. (1947) *The Irish of Ring, Co. Waterford*, Dublin: Dublin Institute for Advanced Studies.

Breen et al. (1990) *Understanding Contemporary Ireland: State, Class and Development in the Irish Republic*, Dublin: Gill and Macmillan.

Burke, K. (1961) *The Rhetoric of Religion: Studies in Logology*, Boston: Beacon Press.

Burke, K. (1964) *Permanency and Change: An Anatomy of Purpose*, California: Hermes.

Burke, K. (1968) "A Dramatistic View of the Origins of Language and Postscripts on the Negative." in *Language as Symbolic Action: Essays on Life, Literature and Method,* Berkeley: University of California Press.

Burke, P. (1978) *Popular Culture in Early Modern Europe*, London: Temple Smith.

Cairns, D. and Richards, S. (eds.) (1990) *Writing Ireland: Colonialism, Nationalism and Culture*, Manchester: Manchester University Press.

Campbell, D. (1910) *Reminiscences and Reflections of an Octogenarian Highlander*, Inverness: The Northern Counties Newspaper and Printing and Publishing Company.

Campion, E. (1963) *Two Bokes of the Histories of Ireland*, Assen: Van Gorcum.

Canny, N. (1973) "The Ideology of English Colonisation from Ireland to America", *William and Mary Quarterly*, 30: 581–596.

Cardoso, C. (1971) "Die Flucht nach Agypten in der mundlichen portugiesischen Uberlieferung", *Fabula*, 12.

Carney, J. (1967) *The Irish Bardic Poet*, Dublin: Dolmen Press.

Cauley, W. and Ó hAodha, M. (2005) *Canting with Cauley*, Dublin: A. & A. Farmar.

Cauley, W. and Ó hAodha, M. (ed.) (2004). *The Candlelight Painter: The Life and Work of Willy Cauley, Traveller, Painter and Poet*, Dublin: A. and A. Farmar.

Charny, I. (ed.) (1999) *Encyclopaedia of Genocide*, Santa Barbara, California: ABC-CLIO.

Chatard, M. et al. (eds.) (1959) *Zanko, Chef Tribal*, Paris: Le Vieux Colombier.

Chatwin, B. (1987) *The Songlines,* London: The Picador Press.

Cheng, V. (1995) *Joyce, Race, and Empire*, Cambridge: Cambridge University Press.

Chowers, E. (2000) "Narrating the Modern's Subjection: Freud's Theory of the Oedipal Complex", *History of the Human Sciences*, Vol. 13, No. 3, pp. 23–45.

Cixous, H. (1975) *La Jeune Née*, Paris: U.G.É.

Clancy, P. et al. (eds.) (1986), *Ireland, A Sociological Profile,* Dublin: Institute of Public Administration.

Clébert, J-P. (1963) *The Gypsies,* London: Penguin.

Cohn, W. (1973) *The Gypsies*, London: Addison-Wesley.

Colie, R. (1966) *Paradoxia Epidemica: the Renaissance Tradition of Paradox,* New Jersey: Princeton University Press.

Collins, M. (1994) "The Sub-Culture of Poverty: A Response to McCarthy" in S. Ó Síocháin et al. (eds.), *Irish Travellers: Culture and Ethnicity*, Belfast: The Institute of Irish Studies, The Queen's University of Belfast.

Commission on Itinerancy (1963) *Report of the Commission on Itinerancy*, Dublin: The Stationery Office.

Conners, G. (2000) "Gerry Conners" in Hines and Keenan (eds.), *In Our Own Way: Tales from Belfast Travellers*, Belfast: Belfast Traveller Support Group.

Corner, J. and Hawthorn, J. (eds.) (1994) *Communication Studies*, London: Edward Arnold.

Cottaar, A. et al. (eds.) (1998) *Gypsies and Other Itinerant Groups: A Socio-Historical Approach*, London: Macmillan Press.

Court, A. (1985) *Puck of the Droms: The Lives and Literature of the Irish Tinkers*, California: University of California Press.

Cox, H. (1970) *The Feast of Fools: A Theological Essay on Festivity and Fantasy,* New York: Harper and Row.

Crawford, M. (1976) "Genetic Affinities and Origin of Irish Tinkers" in G. Lasker, *Biosocial Interrelations in Population Adaptation*, The Hague: Mouton.

Crawford, M. and Gmelch, G. (1974) "The Human Biology of Irish Tinkers: Demography, Ethnohistory and Genetics", *Social Biology*, 21: pp. 321–31.

Cronin, M. (1996) *Translating Ireland*, Cork: Cork University Press.

Culler, J.D. (1983) *On Deconstruction: Theory and Criticism after Structuralism*, London, Routledge & Kegan Paul.

Curtin, C. et al. (eds.) (1990) *Ireland from Below: Social Change and Local Communities*, Galway: Galway University Press.

Curtis, L. (1984) *Nothing but the Same Old Story: The Roots of Anti-Irish Racism*, London: Information on Ireland.

Curtis, L.P. (1968) *Anglo-Saxons and Celts: A Study of Anti-Irish Prejudice in Victorian England*, Connecticut: University of Bridgeport.

Curtis, L.P. (1997) *Apes and Angels: The Irishman in Victorian Caricature*, Washington: Smithsonian Institute Press.

Dahnhardt, V. (1909*) Natursagen II: Eine Sammlung naturdeutender Sagen, Marchen, Fabeln und Legenden*, Leipzig: B.G. Teubner.

Davis, K. (1975) *Administrative Law and Government*, St. Paul: West Pub. Co.

Davis, N.Z. (1975) *Society and Culture in Early Modern France*, Stanford: Stanford University Press.

de Beauvoir, S. (1972) *The Second Sex*, London: Penguin Books.

de Bhaldraíthe, T. (1959) *English-Irish Dictionary*, Baile Átha Cliath: Oifig an tSoláthair.

de Vaux de Foletier, F. (1961) *Les Tsiganes dans l'Ancienne France*, Paris: Connaissance du Monde.

Degh, L. (1965) *Folktales of Hungary*, London: Routledge and Kegan Paul.

Delaney, P. (2000) "Migrancy and Cultural Disappearance" in P.J. Mathews (ed.), *New Voices in Irish Criticism*, Dublin: Four Courts Press.

Delargy, J. (1942) "The Study of Irish Folklore", *Dublin Magazine*, Vol. XVII, No. 3, pp. 19–26.

Demetz, M. (1987) *Hausierhandel, Hausindustrie und Kunstgewerbe im Grodental*, Innsbruck: Universitätsverlag Wagner.

Derrida, J. (1974) "White Mythology: Metaphor in the Text of Philosophy", *New Literary History,* 6, pp. 5–74.

Derrida, J. (1976) *Of Grammatology*, London: Johns Hopkins University Press.

Derrida, J. (1978) *Writing and Difference*, London: Routledge and Kegan Paul.

Derrida, J. (1982) *Margins of Philosophy*, Chicago: University of Chicago Press.

Détienne, M. (1989) *Dionysos Slain*, Michigan: UMI Out-of-Print Books on Demand.

Diamond, S. (n.d.) "The Primitive and the Civilised", *Tract*, 18, pp. 3–44.

Dillman, A. (1905) *Zigeuner-Buch: Herausgegeben zum amtlichen Gebrauche im Auftrage des K.B. Staatsministeriums des Innern vom Sicherheitsbureau der K. Polizeidirektion München*, München: Dr. Wild'sche Buchdruckerei.

Donahue, N. and Gmelch, S. (eds.) (1986) *Nan: The Life of an Irish Travelling Woman*, London: Souvenir.

Donaldson, I. (1970) *The World Upside Down: Comedy from Jonson to Fielding,* London: Oxford University Press.

Douglas, M. (1966) *Purity and Danger: An Analysis of Concepts of Pollution and Taboo*, London Routledge & Kegan Paul.

du Gay, P. et al. (eds.) (1997) *Doing Cultural Studies: The Story of the Sony Walkman*, London: Sage in association with the Open University.

Dunne, P. and Ó hAodha, M. (eds.) (2004) *Parley-Poet and Chanter: A Life of Pecker Dunne*, Dublin: A. & A. Farmar Publishing.

Durkheim, É. (1954) *The Elementary Forms of the Religious Life*, London: Allen and Unwin.

Durkheim, É. (1938) *The Rules of Sociological Method*, Chicago: Chicago University Press.

Durkheim, E. et al. (eds). (1964) *Essays on Sociology and Philosophy*, London: Harper & Row.

Dymmok, J. (1842) *A Treatice of Ireland*, Dublin: Irish Archaelogical Society.

Eagleton, T. (1988) *Nationalism, Colonialism and Literature: Nationalism, Irony and Commitment,* Derry: Field Day Pamphlets.

Eagleton, T. (1991) *Ideology*, London: Verso.

Ennis, M. (1984) *The Victims*, Dublin: Committee for the Rights of Travellers.

Fanning, Bryan (2002), *Racism and Social Change in the Republic of Ireland*, Manchester and New York: Manchester University Press.

Fanon, F. (1986) *Black Skin, White Masks*, London: Pluto.

Faubion, James (1994) *Power: Michel Foucault, Essential Works of Foucault 1954–1984*, London: Penguin.

Fay, R. (1992) *Minorization of Travelling Groups and their Cultural Rights*, Dublin: Pavee Point Publications.

Finlay, T. (1893) "The Jew in Ireland", *The Lyceum*, VI, 70, pp. 215–18.

Fisher, S. (ed.) (1958) *Body Image and Personality*, Princeton: Van Nostrand.

Fitzgerald, G. (1992) *Repulsing Racism: Reflections on Racism and the Irish*, Dublin: Attic Press.

Flower, R. (1957) "Measgra ón Oileán Tiar", *Béaloideas*, Iml. XXV, p. 71.

Forgacs, D. (ed.) (1985) *Antonio Gramsci: Selections from Cultural Writings*, London: Lawrence and Wishart.

Foster, R. (1988) *Modern Ireland 1600–1972*, London: Allen Lane.

Foucault, M. "Theatrum Philosopicum", *Critique*, 282: pp. 885–908.

Foucault, M. (1977) *Discipline and Punish: The Birth of the Prison*, New York: Pantheon Books.

Foucault, M. (1979) *The History of Sexuality*, London: Allen Lane.

Foucault, M. (1981) "The Order of Discourse" in R. Yang (ed.) *Untying the Text*, London: Routledge.

Foucault, M. (1984) *The Archaelogy of Knowledge*, London: Tavistock Press.

Foucault, M. (1985a) *The History of Sexuality, Volume 1: An Introduction*, London: Allen Lane.

Foucault, M. (1985b) *The Use of Pleasure: The History of Sexuality, Volume 2*. London: Penguin.

Fraser, A. (1995) *The Gypsies*, Oxford: Blackwell.

Freire, P. (1970) *Cultural Action for Freedom*, Massachusetts: MIT Press.

Freud, S. (1938) *The Basic Writings of Sigmund Freud*, New York: The Modern Library.

Freud, S. (1950a) "Negation" in J. Strachey (ed.) *Collected Papers,* London: Hogarth Press, Vol. 5, pp. 181–85.

Freud, S. (1950b) *Totem and Taboo*, London: Routledge.

Freud, S. (1957) *Collected Papers*, London: Hogarth Press.

Frisbe, C. (1980) *Southwestern Indian Ritual Drama*, Albuquerque: University of New Mexico Press.

Fyfe, H. (1998) *Drama as Structure and Sign*, PhD, University of Limerick.

Gaster, M. (1923) "Rumanian Popular Legends of the Virgin Mary", *Folklore*, 34, pp. 45–85.

Geertz, C. (1966) *Person, Time and Conduct in Bali: An Essay in Cultural Analysis*, New Haven: Yale University Press.

Geertz, C. (1986) *The Uses of Diversity*, Massachusetts: Tanner.

Geremek, B. (1992) *The Idea of a Civil Society*, New York: National Humanities Center.

Gluckman, M. (1965) *Politics, Law and Ritual Tribal Society*, Oxford: Basil Blackwell.

Gmelch, G. (1977) *Tinkers and Travellers: The Urbanisation of an Itinerant People*, California: Cummings.

Gmelch, G. (1985) *The Irish Tinkers: The Urbanisation of an Itinerant People*, California: Waveland Press.

Gmelch, G. and Gmelch S. (eds.) (1976) "The Emergence of an Ethnic Group: The Irish Tinkers", *Anthropological Quarterly*, 6(3), pp. 225–38.

Gmelch, G. and Kroup, B. (eds.) (1978) *To Shorten the Road: Travellers' Folktales from Ireland*, Dublin: O'Brien Press.

Gmelch, S.B. (1974) *The Emergence and Persistence of an Ethnic Group: The Irish "Travellers"*, PhD, Santa Barbara: University of California.

Gmelch, S.B. (1975) *Tinkers and Travellers: Ireland's Nomads*, Dublin: O'Brien Press.

Gmelch, S.B. (1990) "From Poverty Subculture to Political Lobby: The Traveller Rights Movement in Ireland" in Curtin and Wilson (eds.), *Ireland from Below: Social Change and Local Communities*, Galway: Galway University Press.

Gorman, Bartley (with Peter Walsh) (2002) *King of the Gypsies: Memoirs of the Undefeated Bareknuckle Champion of Great Britain and Ireland*, Bury, UK: Milo Books.

Graham, C. and Hooper, G. (eds.) *Irish and Postcolonial Writing*, UK: Palgrave Macmillan.

Graham, C. and Kirkland, J. (eds.) (1999) *Ireland and Cultural Theory*, Basingstoke: Macmillan Press.

Gramsci, A. (1971) *Selections from Prison Notebooks*, London: Lawrence and Wishart.

Grant, A. (1994) "Shelta: The Secret Language of Irish Travellers viewed as a Mixed Language" in M. Mous (ed.) *Mixed Languages: 15 Case Studies in Language Intertwining,* Amsterdam: Uitgave IFOTT, pp. 123–50.

Great Britain, Commissioners for inquiring into the condition of the poorer classes in Ireland (1835–36) *First Report from His Majesty's Commissioners for inquiring into the condition of the poorer classes in Ireland (with Appendix (A.) and supplement,* London: Ordered, by the House of Commons, to be printed, 8 July 1835.

Greenblatt, S. (1980) *The Improvisation of Power,* Chicago: University of Chicago Press.

Greenblatt, S. (1984) *Renaissance Self-Fashioning,* Chicago: University of Chicago Press.

Greene, D. (1954) "Early Irish Society" in M. Dillon (ed.) *Early Irish Society,* Dublin: Published for the Cultural Relations Committee of Ireland at the Sign of the Three Candles.

Gregory, A. (1974) *Poets and Dreamers: Studies and Translations from the Irish; Lady Augusta Gregory, including [translations of] nine plays by Douglas Hyde,* UK: Colin Smythe.

Grellmann, H. (1783) *Historischer Versuch uber die Zigeuner,* Gottingen: J. Dieterich.

Grellmann, H. (1787) *Dissertation on the Gipsies: being an historical enquiry, concerning the manner of life, family economy, customs and conditions of these people in Europe, and their origin,* London: G. Bigg.

Griffin, C. (1999) "Pollution Concepts and Purity Practices among Irish Travellers: The Outcasts of Ireland and Britain", Paper presented to the 86th Indian Science Congress, Chennai, January.

Gronemeyer, R. (1987) *Zigeuner im Spiegel früher Chroniken und Abhandlungen: Quellen vom 15. bis zum 18. Jahrhundert.* Giessen: Focus.

Groome, F.H. (1880) *In Gipsy Tents,* Edinburgh: William P. Nimmo.

Halifax, J. (1982) *Shaman, The Wounded Healer,* London: Thames and Hudson.

Hall, S. (1997) "The Spectacle of the 'Other'" in S. Hall (ed.) *Representation: Cultural Representations and Signifying Practices,* London: Sage Publications.

Hall, S. (1997) *Representation: Cultural Representations and Signifying Practices.* London: Sage in association with the Open University.

Halliday, M. (1976) in G. Kress (ed.) *Halliday, System and Function in Language,* London: Oxford University Press.

Hamnett, I. (1967) "Ambiguity, Classification and Change: The Function of Riddles", *Man,* 2, pp. 279–92.

Hancock, I. (1987) *The Pariah Syndrome: An Account of Gypsy Slavery and Persecution*, Michigan: Karoma Publishers.

Hancock, I. (1989) "Gypsy History in Germany and Neighboring Lands: A Chronology Leading to the Holocaust and Beyond" in Crowe and Kenrick (eds.) *The Gypsies of Eastern Europe*, Armonk: E.C. Sharpe.

Hancock, I. (1992) "The Roots of Inequity: Romani Cultural Rights in their Historical and Cultural Context", *Immigrants and Minorities*, Vol. 11, No. 1.

Hancock, I. (1999) "The Roma: Myth and Reality", *Patrin Web-Journal*, pp. 1–13.

Handleman, D. (1981) "The Ritual Clown: Attributes and Affinities", *Anthropos*, 76, pp. 321–70.

Hannaford, I (1996) *Race: The History of an Idea in the West*, Washington, DC: Woodrow Wilson Center Press.

Harper, J. (1977) *The Irish Travellers of Georgia*, MA, University of Georgia.

Harrison, A. (1989) *The Irish Trickster*, Sheffield: Sheffield Academic Press for the Folklore Society.

Hawthorn, G. (1994) *Enlightenment and Despair: A History of Social Theory*, Cambridge: Cambridge University Press.

Healy, T. (1992) *New Latitudes: Theory and English Renaissance Literature*, London: Edward Arnold.

Hegel, G. (1910) *The Phenomenology of Mind*, London: Swan Sonnenschein.

Helleiner, J. (1998) *The Travelling People: Cultural Identity in Ireland*, PhD, University of Toronto.

Helleiner, J. (2000) *Irish Travellers: Racism and the Politics of Culture*, Toronto: University of Toronto Press.

Henderson, W. (1879) *Notes on the Folk-Lore of the Northern Counties of England and the Borders,* London: W. Satchell, Peyton and Co. for the Folk-Lore Society.

Henry, G. (1992), *The Irish Military Community in Spanish Flanders 1586–1621*, Dublin: Irish Academic Press.

Heymowski, A. (1969) *Swedish "Travellers" and their Ancestry: A Social Isolate or an Ethnic Minority?,* Uppsala: Almqvist and Wiksell.

Hieb, L. (1972) "Meaning and Mismeaning: Towards an Understanding of the Ritual Clown" in A. Ortiz (ed.) *New Perspectives on the Pueblos,* Albuquerque: University of New Mexico Press.

Hill, C. (1970) *God's Englishman: Oliver Cromwell and the English Revolution*, London: Weidenfeld and Nicholson.

Hughes, K. (1967) "The Golden Age of Early Christian Ireland" in T. Moody (ed.) *The Course of Irish History,* Cork: Mercier Press.

Husband, C. (1982) *"Race" in Britain: Continuity and Change*, London: Hutchinson.

Hyland, J. (ed.) (1993) *Do You Know Us At All?* Dublin: Parish of the Travelling People.

Inglis, Tom (1998), *Moral Monopoly: The Rise and Fall of the Catholic Church in Modern Ireland*, Dublin: University College Press.

Jameson, F. (1981) *The Political Unconscious: Narrative as a Socially Symbolic Act*, London: Methuen.

Jennings, S. (1995) *Theatre, Ritual and Transformation*, London: Routledge.

Johnson, P. (1980) *Ireland: a History from the Twelfth Century to the Present Day*, London: Eyre Methuen.

Jones, J. and Hanham, R. (1995) "Contingency, Realism, and the Expansion Method", *Geographical Analysis*, 27, pp. 185–207.

Joyce, N. (1985) *Traveller: An Autobiography*, Dublin: Gill and Macmillan.

Joyce, P. (1994) *Democratic Subjects: The Self and the Social in Nineteenth-Century England*, Cambridge: Cambridge University Press.

Jusserand, J.J. (1889) *English Wayfaring Life in the Middle Ages*, London: Ernest Benn.

Kamen, H. (1986) *European Society 1500–1700*, London: Hutchinson.

Kayser, W. (1963) *The Grotesque in Art and Literature*, Bloomington, Indiana: Indiana University Press.

Kealinohomoku, J. (1980) "The Drama of the Hopi Ogres" in C. Frisbe (ed.), *Southern Indian Ritual Drama*, Albuquerque: University of New Mexico Press.

Keenan, M. (2000) "Molly Keenan" in Hines and Keenan (ed.), *In Our Own Way: Tales from Belfast Travellers*, Belfast: Belfast Traveller Support Group.

Kenny, M. (1996) *The Routes of Resistance: Travellers and Second-level Schooling*, PhD, Trinity College Dublin.

Kenrick, D. and Puxon, G. (eds.) (1972) *The Destiny of Europe's Gypsies*, London: Sussex University Press in association with Heinemann.

Keogh, D. (1998) *Jews in Twentieth-Century Ireland: Refugees, Anti-Semitism and the Holocaust*, Cork: Cork University Press.

Kephart, W. (1982) *Extraordinary Groups*, New York: St. Martin's Press.

Kerry Traveller Development Project (1996) *Towards Inclusion*, Kerry: Kerry Traveller Development Project.

Khazanov, A. (1995) *After the USSR: Ethnicity, Nationalism and Politics in the Commonwealth of Independent States*, Wisconsin: The University of Wisconsin Press.

Kiberd, D. (1995) *Inventing Ireland*, London: Jonathan Cape.

Kierkegaard, S. (1968) *The Concept of Irony,* Bloomington, Indiana: Indiana University of Press.

Klaar, M. et al. (eds.) (1963) *Christos und das verschenkte Brot. Neugriechische Volkslegenden und Legendenmarchen*, Germany: Kassel.

Klein, M. (1957) *Envy and Gratitude: A Study of Unconscious Sources*, London: Tavistock Publications.

Klein, M. (1960) *Our Adult World and its Roots in Infancy,* London: Tavistock.

Klein, M. (1997) *Envy and Gratitude and Other Works 1946–1963,* London: Vintage.

Koestler, A. (1964) *The Act of Creation*, London: Hutchinson.

Kohler-Zulch, I. (1993) *Die Geshichte der Kreutznagel: Version und Gegenversion? Uberlegungen zur Roma-Varianten* in *Telling Reality. Folklore Studies in memory of Bengt Holbeck*. Copenhagen: M. Chestnutt.

Kristeva J. (1974) *Des Chinoises,* Paris: Éditions des Femmes.

Kristeva, J. (1982) *Powers of Horror*, New York: Columbia University Press.

Kristeva, J. (1991) *Strangers to Ourselves*, New York: Columbia University Press.

Kunzle, D. (1978) "World Upside Down: The Iconography of a European Broadsheet Type" in B. Babcock (ed.) *The Reversible World: Symbolic Inversion in Art and Society*, London: Ithaca.

Lacan, J. (1966) *Écrits 1*, Paris: Editions du Seuil.

Lacan, J. (1971) *Écrits 2*, Paris: Editions du Seuil.

Lacan, J. (1977) *The Four Fundamental Concepts of Psycho-analysis*, London: Hogarth Press.

Laclau, E. (1977) *Politics and Ideology in Marxist Theory: Capitalism, Fascism, Populism*, London: Verso Editions.

Laclau, E. and Mouffe, C. (eds.) (1985) *Hegemony and Socialist Strategy: Towards a Radical Democratic Politics*, London: Verso.

Lash, S. and Urry, J. (eds.) (1994) *The Polity Reader in Cultural Theory*, Cambridge: Polity Press in association with Blackwell Publishers.

Leach, E. (1968) *A Runaway World?* London: Oxford University Press.

Leach, E. (1969) *Genesis as Myth and Other Essays*, London: Jonathan Cape.

Lebow, N. (1973) "British Historians and Irish History", *Éire-Ireland*, Vol. VIII, No. 4.

Lee, J. (1989) *Politics and Society in Ireland 1912–1985*, Cambridge: Cambridge University Press.

Leerssen, J. (1996) *Mere Irish and Fíor-Ghael: Studies in the Idea of Irish Nationality, its Development and Literary Expression prior to the Nineteenth Century*, Cork: Cork University Press.

Leland, C. (1882) *The Gypsies*, Boston: Houghton, Mifflin and Company.

Leland, C. (1891) "Shelta", *Journal of the Gypsy Lore Society*, 2(4), pp. 321–3.

Lentin, R. and and McVeigh, R. (eds.) (2002) *Racism and Anti-Racism in Ireland*, Belfast: BTP Publications.

Lévinas, E. (1961) *Totalité et Infini: Essai sur l'Extériorité*, La Haye: M. Nijhoff.

Lévinas, E. (1969) *Totality and Infinity: An Essay on Exteriority*, Pittsburgh: Duquesne University Press.

Lévinas, E. (1996) *Basic Philosophical Writings: Emmanuel Levinas*, Bloomington, Indiana: Indiana University Press.

Lévi-Strauss, C. (1964) *Mythologiques*, Paris: Plon.

Lévi-Strauss, C. (1971) *L'Homme Nu,* Paris: Plon.

Lewis, O. (1963) *Life in a Mexican Village: Tepoztlán Re-studied,* Urbana: University of Illinois Press.

Liégeois, J-P. (1987) *Gypsies and Travellers: Socio-Cultural Data, Socio-Political Data,* Council for Cultural Cooperation, Council of Europe.

Liégeois, J-P. (1994) *Roma, Gypsies, Travellers,* Strasbourg: Council of Europe.

Lis, C. and Hugo, S. (1979) *Poverty and Capitalism in Pre-Industrial Europe*, London: Humanities Press.

Lofgren, O. (1993) *The Cultural Grammar of Nation-Building* in R. Kvideland et al. *Nordic Frontiers*, Turku: Nordic Institute of Folklore.

Lombroso, C. (1918) *Crime: Its Causes and Remedies*, Boston: Little Brown and Co.

Longley, E. (1994) *The Living Stream: Literature and Revisionism in Ireland,* Newcastle-upon-Tyne: Bloodaxe Books.

Lucassen, J. (1987) *Migrant Labour in Europe between 1600 and 1900: The Drift to the North Sea*, Beckenham: Croom Helm.

Lyotard, J-F. (1984) *The Postmodern Condition: A Report on Knowledge*, Manchester: Manchester University Press.

Macalister, R.A.S. (1937) *The Secret Languages of Ireland, with special reference to the origin and nature of the Shelta language: partly based upon collections and manuscripts of the late John Sampson,* Cambridge: Cambridge University Press.

Mac Cana, P. (1970) *Celtic Mythology*, London: Chancellor.

McCarthy, P. (1971) *Itinerancy and Poverty: A Study in the Sub-Culture of Poverty*, MA, University College Dublin.

McCarthy, P. (1994) "The Sub-Culture of Poverty Reconsidered" in S. Ó Síocháin et al. (eds.) *Irish Travellers: Culture and Ethnicity*, Belfast: Institute of Irish Studies, Queen's University.

McCormick, A. (1907) *The Tinkler Gypsies*, Dumfries, Scotland: Maxwell.

McDonagh, M. (1994) "Nomadism in Irish Travellers' Identity", in S. Ó Síocháin et al. (eds.) *Irish Travellers: Culture and Ethnicity*, Belfast: Institute of Irish Studies, Queen's University.

McDonagh, M. (2000a) "Nomadism", in E. Sheehan (ed.) *Travellers: Citizens of Ireland*, Dublin: Parish of the Travelling People.

McDonagh, M. (2000b) "Origins of the Travelling People", in E. Sheehan (ed.) *Travellers: Citizens of Ireland*, Dublin: Parish of the Travelling People.

McDonagh, M. (2000c) "Ethnicity and Culture", in E. Sheehan (ed.) *Travellers: Citizens of Ireland*, Dublin: Parish of the Travelling People.

McDonagh, M. and McDonagh, W. (1993) "Nomadism" in J. Hyland (ed.), *Do You Know Us At All?* Dublin: Parish of the Travelling People.

McDonagh, M. and McVeigh, R. (eds.) (1996) *Minceir Neeja in the Thome Munkra: Irish Travellers in the USA,* Belfast: Belfast Travellers Education and Development Group.

McGrath, S. (1955) *Miscellaneous Information on Tinkers, particularly in County Clare*, Irish Folklore Commission.

MacGréil, M. (1996) *Prejudice in Ireland Revisited*, Dublin: Survey and Research Unit, St Patrick's College, Maynooth.

MacGréil, M. (1977) Prejudice and Tolerance in Ireland, Dublin: Research Section, College of Industrial Relations.

MacGréine, P. (1931) "Irish Tinkers or 'Travellers', Some Notes on their Manners and Customs, and their Secret Language or 'Cant'", *Béaloideas: the Journal of the Folklore of Ireland Society*, Vol. 3 (1), pp. 170–81.

MacGréine, P. (1932) "Irish Tinkers or 'Travellers'", *Béaloideas: the Journal of the Folklore of Ireland Society*, Vol. 3 (2), pp. 170–86.

MacGréine, P. (1932) "Further Notes on Tinkers' 'Cant'", *Béaloideas: the Journal of the Folklore of Ireland Society*, Vol. 3 (3), pp. 290–303.

MacGréine, P. (1934) "Some Notes on Tinkers and their 'Cant'", *Béaloideas: the Journal of the Folklore of Ireland Society*, Vol. 4 (3), pp. 259–63.

MacLachlan, M. and O'Connell, M. (eds.) (1999) *Cultivating Pluralism: Psychological, Social and Cultural Perspectives on a Changing Ireland*, Dublin: Oak Tree Press.

MacLaughlin, J. (1995) *Travellers and Ireland: Whose Country, Whose History?* Cork: Cork University Press.

MacLaughlin, J. (1996) "Travellers are still Victims of a Victorian Image of Society", *Sunday Tribune*, 12 September.

MacLean, E. et al. (1995) *Selected Works of Gayatri Chakravorty Spivak*, London: Routledge.

McLoughlin, D. (1994). "Ethnicity and Irish Travellers: Reflections on Ní Shúinéar" in S. Ó Síocháin et al. (eds.) *Irish Travellers: Culture and Ethnicity*, Belfast: Institute of Irish Studies, Queen's University.

MacMahon, B. (1971) "A Portrait of Tinkers", *Natural History*, Vol. 80, No. 10.

Mac Neill, E. (1919) *Phases in Irish History*, Dublin: M.H. Gill.

MacRitchie, D. (1889) "Irish Tinkers and their Language", *Journal of the Gypsy Lore Society*, Vol. 1(6), pp. 350–7.

McVeigh, R. (1992a) "The Specificity of Irish Racism", *Race and Class*, Vol. 33, No. 4, pp. 31–45.

McVeigh, R. (1992b) *Racism and Travelling People in Northern Ireland*, 17th Report of the Standing Advisory Commission on Human Rights.

McVeigh, R. (1994) "Theorising Sedentarism: The Roots of Anti-Nomadism", Paper for ESRC Romani Studies Seminar, University of Greenwich, Belfast: Campaign for Research and Documentation.

McVeigh, R. (1996) *The Racialisation of Irishness: Racism and Anti-Racism in Ireland*, Belfast: Campaign for Research and Documentation.

McVeigh, R. (1997) "Theorising Sedentarism: The Roots of Anti-Nomadism" in T. Acton (ed.) *Gypsy Politics and Traveller Identity*, UK: University of Hertfordshire Press.

Maffesoli, M. (1993a) "Introduction", *Current Sociology*, Vol. 41(2), pp. 1–6.

Maffesoli, M. (1993b) *The Shadow of Dionysus: A Contribution to the Study of the Orgy*, Albany: State University of New York Press.

Maher, S. (1972) *The Road to God Knows Where*, Dublin: Talbot Press.

Mahr, A. (1943) "The Gypsy at the Crucifixion of Christ", *Ohio Journal of Science*, Vol. 43, pp. 17–21.

Malik, K. (1996) *The Meaning of Race: Race, History and Culture in Western Society*, Basingstoke: Macmillan.

Mariani, E. et al. (1989) *Remaking History*, Seattle: Bay Press.

Marx, K. (1965) *Pre-Capitalist Economic Formations*, New York: International Publishers.

Maxwell, C. (1923) *Irish History from Contemporary Sources, 1509-1610*, London: George Allen & Unwin.

Mayall, D. (1982) *Itinerant Minorities in England and Wales in the Nineteenth and Early Twentieth Centuries: A Study of Gypsies, Tinkers, Hawkers and Other Travellers*, PhD, University of Sheffield.

Mayall, D. (1988) *Gypsy-Travellers in Nineteenth-Century Society*, Cambridge: Cambridge University Press.

Mayall, D. (2004) *Gypsy Identities 1500–2000: From Egipcyans and Moon-men to the Ethnic Romany*, London: Routledge.

Mercer, K. (1994) *Welcome to the Jungle: New Positions in Black Cultural Studies*, London: Routledge.

Meyer, K. (1891) "On the Irish Origin and Age of Shelta", *Journal of the Gypsy Lore Society*, Vol. 2, pp. 257–66.

Meyer, K. (1909) "The Secret Languages of Ireland", *Journal of the Gypsy Lore Society*, New Series, Vol. 2 (3), pp. 241–6.

Middleton, J. (1960) *Lugbara Religion*, Oxford: Oxford University Press.

Miege, G. (1715) *The Present State of Great Britain and Ireland*, London: J. Nicholson.

Miles, R. (1989) *Racism,* London: Routledge.

Mitchell, S. and Black, A. (eds.) (1995) *Freud and Beyond: A History of Modern Psychoanalytic Thought*, New York: Basic Books.

Mitchell, T. (1994) *Flamenco Deep Song*, New Haven: Yale University Press.

Mongan, B. (2000) "Bernie Mongan" in Hines and Keenan (ed.), *In Our Own Words: Tales from Belfast Travellers,* Belfast: Belfast Traveller Support Group.

Mongia, P. (1996) *Contemporary Postcolonial Theory: A Reader*, London: Arnold.

Montagu, A. (1972) *Statement on Race*, Oxford: Oxford University Press.

Moore, R.I. (1987) *The Formation of a Persecuting Society: Power and Deviance in Western Europe, 950–1250*, Oxford: Basil Blackwell.

Moore-Gilbert, B. (ed.) (1983) *Literature and Imperialism: A Conference Organised by the English Department of the Roehampton Institute in February 1983*, London: English Department of the Roehampton Institute of Higher Education.

Moore-Gilbert, B. (1997) *Postcolonial Theory: Context, Practices, Politics*, London: Verso.

Moore-Gilbert, G. and Colwell, D. (eds.) (1998) *Empire and Literature*, London: University of London.

Moryson, F. (1617) *An Itinerary Written by Fynes Moryson Gent*, Glasgow: James MacLehose.

Mudimbe, V. (1988) *The Invention of Africa: Gnosis, Philosophy and the Order of Things*, Indianapolis: Indiana University Press.

Mudimbe, V. (1994) *The Idea of Africa*, Indianopolis: Indiana University Press.

Myerhoff, B. (1982) "Rites of Passage: Process and Paradox", in V. Turner (ed.) *Celebration: Studies in Festivity and Ritual*, Washington: Smithsonian Institution Press.

Nandy, A. (1983) *The Intimate Enemy*, Delhi: Oxford University Press.

Neat, T. (1996) *The Summer Walkers: Travelling People and Pearl-Fishers in the Highlands of Scotland*, Edinburgh: Canongate Books.

Needham, R. (1963) "Introduction" in Durkheim and Mauss (eds.) *Primitive Classification*, London: Cohen and West.

Needham, R. (ed). (1973) *Right and Left: Essays on Dual Symbolic Classification*, Chicago: University of Chicago Press.

Ní Shúinéar, S. (1994) "Irish Travellers, Ethnicity and the Origins Question" in S. Ó Síocháin et al. (eds.) *Irish Travellers: Culture and Ethnicity*, Belfast: Institute of Irish Studies, Queen's University.

Norbeck, E. (1963) "African Rituals of Conflict", *American Anthropologist*, 65, pp. 1254–1279.

Ó Baoill, D.P. (1994) "Travellers' Cant: Language or Register?" in S. Ó Síocháin et al. (eds.) *Irish Travellers: Culture and Ethnicity*, Belfast: Institute of Irish Studies, Queen's University.

O'Boyle, M.B. (1990) *The Alienation of Travellers from the Education System: A Study in Value Orientations*, M.Ed Thesis (Unpublished), National University of Ireland, Maynooth.

O'Connell, J. (1992a) "Working with Irish Travellers" in *DTEG File*, Dublin: Pavee Point Publications.

O'Connell, J. (1992b) "The Need for Imagination in Work with Irish Travellers", in *DTEDG File*, Dublin: Pavee Point Publications.

O'Connell, J. (1994a) *Reach Out: Report on the "Poverty 3" Programme, 1990-94*, Dublin: Pavee Point Publications.

O'Connell, J. (1994b) "Ethnicity and Irish Travellers" in S. Ó Síocháin et al. (eds.) *Irish Travellers: Culture and Ethnicity*, Belfast: Institute of Irish Studies, Queen's University.

O'Connell, J. (1995) "Travellers and History" in N. Ní Laodhóg (ed.) *A Heritage Ahead: Cultural Action and Travellers*, Dublin: Pavee Point Publications.

O'Connell, J. (1997) *Travellers, Gypsies, Roma*, Dublin: Pavee Point .

Ó Dónaill, N. (eag). (1977) *Foclóir Gaeilge-Béarla*, Baile Átha Cliath: Oifig an tSoláthair.

O'Dowd, A. (1987) *Migratory Agricultural Workers*, PhD, University College Dublin.

Ó Duilearga, S. (1977) *Leabhar Sheáin Í Chonaill: Sgéalta agus Seanchas ó Íbh Ráthach,* Baile Átha Cliath: Comhairle Bhéaloideas Éireann.

Ó Fearadhaigh, M. and Wiedel, J. (eds.) (1976) *Irish Tinkers*, London: Latimer New Dimensions Ltd.

Ó Floinn, B. (1995) "Travellers and the Oral Tradition", in N. Ní Laodhóg (ed.) *A Heritage Ahead: Cultural Action and Travellers,* Dublin: Pavee Point Publications.

Ó Giolláin, D. (2000) *Locating Irish Folklore: Tradition, Modernity, Identity*, Cork: Cork University Press.

Ó hAodha, M. (2001) "Teanga an Lucht Siúil: Cad atá i nDán di?" in Ó hUigínn agus MacCóil (eag.) *Bliainiris, 2001*, Meath: Carbad.

Ó hAodha, M. (2002a) "Travellers' Language: Some Irish Language Perspectives", in Kirk and Ó Baoill (eds.) *Travellers and their Language,* Belfast: Cló Ollscoil na Banríona.

Ó hAodha, M. (2002b) "Exoticising the Gypsies: The Case of Scott Macfie and the Gypsilorists" in Kirk and Ó Baoill (eds.), *Travellers and their Language,* Belfast: Cló Ollscoil na Banríona.

Ó hAodha, M. (2002c). "Tionchar na Gaeilge ar Shelta Lucht Taistil", in Ó hUigínn agus MacCóil (eag.) *Bliainiris, 2002*, Meath: Carbad.

Ó Héalaí, P. (1977) "Moral Values in Irish Religious Tales", *Béaloideas: The Journal of the Folklore of Ireland Society*, 42–44, pp. 176–212.

Ó Héalaí, P. (1985) "Tuirse na nGaibhne ar na Buachaillí Bó: Scéal Apacrafúil Dúchasach", *Béaloideas*, 53, pp. 87–129.

Ó hÓgáin, D. (1982) *An File: Staidéar ar Ósnádúrthacht na Filíochta sa Traidisiún Gaelach*, Baile Átha Cliath: Oifig an tSoláthair.

Ó hÓgáin, D. (1985) *The Hero in Irish Folk History*, Dublin: Gill and Macmillan.

Okely, J. (1975) "Gypsies Travelling in Southern England" in E.F. Rehfisch (ed.) *Gypsies, Tinkers and Other Travellers*, London: Academic Press.

Okely, J. (1983) *The Traveller-Gypsies*, Cambridge: Cambridge University Press.

Okely, J. (1984) "Ethnic Identity and Place of Origin: The Traveller Gypsies in Great Britain" in J. Vermeulen (ed.) *Ethnic Challenge: The Politics and Ethnicity of Europe*, Gottingen: Edition Herodot.

Okely, J. (1994) "An Anthropological Perspective on Irish Travellers." in S. Ó Síocháin et al. (eds.) *Irish Travellers: Culture and Ethnicity*, Belfast: Institute of Irish Studies, Queen's University.

O'Meara, J.J. (1982) *The History and Topography of Ireland, Gerald of Wales*, Harmondsworth: Penguin.

Ó Muirithe, D. and Nuttall, D. (eds.) (1999) *Folklore of County Wexford*, Dublin: Four Courts Press.

Ó Nualláin, S. and Forde, M. (1992) *Changing Needs of Irish Travellers: Health, Education and Social Issues*, Galway: Woodlands Centre.

O'Reilly, M. and Kenny, M. (eds). (1994) *Black Stones around Green Shamrock*, Dublin: Blackrock Teachers Centre.

Ó Riain, S. (2000) *Solidarity with Travellers: A Story of Settled People Making a Stand for Travellers*, Dublin: Roadside Books.

Ó Síocháin, S. et al. (eds.) *Irish Travellers: Culture and Ethnicity*, Belfast: Institute of Irish Studies, Queen's University.

Ó Súilleabháin, S. (1942) *A Handbook of Irish Folklore*, Dublin: Folklore of Ireland Society.

Ó Súilleabháin, S. (1970) *A Handbook of Irish Folklore*, Detroit: Singing Tree Press.

Ó Súilleabháin, S. (1977) *Legends from Ireland*, London: Batsford.

O'Toole, E.B. (1972) *An Analysis of the Life Style of the Travelling People of Ireland*, M.Phil., New York University.

O'Toole, Electa Bachman (1973) "An Analysis of the Life Style of the Travelling People of Ireland" in *Journal of the Gypsy Lore Society*, 3rd series, Vol. LI, July/October, pp. 54–80.

Partridge, A. (1983) *Caoineadh na dTrí Muire: Téama na Páise i bhFilíocht Bhéil na Gaeilge*, Baile Átha Cliath: An Clóchomhar Tta.

Pavee Point (1992a) "Anti-Racist Law and the Travellers" in *DTEDG File*, Dublin: Pavee Point Publications.

Pavee Point (1992a) *Traveller Ways, Traveller Words*, Dublin: Pavee Point.

Pavee Point (1994) *Nomadism, Now and Then*, Dublin: Pavee Point.

Peacock, J. (1968) "Society as Narrative" in R.F. Spencer (ed.) *Forms of Symbolic Action*, Washington: Washington University Press.

Peart, S.A. (2001) *English Images of the Irish 1570-1620,* PhD, University of Limerick.

Peart, S.A. (2002) *English Images of the Irish 1570–1620*, Wales: The Edwin Mellen Press.

Phipps, A. (1986) *The Adult Traveller: An Unknown Species (A Study of Traveller People as an Ethnic Group)*, privately circulated, Dublin.

Platinga, C. (1995) *Not the Way It's Supposed to Be: A Breviary of Sin*, Michigan: Eerdmans.

Plumb, J.H. (1969) *England in the Eighteenth Century (1714–1815)*, London: Penguin.

Porter, B. (1983) *Britain, Europe and the World 1850–1982: Delusions of Grandeur*, London: Allen & Unwin.

Pound, J. (ed.) (1971) *The Norwich Census of the Poor, 1570*, Norfolk: Norfolk Record Society.

Power, C. (2004) *Room to Roam: England's Irish Travellers*, London: Action Group for Irish Youth.

Puxon, G. (1967) *The Victims (Itinerants in Ireland)*, Dublin: ITM.

Quinn, D.B. (1966) *The Elizabethans and the Irish*, New York: Ithaca.

Quintana, B. and Floyd, L. (eds.) (1972*) Qué Gitano: Gypsies of Southern Spain*, New York: Rinehart and Winston.

Ranelagh, J. (1981) *Ireland: An Illustrated History*, London: Collins.

Ricoeur, P. (1992) *Oneself as Another*, Chicago: University of Chicago Press.

Ritter, R. (1937) *Ein Menschenschlag*, Leipzig: Georg Thieme.

Ritter, R. (1938) "Zur Frage der Rassenbiologie und Rassenpsychologie der Zigeuner in Deutschland", *Reichgesundheitsblatt,* No. 22, pp. 425–6.

Ritter, R. (1941) "Die Asozialen, ihre Vorfahren und ihre Nachkommen", *Fortschritte der Erbpathologie, Rassenhygiene und ihrer Grenzgebiete,* Vol. V, No. 4, pp. 137–55.

Roberts, S. (1836) *The Gypsies,* London: Longmans.

Roinn Béaloideasa Éireann (1952) *IFC Tinker Questionnaire,* Baile Átha Cliath: UCD Collection.

Rokala, K. (1973) *A Catalogue of Religious Legends in the Folklore Archive of the Finnish Literature Society,* Turku: Finnish Literature Society.

Rose, Nicholas (1996) "Identity, Genelaogy, History" in du Gay, P. and Hall, S. (eds.) *Questions of Cultural Identity,* London: Sage.

Rubenstein, J. (1975) *Structual Ambivalence in Ritual Drama,* PhD, New School of Social Research, New York.

Said, E. (1978) *Orientalism,* London: Penguin.

Said, E. (1986) *Literature and Society,* Baltimore: Johns Hopkins University Press.

Said, E. (1989) "Yeats and Decolonization", in P. Kruger (ed.), *Remaking History,* Seattle: Bay Press.

Said, E. (1993) *Culture and Imperialism,* London: Chatto and Windus.

Sales, R. (1983) *English Literature in History 1780–1830: Pastoral and Politics,* London: Hutchinson.

Salgado, G. (ed.) (1972) *Cony-Catchers and Bawdy Baskets: An Anthology of Elizabethan Low Life,* Harmondsworth: Penguin.

Sampson, J. (1891) "Tinkers and their Talk", *Journal of the Gypsy Lore Society,* Vol. 2, pp. 204–21.

Schroeder, J. "Gypsy Crime in America", *Centurion: A Police Lifestyle Magazine,* 1 (6).

Schubert, K. and Schubert, U. (eds.) (1983) *Judische Buchkunst,* Graz: Akademische Druck-U. Verlagsanstalt.

Schurtz, H. (1902) *Altersklassen und Mannerbunde: Eine Darstellung der Grundformen der Gesellschaft,* Berlin: G. Reimer.

Segal, H. (1997) *Reason and Passion: A Celebration of the Work of Hanna Segal,* New York: Routledge.

Sheehan, E. (2000) *Travellers: Citizens of Ireland,* Dublin: Parish of the Travelling People.

Sibley, D. (1981) *Outsiders in Urban Society*, Oxford: Basil Blackwell.

Sinclair, A. (1908) "Irish Stonemasons in America", *Journal of American Folklore*, Vol. 16(2), pp. 12–17.

Spivak, G.C. (1996) *The Spivak Reader*, New York: Routledge.

Spivak, G.C. (1996) "Can the Subaltern Speak?" in G. Landry et al. (eds.) *The Spivak Reader*, London: Routledge.

Spivak, G.C. (1996) "Deconstructing Historiography" in G. Landry et al. (eds.) *The Spivak Reader,* London: Routledge.

Spivak, G.C. (1997) "More on Power/Knowledge: Outside in the Teaching Machine", in B. Moore-Gilbert (ed.) *Postcolonial Theory: Contexts, Practices, Politics*, London: Verso.

Stallybrass, P. and White A. (ed.) (1986) *The Politics and Poetics of Transgression*, London: Methuen.

Staples, R. (1982*) Black Masculinity: The Black Male's Role in American Society*, San Francisco: Black Scholar Press.

Sutherland, A. (1975) *Gypsies: the Hidden Americans*, London: Tavistock Publications.

Sutherland, A. (1975). "The American Rom: A Case of Economic Adaptation" in E.F. Rehfisch (ed.), *Gypsies, Tinkers and Other Travellers*, London: Academic Press.

Synge, J.M. (1980) *In Wicklow, West Kerry and Connemara*, Dublin: O'Brien Press.

Takaki, R. (1979) *Iron Cages: Race and Culture in Nineteenth-Century America*, New York: Knopf.

Task Force of the Travelling Community (1995) *Report of the Task Force on the Travelling Community*, Dublin: Stationery Office.

Thompson, D (1978) *The Voice of the Past: Oral History*, Oxford: Oxford University Press.

Thompson, S. (1955) *Motif-Index of Folk-Literature: A Classification of Narrative Elements in Folktales*, Bloomington: Indiana University Press.

Thomson, P. (1972) *The Grotesque*, London: Methuen.

Toelken, B. (1979) *The Dynamics of Folklore*, Boston: Houghton Mifflin.

Tolson, A. (1996) *Mediations*, London: Edward Arnold.

Tong, D. (1989) *Gypsy Folk Tales*, New York: Harcourt Brace and Co.

Travelling People Review Body (1985) *Report of the Travelling People Review Body*, Dublin: Stationery Office.

Turner, V. (1968) *The Drums of Affliction: A Study of Religious Processes among the Ndembu of Zambia,* Oxford: Oxford University Press.

Turner, V. (1974) *The Ritual Structure: Structure and Anti-Structure,* Hardmondsworth: Penguin.

Turner, V. (1982) *Celebration: Studies in Festivity and Ritual,* Washington, D.C.: Smithsonian Institution Press.

Turner, V. (1986) *The Anthropology of Performance,* New York: PAJ Publications.

Turner, V. (1992) *From Ritual to Theatre: The Human Seriousness of Play,* New York: New York City Performing Arts Journal Publications.

Ua Duinnín, An tÁth Pádraig (1901) *Amhráin Eoghain Ruaidh Uí Shúilleabháin,* Baile Átha Cliath: Oifig Dìolta Foilseacháin Rialtais.

Van Dijk, T. (1977) *Text and Context: Explorations in the Semantics and Pragmatics of Discourse,* London: Longman.

Van Dijk, T. (1993) *Elite Discourse and Racism,* London: Sage.

Van Gennep, A. (1960) *The Rites of Passage,* London: Routledge and Paul.

Vansina, J. (1961) *Oral Tradition: A Study in Historical Methodology,* Chicago: Aldine Publishing Company.

Vansina, J. (1985) *Oral Tradition as History,* London: Heinemann.

Vesey-Fitzgerald, B. (1973) *Gypsies of Britain: An Introduction to their History,* Newton Abbot: David and Charles.

Volf, M. (1996) *Exclusion and Embrace,* Nashville: Abingdon Press.

Walens, S. (1982) "The Weight of my Name is a Mountain of Blankets: Potlatch Ceremonies" in Turner, V. (ed.) *Celebration: Studies in Festivity and Ritual,* Washington: Smithsonian Institution Press.

Ward, C. (1992) "Chrissie Ward" in *Traveller Ways, Traveller Words,* Dublin, Pavee Point.

Warf, Barney (2002) "The Way it Wasn't: Alternative Histories, Contingent Geographies" in Kitchin, R. and Kneale, J. (eds.), *Lost in Space: Geographies of Science Fiction,* London: Continuum.

Warner, M. (1995) *From the Beast to the Blonde: On Fairy Tales and their Tellers,* London: Vintage.

Watson, H.F. (ed.) (1978) *The Concise Oxford Dictionary of Current English,* (6th edition), Oxford: Oxford University Press.

Waugh, P. (1989) *Feminine Fictions: Revisiting the Postmodern,* London: Routledge.

Wehler, H.U. (1987) *Deutsche Gesellschaftsgeschichte. Vom Feudalismus des Alten Reiches bis zur defensiven Modernisierung der Reformara 1700-1815*, Munich: Beck.

Welch, R. (1993) *Changing States: Transformations in Modern Irish Writing*, London: Routledge.

Welker, M. (1995) *Kirche im Pluralismus*, Gutersloh, Germany: Kaiser Taschenbuch.

White, H. (1973) *Metahistory*, Baltimore: Johns Hopkins University Press.

Willeford, W. (1969) *The Fool and his Sceptre*. London: Edward Arnold.

Willems, W. (1997) *In Search of the True Gypsy: From Enlightenment to Final Solution*, London: Frank Cassells.

Wilson, T. (1567) *The Rule of Reason: Conteinying the Arte of Logike*, London: Ihon Kingston.

Wolfe, A. (1992) *"Democracy versus Sociology: Boundaries and their Political Consequences"* in M. Fournier et al. (eds.) *Cultivating Differences: Symbolic Boundaries and the Making of Inequality*, Chicago: University of Chicago Press.

Yinger, J.M. (1982). *Countercultures: The Promise and Peril of a World Turned Upside Down*, New York, The Free Press.

Yoors, J. (1967) *The Gypsies*, New York: Simon and Schuster.

Young, R. (1990) *White Mythologies: Writing History and the West*, New York: Routledge.

Ziff, T. (1995) *Distant Relations: Cercanias Distantes: Clann i gCéin,* Santa Monica: Smart Art Press.